Tomorrowland

Tomorrowland

OUR JOURNEY FROM SCIENCE FICTION TO SCIENCE FACT

STEVEN KOTLER

Published by Amazon Publishing, New York

www.apub.com

Amazon, the Amazon logo and Amazon Publishing are trademarks of
Amazon.com, Inc. or its affiliates.

ISBN-13: 9781477827949
ISBN-10: 1477827943

Cover design by Dave Stanton / Faceout Studio
Author photograph by Ryan Heffernan

For my mother and father

Sure this is magic, but not necessarily fantasy.

—Thomas Pynchon

Contents

Part Three: The Future Uncertain

The Future Is Here

It was early spring of 1997, about five years into my career as a journalist, a day of dark skies and cold rain. Peter Diamandis and I had gotten together for the very first time at a rundown diner on the outskirts of Chinatown, San Francisco. The diner was long and narrow, and we were seated toward the rear of the room. I was sitting with my back to the building's far corner, Peter with his back to the rest of the restaurant. And the rest of the restaurant was staring at him.

For twenty minutes, Peter had been getting more and more excited while telling me about his newly launched endeavor: the XPRIZE, a ten-million-dollar competition for the first team to build a private spaceship capable of taking three people into space twice in two weeks. Already, the Sharpie had come out. There were charts on napkins, graphs on placemats, a healthy rearrangement of condiments—the ketchup marking the end of the troposphere, the mustard the beginning of the mesosphere. About the time he got loud about how some maverick innovator working out of a garage somewhere was going to "take down NASA," people began to stare. Peter couldn't see them; I could. Twenty folks in the restaurant, all looking at him like he was stark raving mad. And I remember this: I remember thinking they were wrong.

It's hard to put my finger on why. Part of it was a strange hunch. Journalists tend to be cynical by nature and disbelieving by necessity. The job requires a fairly healthy bullshit detector, and that was the thing — mine wasn't going off.

More of it was that I had just come from a month in the Black Rock Desert, outside of Gerlach, Nevada, watching Craig Breedlove try to drive a car through the sound barrier. Breedlove's effort was terrestrial-bound rocket science, for sure. The *Spirit of America*, his vehicle, was pretty much a miniature *Saturn V* — 40 feet long, 8 feet wide, 6 feet high, and powered by a turbojet engine that burned, well, rocket fuel.

During those long days in the desert, I spent a lot of time talking to aerospace engineers. They all made one thing clear: Driving a car through the sound barrier was a lot harder than sending a rocket ship into low-earth orbit. In fact, when I asked Breedlove's crew chief, former Air Force pilot turned aerospace engineer Dezso Molnar — who we'll meet again later as the inventor of the world's first flying motorcycle — what he was going to work on when all this was over, he said, "I want to do something easy, something relaxing. I think I'm going to build a spaceship."

He wasn't kidding.

Plus, Breedlove's effort was exactly the kind of big-budget project you would expect an agency like NASA to get behind. Except there was no budget. And no NASA. The *Spirit of America* had a crew of seven working out of an oversized tool shed. And while they never did break the sound barrier, they got really close — 670 mph (700 was the barrier) — and then ran out of cash. They were literally one sponsorship check away from making history.

So, that day in the diner — despite Peter's exuberance, despite the fact that, back then, the XPRIZE had no major sponsors and no money in the bank, and despite the fact that NASA had called his idea utterly impossible and the entire aerospace industry had agreed — from where I was sitting, some maverick opening the space frontier didn't seem too outlandish.

Of course, today, with the XPRIZE won, with the private space industry worth more than a billion dollars, none of this may seem incredibly shocking. But it was. In 1997, space was off-limits to anyone but big government. This much was gospel. Yet I left that diner absolutely certain that sometime in the next decade, the far frontier would open for business.

I also left the diner a little gobsmacked. In less time than it took to drink a cup of coffee, a paradigm had shattered — science fiction had become science fact. On the way home, I started to wonder about other paradigms. After all, if private spaceships were possible, what about all the other sci-fi mainstays? What about bionics? Robotics? Flying cars? Artificial life? Life extension? Asteroid mining? What about those more ephemeral topics: the future of human evolution, the possibilities of downloadable consciousness? I made a long list — and that list defined large parts of the next two decades of my career.

Tomorrowland is the result of that journey. The pieces in this book come from an assortment of major publications — the *New York Times, Wired, Atlantic Monthly,* to name a few — and all were penned between 2000 and 2014. They are all investigations into those moments when science fiction became science fact and the massively disruptive impact those moments have on culture. Because of the blitzkrieg rate of change in today's world, few of these stories appear exactly as they ran. Instead, I've updated the science and technology so — unless the tale is historical in nature — the information contained in this book is as current as possible.

Furthermore, to help make better sense of things, I've also broken these stories into three categories. The first grouping — The Future In Here — is about us, an examination of the ways science and technology are fundamentally altering you and me. Here we'll explore artificial senses (the world's first artificial vision implant), bionic limbs (the world's first bionic soldier), and evolution's future (say good-bye to *Homo sapiens*), among other seismic shifts in what it means to be human. The second section — The Future Out There — is about the ways science and technology are radically reshaping our world. Here we'll cover everything from on-world paradigm shifts, like the birth of the world's first genetically engineered insect, to off-world paradigm shifts, like the birth of the asteroid mining industry. Finally, in The Future Uncertain, we'll examine the gray areas, those explosive collisions between science and culture — for example, the use of steroids for life extension or the use of synthetic biology for the creation of bioweapons — where lines are being crossed and controversy reigns, and no one is certain what tomorrow brings.

This last bit is no small thing. All of the technologies described in this book are disruptive technologies, though not as we traditionally define the word. Typically, disruptive technologies are those that displace an existing technology and disrupt an existing market, but the breakthroughs described herein do more than dismantle value chains — they destroy longstanding beliefs. You will, for example, come across an article about William Dobelle, inventor of the world's first artificial vision implant. Dobelle was extremely paranoid about talking to the press. This isn't that uncommon, but it's usually about protecting intellectual property. That wasn't Dobelle's problem. When I asked him about his reticence, his answer surprised me: "Jesus cured blindness. People don't like it when mortals perform miracles."

It was an offhand comment, but one that stayed with me. Consider the enormous influence that our spiritual traditions exert in today's world. Think about the blood that has been spilled in the name of religion in just these past hundred years. Think about the ongoing hubbub surrounding the — shall we say — "philosophical question" of millions of years of evolution, versus the more economic six-day approach. Now, think about what's coming.

Right now, researchers are storming heaven from every direction. In "Extreme States," we'll see how things like trance states, out-of-body experiences, and cosmic unity — all core mystical experiences that underpin our spiritual traditions—are now understood as the product of measurable biology. The hard science has been done; the disruptive technologies are what come next. So forget about science putting something as flimsy as "philosophical" pressure on religion—pretty soon the direct experience of the numinous is going to be available via video game.

And that's just the beginning of the storm. How many spiritual traditions rely on the premise of the hereafter to steer morality? Yet, as you'll see in "The Genius Who Sticks Around Forever," we are already poking at the possibility of downloadable consciousness—the idea that we can store self in silicon, loading consciousness onto a chip and loading that chip onto a computer, allowing us to hang on to our personalities forever—so what happens to morality in the face of immortality?

Or take synthetic biology, a technology explored in "Hacking the President's DNA," that allows us to write genetic code much like we write computer code, a development that gives us the power to create life from scratch. So now we can cheat death and jumpstart life and, as e.e. cummings once said, "Listen, there's a hell of a good universe next door; let's go."

Well, folks, we're already gone.

Of course, some might not be moved by the above "spiritual" arguments, so it's worth taking a moment to examine these ideas in more secular terms. One of the most well-established facts in psychology is that the burden of consciousness confers on every human being an innate fear of death. In 1974, psychologist Ernest Becker won a Pulitzer Prize for *The Denial of Death*, arguing that death anxiety is the most fundamental of all our motivational drivers—more powerful than our need for food, drink, or sex. In fact, Becker claimed, everything we consider "culture" is nothing more than an elaborate defense mechanism against the awful knowledge of our own mortality. A great many researchers now agree. Fear of death is the fundamental human experience, the very cornerstone of our psychological foundation. Yet, right now, in labs all over the world, researchers are chipping away at this cornerstone, hollowing out our very essence. So what happens when they succeed?

Who knows.

What we can say for sure is that the future that's coming is unlike anything we've ever seen. I've heard it called the Age of Prometheus, I've heard it called the Age of Icarus, but either way the part that strikes me as truly strange is these mythic metaphors are no longer metaphors. We actually are stealing fire from the gods; we really might be flying too close to the sun.

Another thing I can say is that it's been an astounding ride. On a number of occasions, I've been lucky enough to be in the room when history happens. In fact, when William Dobelle switched on his artificial vision implant for the first time, I wasn't just in that room — I was what was seen.

That wasn't my intention. Twenty seconds before Dobelle switched on the device, I realized that I was sitting directly across from Patient Alpha, smack in the middle of his line of sight. I didn't feel right about what was about to happen, so I actually tried to get out of the way. In the final moments of the countdown to curing blindness, I slid back my chair, got up, and took a couple of quick steps to the left. What was I thinking? Patient Alpha was blind. He'd spent his entire life tracking motion through sound. Of course, when I moved, he tracked the sound and turned his head and that, as they say, was that.

I've come to see that moment as emblematic of these past few decades. Despite my best intentions and best efforts, I wasn't stealthy enough. I wasn't fast enough. I couldn't duck. No matter what I did, there was no way to get out of the way of the future.

And so it is for all of us.

These are exponential times. The far frontier is no longer a distant dream. It is there today and here tomorrow, and that's the thing: Luddite revolutions don't seem to hold for long. Resisting the lure of technology isn't really in us. In *What Technology Wants*, *Wired* cofounder Kevin Kelly argues that this is because technology is actually another form of life — a living, natural system with ancient origins and deep desires. And while Kelly has a point, I also think there's simpler truth at work. Life is tricky sport. It can be hard here, often harder than we want it to be, sometimes harder than we can take. And that strikes me as the emotional core of the story, the real reason we can't put Pandora back in the box. When you strip everything else away, technology is nothing more than the promise of an easier tomorrow. It's the promise of hope. And how do you stop hope?

Right now, in a deep forest in the South of France, researchers are completing work on the International Thermonuclear Experimental Reactor, which is far and away the most complex machine ever built. When switched on, the reactor will ionize hydrogen to temperatures over two million degrees — which is ten times hotter than the sun. In other words, when ITER is switched on, we will be turning on a star. How far has hope taken us? From the very first time one of our primate progenitors sharpened a stick to a star. A freaking star. In a lab. Created by us.

Let there be light.

PART ONE

THE FUTURE IN HERE

Bionic Man

THE WORLD'S FIRST BIONIC MAN

Future technology has always been about pushing limits. Now, unless we're talking about defying the fundamental laws of physics, then the limits that interest us most are the ones imposed by our biology. And there is no greater reminder of those limits than age-related decline, the loss of the use of our own limbs, the undeniable signal that the clock called life is winding down.

Bionics, of course, marks the beginning of the end for this particular trend. The creation of artificial limbs not only ushers in a new era of radically enhanced prosthetics – itself a boon for anyone who has suffered the horrors of amputation – but opens the door for a new era of rebirth, where platitudes about second childhoods can now be reinforced by some serious mechanistic heft. This means, I suspect, that the true impact of bionics is going to be as much mental as physical. We think we're building new bodies, but my guess is we're going to end up with new brains as well. Or, to put this in slightly different terms, I know very few adults who don't share George Bernard Shaw's opinion: "Youth is wasted on the young." Well, not for long.

1.

The first thing David Rozelle did after the insurgents put a price on his head was up the ante. After all, this was Captain David Rozelle, the one they called Iron Man or Killer 6 or Kowboy 6 — the 6 being short for "six-shooter," as in gunslinger, ass kicker, take your pick. His head for a measly thousand bucks? It was insulting.

This all went down in the summer of 2003, in a police station in the city of Hit (pronounced "Heat"), Iraq. Rozelle and the 139 men under his command, the Army's Third Armored Cavalry Regiment K Troop, had already battled their way from Kuwait to Syria. They had followed the men on Thunder Run and scrapped beside the marines in Fallujah, and when they were done there, the brass had told Rozelle to secure a town in northwestern Iraq. What town? It didn't matter. Everything was a bloody mess up there.

Rozelle started looking at maps. Hit caught his eye. There was no CIA data on the place. Aerial reconnaissance photos showed lots of fancy cars — Mercedeses, Rolls-Royces — but no major industry. All the earmarks of a significant Sunni stronghold. "Major bad guys for sure" is how Rozelle describes it.

So Rozelle and K Troop took Hit. In two months, they restored order. Under Rozelle's command, the members of K Troop taught themselves counterinsurgency tactics: tracking snipers, putting money back into the banks, and restoring the electricity. Rozelle even put a woman on the city council, a fact he likes to brag about: "We were going to be the first town in Iraq to have equal rights for women."

Then, in the sticky weather of early June, at roughly 6:30 p.m.,

Rozelle arrived at the new police station—new because insurgents had already burned down the old one in an attempt to scare off the police force Rozelle had built—for his nightly pre-mission briefing. Something was wrong. There was tension in the room, people talking in whispers. Demanding an explanation, Rozelle was told that Sunni insurgents had put a price on his head. He was not surprised. But he was curious—how much was he worth?

"I asked my translator," says Rozelle. "It was this big moment. The room got quiet. He turned to me and said in a stage whisper, 'One thousand dollars.'"

Rozelle knew there were spies in that room. He knew whatever he said would get back to the insurgents.

"That's bullshit!" he shouted. "Tell those sons of bitches I'm worth way more than that. I'm worth ten thousand dollars. Tell them I'll pay the bounty myself."

No one claimed Rozelle's bounty that first night. Or the next. No one got close for almost two weeks—but that only exacerbated the situation. The insurgents started burying land mines on frequently traveled roads, including the one just outside the soccer stadium. On June 21 Rozelle was leading a convoy down that road. Unwilling to subject his men to dangers he would not face himself, Rozelle had his Humvee take point. He rode shotgun. As was his custom, he held a pistol out the window in his right hand, his left staying firmly atop the Bible his father had given him before he departed for Iraq.

Up ahead, the road looked disturbed, like something had pushed the dirt around. Rozelle halted the convoy and surveyed the area. He told the driver to proceed slowly. Seconds later all hell arrived. The truck hit a land mine. The explosion shot the front end of the Humvee four feet into the air. Doors and windows blew out, scattering debris more than a hundred yards. Rozelle's flak jacket saved his life. He took shrapnel to the face and arms. His left foot was pinned between the ground and the engine block. His right foot? His boot was still on, but blood and bone oozed out of the side. When he tried to step on it, he drove his tibia and his fibula straight into the ground. Wow, did that hurt like a motherfucker.

The first surgery took place in a dusty tent outside Baghdad. The setup looked like something out of *M*∗*A*∗*S*∗*H*. Rozelle couldn't believe anyone would operate under such conditions. Operate they did. Doctors are trained to salvage as much of the limb as possible, so they performed a tricky ankle-joint amputation known technically as a Syme's.

Amputation is one of the greatest possible shocks. Children cannot help staring at amputees, as psychologists have said, because losing a limb is literally the worst thing a child can imagine. Adults may have better manners, but the internal damage is no less severe. The patient must endure a period of heavy grief, as if the mind cannot tell the difference between a lost limb and death itself. "When I woke up from surgery without my foot," says Rozelle, "I had no frame of reference. I had never known an amputee before. It was like being completely reborn."

Not long afterward, Rozelle was loaded onto a transport plane for Ramstein Air Base in Germany. Before departure, his commanding officer, Lieutenant Colonel Butch Kievenaar, paid him a visit. He'd come to deliver a message, telling Rozelle that if he got himself patched up, he could come back to Iraq and be given another command.

Rozelle was pissed. Maybe this was motivational bullshit, something the shrinks dreamed up to keep him from killing himself. But Kievenaar was a straight shooter, so perhaps the offer was good. Either way, at that point, with the bedsheets pressed flat where his foot should have been, all Rozelle could think was, *I have given enough.*

2.

Twenty-one years before anyone put a price on David Rozelle's head, during the winter of 1982, Hugh Herr, then seventeen, and

Jeff Batzer, then twenty, left their homes in Lancaster, Pennsylvania, for an adventure in New Hampshire's White Mountains. Both were experienced rock climbers, Herr already something of a legend. Known as Boy Wonder, he had been the youngest to ascend several North American mountaineering classics, including Mount Temple in the Canadian Rockies, which he scaled at the age of eight.

Herr and Batzer had their sights on Odell's Gully, an ice-climbing route atop Mount Washington, one of the world's most dangerous destinations. Since 1849 more than 135 people have died on this mountain and its surrounding peaks. Freezing temperatures, frequent avalanches. The average wind speed is 35 mph, but in 1934 a weather station on its summit clocked 231 mph — the strongest recorded blow in history.

Herr and Batzer knew all this but still decided to leave their extra backpack — containing food, clothes, and sleeping bags — at the base of the climb. Herr figured that without the added weight they could make it up and back more quickly, an important consideration, as a big storm was heading their way.

They did make good time, climbing four pitches of ice in less than an hour and a half, reaching the top of Odell's before 10 a.m. But the top of Odell's is not the top of Mount Washington. The apex lies some 1,000 feet higher. Not many climbers, at least not in winter, make a summit bid. Herr and Batzer decided to give it a try.

The storm arrived soon after. Temperatures fell far below zero; the wind gusted over 70 mph. Maybe they made it to the summit, maybe they turned back early; in those whiteout conditions it was impossible to tell. What we do know is that they never made it back to their planned descent route, instead trekking into the largest ravine in the White Mountains, a vast icy wildlands known as the Great Gulf.

When nightfall came and they hadn't returned, a search-and-rescue effort was mounted. Over the next three days dozens of people fanned out over Mount Washington. Some went on foot, others by snowmobile. Helicopters canvassed the area. It was a brutal effort. An avalanche caught two members of the North Conway Mountain Rescue Service, Michael Hartrick and Albert Dow. Hartrick walked away from the incident. Dow wasn't so lucky. The slide swept him into a tree: his back snapped, his chest crushed, his death nearly instantaneous. He was twenty-eight years old.

Herr and Batzer, meanwhile, were still lost in the wilderness.

They spent three long days wandering through the Great Gulf, three longer nights huddled in prayer. The temperatures stayed below freezing. In the beginning, they hugged each other for warmth. Later, when they could no longer stand it, they let go of their embrace, wanting the cold, the frozen relief of a quicker death.

On the fourth day, with a turn of fortune that in other times would have been called divine providence, a snowshoer found them hidden beneath a boulder, barely alive. They were medevaced to a hospital that specialized in frostbite and hypothermia, then transferred farther afield. But the gangrene was too severe. Two weeks later, Batzer's doctor amputated his right thumb and four fingers down to the first joint; three days after that they came back and took his left foot and the toes from his right. Herr was in worse shape. Both his feet were black, the skin ragged, his toes fused together. In just over a month's time, he had seven surgeries. None did much good. His feet could not be saved. For his last surgery, doctors performed a pair of standard below-knee amputations — six inches below the knee, to be exact, long considered the right length for plugging stumps into prosthetics.

Herr woke from surgery screaming — his physical pain otherworldly, his psychological torment even worse. He had been an awkward child, shy, not very good at school; his self-worth, his self-image, his entire being was tied to stone. Herr needed rock climbing like most people need air.

Yet, while Herr's fear of never climbing again was overwhelming, even worse was his remorse over Albert Dow's death. Mountaineers live by a strict code: Never endanger another's life. Herr had violated this rule. The guilt was crushing.

3.

The last time an American soldier with injuries as extensive as David Rozelle's returned to active combat duty was during the Civil War. But the army was Rozelle's life.

He was born in Dallas in 1972 and grew up as the child of patriots. His father served with the Air Force, raising him on stories of duty, honor, and the importance of American freedom. But as with so many other Americans, it wasn't only these values that drove Rozelle into the military—it was also the need for a paycheck.

Rozelle went to Davidson College in North Carolina on a football scholarship. Unfortunately, he was also working three jobs and barely making ends meet. A good friend, meanwhile, was in ROTC and having no such trouble. So Rozelle went to talk to the recruiter, who sent him to Fort Benning's Airborne School. "This guy knew his job," says Rozelle. "Sending a nineteen-year-old to go jump out of airplanes? Of course I fell in love with the army."

After graduation, Rozelle went to Fort Knox to train as a tank commander, spent the early years of his career working at Fort Hood, and saw his first operational deployment in 1999, in Kuwait. Afterward, it was on to Korea for top-secret war planning and a second life playing semipro rugby. Finally, he made it back home to a dream job at Fort Carson in Colorado, close to the mountains and the skiing he so loved.

On 9/11 that dream ended. Rozelle reported for duty. And then, after more than a decade in the military, he killed his first man. "As a Christian," he says, "killing went against everything I believed. But this was war and it was either him or me. It was like living a nightmare."

There would be other nightmares. Morphine is just about the only workable shield against the pain of amputation, but opiate addiction is a frequent side effect. After eight excruciating surgeries, a quarantine at the Walter Reed Army Medical Center and phantom pains as severe as those he experienced when he'd first been blown up, Rozelle kicked a morphine habit cold turkey. Now that was a fucking nightmare.

He replaced the habit with another: physical therapy. Rozelle had deployed for Iraq weighing 220. Now he was down to 175. The mirror was not his friend. He wanted his body back, his life back. His wife was about to give birth to their first child; he needed to set an example. Plus, President Bush had told Rozelle that he could come down to the Crawford ranch for a run whenever he was ready.

Rozelle decided to get ready. Half an hour after being fitted with his first pair of prosthetics, with his stumps still raw, Rozelle was outside: running, jumping, doing push-ups. Still, reality was settling in. "Ever since my injury, I was waiting for this magic prosthesis that would make me feel healed. I was ready to be healed. But then I got my first leg and realized how wrong I had been. There was no quick fix. The prosthesis sucked. I had lost my foot and was going to be like this forever."

And herein lies the rub. While prosthetic devices are among mankind's earliest inventions (they date back to Egypt circa 1069 BCE), progress has been exceedingly slow. "At the time I got hurt," says Rozelle, "there was no major difference between the prosthetic limb I was using and the ones soldiers got coming back from Vietnam."

All this, though, was starting to change. "For the first time in history," says Rozelle, smiling and quoting the opening monologue of *The Six Million Dollar Man,* "we can rebuild him. We have the technology."

And the reason we can rebuild him?

There are several. One is the more than 1,400 men and women who have lost limbs in the wars in Iraq and Afghanistan: a sad

parade that reinvigorated our national conscience and sent research dollars flooding back into the field. Additionally, over
the past decade, revolutionary breakthroughs in a bevy of whiz-
bang technologies — robotics, nanotechnology, tissue engineering, machine-brain interfaces, to name but a few — have begun
leaking into the medical arts. But money and technology alone
did not close this gap. To understand how this really came together, you need to start some twenty-one years ago, with a
seventeen-year-old boy named Hugh Herr and his very big debt
to pay.

4.

Ten days after surgery, Herr couldn't wait any longer: He had to
know if he could climb. Herr began sneaking out of his hospital
bed, dragging himself over to the window, trying to do pull-ups
on the ledge. A letter arrived from President Reagan. "I know
you are a young man with a very brave heart," it read. The president didn't know the half of it.

Five weeks after surgery, Herr got his first set of legs. Called
pylons, they were made of plaster and attached by straps above
the knee. The first two times Herr left the hospital, his doctors
refused to let him take the pylons along — for fear he would try to
climb. The third time, less than ten weeks after Herr had lost his
legs, his brother and frequent climbing partner, Tony, drove him
to a Pennsylvania crag called Safe Harbor.

Herr had come to attempt a 60-foot intermediate route that,
before the accident, he could have done blindfolded. Maybe he
could do so again, but first he had to make it up the long hik-
ers' trail that led to the bottom of the cliff. Herr stumbled along
on his canes. Then his brother carried him piggyback. When
the ground steepened further, Herr got down on all fours and
dragged himself up the path.

At the base of the climb, Tony scampered off to set a top rope, leaving Herr alone at the bottom, staring upward. Here, at last, was the stone test he was desperate to pass. He had no idea what would happen next; he only knew that his whole life depended on it.

Herr made his first move. One good hold led to another and then another, and his legs didn't cause much trouble. He rose higher. Getting to that climb had kicked his ass, but as soon as he made his initial moves, he came to a startling realization: He could climb better than he could walk.

It was the first of a series of startling revelations. Herr still had to finish his senior year of high school. He spent much of that time climbing, much of it working in a machine shop at school — building his own prosthetic legs. Lifelike aesthetics play a role in normal prosthetics, but Herr had a different goal in mind. "I realized that I didn't need human feet," he says. "I needed climbing tools. If I could build the right kind of appendage, one customized for a vertical world, I could erase my disability with technology."

Herr built a huge assortment of vertically customized prosthetics: climbing legs with crampons for feet, short legs for certain routes, longer ones for others. One early masterpiece was a pair of bladed, beveled feet, narrow at the toe, wider at the heel, perfect for fitting into cracks.

With these tools, Herr earned himself a new nickname: Mechanical Boy. It wasn't long before he was climbing at his previous level. Pretty soon, he was better than before. In August 1983, in conjunction with a trio of other professional climbers, Herr helped establish one of America's first legitimate 5.13+ climbs — there's no easy translation, but 5.13+ essentially means "very, very expert," or what was then among the toughest grades anyone had yet climbed — on homemade prosthetic limbs.

In the history of the world, no other disabled athlete had ever performed at this level. Herr's success on the rock was merely a proof of concept: "It's where I learned that people aren't disabled," he says. "Technology is disabled." So Herr decided to improve the technology, to devote his life to building better bionic limbs. He had finally figured out a way to pay his debt.

"Climbing taught me to focus," recounts Herr, "to distill problems down to critical components and stick with them until they were solved. So while I wasn't the brightest student, I had a good toolbox and could learn hard subjects."

He excelled at physics at Millersville University in Pennsylvania and displayed genius as an inventor, earning his first patent — for a much more comfortable limb-socket interface built around inflatable bladders — before the end of his senior year. He went on to earn a master's in mechanical engineering from MIT and a doctorate in biophysics from Harvard. Somewhere in between, he stumbled upon the puzzle that would occupy his next fifteen years: human motion.

"Human motion doesn't seem like it should be a puzzle," says Herr. "We've been studying it for a very long time, but it's really a black hole. We can't even give sophisticated answers to simple questions. What does a muscle do? Well, we're not exactly sure."

First as a graduate student and later, in his current role as head of the biomechatronics research group at MIT's Media Lab, Herr decided the best approach was to mimic nature's designs. He started with "embodied intelligence." Amputees had been making do with dumb prosthetics, but our natural limbs are incredibly smart. When your leg moves, all your nervous system needs to do is increase or decrease muscle stiffness, because every other decision is made automatically by the limb's internal design. Herr decided it was time to apply similar principles to prosthetics.

In the late 1990s he began working on a smarter knee. He packed it with microsensors capable of measuring joint angle and load at a rate of a thousand times per second. The data were then fed into a computer chip that regulated a magnetic field that impacted iron particles floating in an oil mixture surrounding the knee joint. The result was the world's first artificially intelligent prosthetic — a knee able to adjust dampening on the fly.

Even better, the knee could learn, so performance improved over time.

The prosthesis was brought to market as the Rheo Knee by the Icelandic firm Ossur. *Time* named it one of 2004's best inventions, and *Fortune* called it one of the best products of the year. "Using artificial intelligence to control the Rheo Knee was a major step forward for the industry," says Dr. Richard Satava, professor of surgery at the University of Washington Medical Center and former program manager for advanced biomedical technology at the Defense Advanced Research Projects Agency (DARPA). But Herr was only getting started.

5.

In the fall of 2003, Rozelle started swimming and began to excel in the weight room. Pretty soon he was bench-pressing 300 pounds. In February, Rozelle did two minutes each of push-ups and sit-ups and swam for 800 yards — passing the army physical training test in the top 19th percentile for his age group. He took the next step at Vail. Skiing turned out to be no problem; neither did snowboarding. By the end of a week in Vail, Rozelle had taken to heart the motto of Disabled Sports USA — "If I can do this, I can do anything."

Top among the things Rozelle was interested in doing was finding a way to provide better support for returning wounded soldiers. At the start of the second Gulf War, there was little in the way of follow-up psychological care. He started visiting wounded soldiers at Walter Reed, began to work with the US Olympic Committee military and veteran programs, and became a representative for Disabled Sports USA. But, as a national spokesman for disabled soldiers, Rozelle knew the best way he could help was to set a great example. Maybe it really was time to take Kievenaar up on his offer.

This was the army, so of course there was paperwork. With the forms and the letters and the meetings, the process to get cleared by the medical evaluation board took time. But Rozelle pushed, and on March 4, 2004, he was declared fit for duty.

Rozelle spent the next few months working at Fort Carson and was given a new command on June 17, 2004, four days before the first anniversary of his injury. Two weeks later, Rozelle was back in Iraq, commanding troops on the same field of battle where he'd sustained his injury.

During his first tour back, Rozelle broke three prosthetic feet. His life was never seriously endangered, but that was mostly a matter of luck. Rozelle was frustrated. In the coming years he wrote dozens of articles about this issue, all of them containing the line "We can send an astronaut into space, but we can't build a better prosthetic device?"

6.

After completing work on the Rheo, Herr set his sights on a much more ambitious challenge: to create an artificial ankle that perfectly mimicked the fluidity of the normal human gait. A lot was at stake. Most amputees walk with a limp. Over time, even the smallest deviations in motion can compound into enormous problems. The constant chafing destroys flesh, nerve, and bone, often requiring surgeries to repair.

Around 2002, Herr went to work on a radically new bionic body part. It would be far smarter than anything ever designed. The Rheo's one computer became five in the new device. He also added a battery pack, more sensors, and Bluetooth. Robotics were used to replicate the action of the foot, Achilles tendon, and calf muscle — creating what Herr calls "powered plantar flexion."

Herr also started rethinking the design. As a climber, especially after his accident, Herr had a flamboyant style. In a sport then dominated by earth tones, he favored dyed red hair, dangling feather earrings, and neon blue tights. Add to that his customized climbing prosthetics — essentially daggers protruding from his legs — and the effect was startling. Herr wanted something similar from his prosthetics. "People kept making devices that were ugly, that screamed disabled. I wanted to make devices that were sexy and scary and powerful, man-machine hybrids that replace the notion of disabled with the healthy reverence we feel for the Terminator."

In 2005 word started leaking out that Hugh Herr was building the world's first bionic ankle. By then, Rozelle was back from his second tour in Iraq, living in Washington, D.C., and helping Walter Reed build a better center for amputees. He definitely heard about Herr's work. "Cyborg limb replacement," he says. "Oh yeah, I knew all about Herr's dream. We all did."

The following year, in June 2006, at a No Limits Foundation event in Lake Tahoe, Nevada, Rozelle met Herr for the first time. They hit it off, sitting poolside, drinking beer. "I gave him a rash of shit about progress on the ankle," recounts Rozelle. "I wanted one. He kept saying it wasn't ready."

Fabricating a bionic body part for a guy like Rozelle was no small matter. Between 2005 and 2007, mostly wearing a carbon-fiber running leg that operated at a 30 percent energy deficit, Rozelle finished more than a dozen sprint- and Olympic-distance triathlons, five marathons, seven half-Ironman events, and his first full-scale Ironman triathlon (2.4-mile swim, 112-mile bike ride, and 26.2-mile run) with a time was fast enough to qualify for the world championships in Kona, Hawaii. There, Rozelle covered the fabled Ironman course in 12 hours and 46 minutes. He saluted as he crossed the finish line, placing in the bottom third of the field but still ahead of dozens of able-bodied competitors. "It's pretty strange to see guys with two legs looking at me with jealousy," says Rozelle, "but that's what happened."

Meanwhile, with all the wounded soldiers returning from

battle, the military continued to fund bionic research. In 2006, DARPA contracted inventor Dean Kamen, who specializes in revolutionary medical devices, to develop a new kind of arm.

As Kamen put it, "DARPA wanted me to build an arm-hand combo that could pick up a grape without breaking it, which requires very fine haptic sensing; lift a raisin without dropping it, which requires fine motor control and wrist, elbow, and shoulder flexibility; be entirely self-contained, including the power supply; weigh less than nine pounds; and fit on a 50th-percentile female frame, 32 inches from the long finger to the shoulder. And even better, I had to finish the job in two years. So, you know, I told them they were completely nuts."

But Kamen's conscience got the better of him, and he took the job. He completed the beta version right on schedule, naming the device the Luke Arm after that fabled *Star Wars* amputee, Luke Skywalker. (The Luke Arm is now undergoing clinical trials.)

"It was an exciting time," says Rozelle. "There was finally some hope for real progress."

7.

In 2007, Herr finished the beta version of the BiOM, as his bionic ankle is now known. Five computers and twelve sensors give the BiOM sufficient intelligence to read and react to differences in terrain and slope—meaning it's the first robotic foot that can be used to walk uphill. Unlike traditional prosthetic devices, to which a person must adapt his walking style, the BiOM gathers gait data to attune itself to the wearer. This is what the Bluetooth is for: The world's first true bionic limb is programmable by means of an Android phone.

Time named the BiOM one of the best inventions of 2007. Other accolades followed, but there was significantly more work to be done before the device was ready for the general public. "The dominant challenge was durability," says Herr. "I was building a prosthetic leg. It's a transportation device. It can't fail. But if it's going to last five years, then it has to be capable of taking six million steps — because that's how many the average person takes in that period. Look, there's nothing like the human body. There are versions that can walk without failure for eighty years. I was trying for just five — but this was not a trivial problem in robotics."

By late 2010 Herr felt the BiOM was durable enough for human trials. Because the military was funding much of the work, soldiers were the obvious crash-test dummies. Plus, Rozelle had challenged Herr to build a device for guys like him — so who better to try it out?

In January 2011 he got his shot. Rozelle became the world's second official bionic man (one other soldier had been fitted before him). As soon as the BiOM was attached, Rozelle went in search of the toughest terrain he could find. "The prosthetists were so happy," he says. "They were used to seeing guys just walk up and down the hallway. I went outside and found a hill to walk up and down at an angle. It was pretty amazing. I immediately felt I had my real foot back."

Over the next year, Rozelle and a couple dozen other veteran amputees put the BiOM through its paces. "It was an incredible process," recalls Tim McCarthy, the CEO of iWalk, the company that builds the BiOM. "Over the past twenty years I've introduced dozens of new products — none like this. People put on the BiOM and burst into tears." Herr had seen it too: "Grizzled truck drivers, guys who haven't shed a tear in twenty years, just sobbing."

But the biggest deal — what many think the BiOM's real legacy will be — is a massive reduction in health care costs. With less pain and exhaustion, amputees don't stop moving around. They lose weight (tens of pounds), reduce their pain meds (some by up to two-thirds), and return to work (for the first time in years). The real proof is that the device costs about $60,000, yet workers' compensation agents are requesting it, feeling that the savings in medical costs later will more than cover the high price tag. "Beyond changing lives," says McCarthy, "this has a huge economic benefit. Over time, it's going to save millions of dollars."

Herr, meanwhile, isn't close to being done. He's beginning to work on an above-the-knee version of the BiOM and is finishing work on the world's first true bionic exoskeleton, a revolutionary kind of knee brace for able-bodied people that he hopes will be commercially available by 2015. "Right now," he says, "one of the worst parts of growing old is losing the ability to move around. So imagine taking the bionics in the BiOM and turning it into a strap-on device, something that can restore strength and function to the elderly or anyone with a bum knee."

Over the past thirty years, Hugh Herr became the first disabled athlete to outperform able-bodied ones at an expert level. He then helped bring prosthetics into the modern age; next he became the first to forge ahead into the bionic era. Already he has bettered thousands of lives. In light of all this, the assumption might be that his debt to Albert Dow — the rescuer who perished so many years ago on Mount Washington — would be paid. But Herr would disagree.

"If you ask me if I've done great things in my life, well, I'm very self-critical, so the answer is, 'Not yet,'" he says. "But that's almost beside the point. Has that debt been paid? I would say no, never. That debt can never be repaid."

8.

On a rainy day in February 2012, David Rozelle and a couple of friends approach the curb of a busy three-lane street in Denver. Rozelle, wearing his BiOM, is lost in conversation, not really thinking about what he's doing. There's a momentary break in traffic, and he decides to make a run for it. Leaving his friends behind, he bounces off the curb and darts across the first lane, freezes midstride to let an oncoming car pass, then dashes across the next lane, pausing to make sure he's still clear, and across the final lane, even jumping over a puddle as he hops back onto the sidewalk. Rozelle didn't even realize that he'd jaywalked until it was pointed out later.

Herr smiles when he hears this story. "Everything I've done has been to copy nature. That's the true definition of bionics — using technology for the emulation or extension of natural biological function. And we humans are spinal animals. To hear that David could pull off this kind of ballet without thinking about it — that's exactly a spinal animal phenomenon. It worked. Somehow we captured lightning in a bottle."

"Yeah," says Rozelle, "but the mad scientists who designed the jet pack, they're never remembered. The crazy son of a bitch who flew it? He'll be celebrated forever."

The Genius Who Sticks Around Forever

THE SCIENCE OF MIND UPLOADING

In his novel *Terra Nostra,* author Carlos Fuentes writes: "Incredible the first animal that dreamed of another animal." Quite an idea, right? Both the origin story for dreaming and the initial step up the ladder that scientists describe with the phrase "theory of mind": our ability to attribute mental states – beliefs, intents, desires – to oneself and others. It is, without question, an extraordinary ability.

Now consider the opposite end of the spectrum, the farthest rung up the theory-of-mind ladder: the ability to share the mind of another. This is the frontier known as mind uploading, and it is a truly wild frontier. In the previous chapter, we explored using technology to battle back decrepitude. In this chapter, we're using technology to battle death itself. Where will this lead? A place we've never ever been before. Descartes told us: "I think, therefore I am." But what happens when someone else thinks you? Seriously, who are you now?

1.

They say that wisdom accumulates, that perhaps it is not subject to the same tick-tock corrosion that renders bones frail and hair thin. They say it is our one real treasure, this thing to be passed on, generation to generation, to grant us a stay against a dark, dim future. And so we have Greek lectures transcribed by diligent pupils, sketches by Leonardo da Vinci, a collection of Gertrude Stein's writings, the fireside scratch of a chatty F.D.R., a cinematic tour of Stephen Hawking's universe, and, of course, Timothy Leary's Internet broadcast of his last days on earth.

But what we don't have is the people themselves; we don't have their consciousness, and that, many feel, is the real loss. And, if you believe the believers, that is about to change.

They're calling it the Soul Catcher, a pet name really, as if the soul were something that could be caught like a fish. It's the brainchild of Dr. Peter Cochrane, chief technical officer for British Telecommunications: a micromemory chip implanted in the human brain, implanted for the whole of a lifetime, meant to record the whole of that lifetime.

As future-forward as this chip may sound, the first step — integrating it with the body — already shows great promise. And has for some time. Back in the late 1990s, researchers at Stanford University found a way to splice nerves and, using a chip, grow them back together. A few years later, in a Georgia hospital, electrodes were successfully embedded in the brain of a completely paralyzed man, translating thoughts into cursor movement. This was also when we learned that, unlike the rest of the body, which tends to reject foreign implants, the nervous system is incorporative — meaning that the act of placing a chunk of metal into the brain is more like rewiring a light switch than reinventing the wheel.

The technical name for this first step is "brain-computer interface," or BCI. There are now hundreds of researchers pioneering BCI science, with the aforementioned efforts being merely the initial drops in what has since become a much larger ocean. Many of them share Cochrane's interest in memory. Theodore Berger, for example, a neural engineer at the University of Southern California, is working on an artificial hippocampus, one of the core neuronal structures implicated in this process. Berger's device records the electrical activity that arises whenever we encode short-term memories — for example, learning to play scales — then translates them into digital signals. These signals are sent to a computer, transformed once again, and then re-fed into the brain, where they're then stored as long-term memories. While the device is far from done, Berger has run successful tests with monkeys and rats and is now working with humans.

Cochrane also has to invent new gear to pioneer the Soul Catcher, but it's based on older gizmos. By using variations of existing technologies — the silicon retina, artificial cochlea, artificial tongue — scientists have successfully documented the activity of each of the five senses. Each time we have a sensory experience, a chemical reaction is triggered in the brain, which we interpret as emotion. Thus Cochrane's next goal — which he thinks will take about five years to achieve — is the creation of microneurochemical sensors capable of measuring, tracking, and recording these reactions, eventually creating a record of a lifetime's worth of experience and feeling.

Now that would be quite a record.

Throughout the typical seventy-year human life span, the brain processes something akin to 50 terabytes of memory, a data accumulation equivalent to millions of books. In about ten years, Cochrane says, computers will be so advanced that they will be capable of reassembling millions of bits of recorded experience into a facsimile of individual perspective. Think, for instance, of

a chip that could record everything that a person ever ate—a lifetime of fast food and gourmet snacks and all the rest. Now add
to that a record of the chemical reactions set in motion by eating these meals. A computer powerful enough to synthesize this
data could end up with a pretty good idea of that person's taste.
Multiply this by all sensory experiences, and you have a machine
capable of reproducing all experience, over and over again. Certainly, it's not quite immortality, but it is, most definitely, as the
saying now goes: "an interim solution."

2.

It was University of Washington biogerontologist George M.
Martin who first proposed this interim solution, in his aptly
named 1971 *Perspectives in Biology and Medicine* paper, "Brief
proposal on immortality: an interim solution." Or, at least, this
was the first time the idea was proposed in an academic setting.

In the nonacademic world, the concept of saving self in silicon,
of storing our personalities on a computer chip—what is technically termed "mind uploading"—stretches back further. The
concept made its first minor appearance in Frederik Pohl's 1955
story "The Tunnel Under the World," then a more major debut
the following year, showing up in both Arthur C. Clarke's novel
The City and the Stars and Isaac Asimov's short story "The Last
Question." In philosopher Bertil Martensson's 1968 novel, *This Is
Reality,* the notion took a darker turn—people are uploaded into
computers as a way of combating global overpopulation—and
this darker turn was also the turning point. Afterward, mind uploading went wide, becoming a pervasive and perennial meme,
appearing in nearly one major sci-fi offering a year, with James
Cameron's *Avatar* and Christopher Nolan's *Inception* being only
two of the more recent examples.

At the same time this science fiction lineage has been unfolding, so has one of scientific fact. Recently, a bevy of new players

have gotten involved. In May 2005, for example, IBM and the Swiss Federal Institute of Technology in Lausanne announced the Blue Brain project, whose goal is to create a computer simulation of a mammalian cortical column down to the molecular level. A few years later, in July 2009, the NIH entered the game with the Human Connectome Project, the idea here being to construct a "network map" of the brain's synaptic connectivity — and a big deal in mind downloading, as researchers now believe that memories are encoded at the synaptic level and mapping those connections is the necessary first step to preserving those memories. Then there's Google's efforts to build conscious computers, real AI, and, at least in their minds, the end-all-be-all search system if there ever was one.

When will all this work be completed remains an open question. Peter Cochrane — who is arguably taking a more limited approach to the problem, believing that the combination of sensory experience and the resulting neurochemistry is enough to recreate memory — thinks the Soul Catcher will be working by 2025. In *The Singularity is Near,* futurist, author, inventor, and director of engineering at Google — and thus the man in charge of building a conscious computer — Ray Kurzweil almost agrees with this timing, arguing that 2029 is the year man and machine will truly merge.

To many, these predictions seem overly optimistic. For certain, there are long and complicated arguments about the true nature of consciousness and our ability to capture it in a computer. There are even more arguments about whether a self stored in silicon would be our actual essence or some sorely diminished version. Both are fair points. Yet it is worth noting that Moore's Law states that computers double in power every twelve months, and this is the reason that the cell phone in our pocket is a million times more powerful, and a thousand times cheaper, than a supercomputer from the 1970s. Biotechnology, meanwhile, the field where mind uploading most squarely sits, is currently progressing at five times the speed of Moore's Law. With this in mind, it is not inconceivable to say that there are people alive today who will live long enough to see their selves stored in silicon and thus, by extension, see themselves live forever.

3.

No one knows, exactly, when our omnipresent sense of self-awareness (aka consciousness) first arose, yet we do know that once it appeared, awareness of mortality was not far behind. Sure, the debate rages back and forth about whether animals are aware of death and its, shall we say, lengthy consequences — more and more evidence points to yes — but among our own species there is no discussion. We come with a use-by date and a built-in awareness of this date.

This terrible knowledge of our eventual end is the so-called human condition. And it is quite a condition. In 1974, psychologist Ernest Becker won the Pulitzer Prize for his book *The Denial of Death,* wherein he argues that everything we think of as society — from the cities we construct to the religions we believe in — is nothing more than an elaborate psychological defense mechanism against this knowledge. And a great many researchers agree. Today, our fear of death, what is technically called "death anxiety," is considered the most fundamental of human motivators, the very drive that drives us most.

So what happens when we remove that drive?

Consider how many of our wisdom traditions use the threat of the hereafter to shape behavior in the here and now. Judgment day and all that. But what happens when judgment is suspended indefinitely? What happens to our morality when we achieve immortality?

Perhaps nothing. After all, for those who toe the Judeo-Christian line, believing that there is a kernel of immortality inside our mortality — that is, a soul — this problem is already solved. It is also solved for those who take the Eastern view — that we are already immortal and must merely remember this fact. Yet, for everyone beyond the truest of true believers, the promise of immortality needs to rest on something stronger than faith. Something tangible and tactile and testable. Something like silicon.

And silicon is coming.

So, again, what happens then? We don't really know. But we do know that with biotechnology accelerating exponentially, sooner or later, we are going to find out.

4.

Immortality is one thing — playback is another. See, Cochrane's idea is not simply to capture a life. He also wants to make that life available to others. Education is the real point of the Soul Catcher. And it will be an education unlike any other.

Take the late, great physicist Richard Feynman, considered one of the most brilliant minds in recent history. According to biographers, Feynman's genius was not linear and orderly but rather radical and intuitive. In his mind, A + B did not equal C. It equaled Z. How Feynman's brain produced such leaps is unknown. But if the physicist had been hooked up to the Soul Catcher — which would record his life — and the Soul Catcher was further connected to some sort of total experience playback device, this might make his A + B = Z intuition not just knowable, but experienceable — meaning teachable.

Of course, it would have to be a really powerful playback device like, say, the virtual reality systems that are now hitting the market. Cochrane envisions a Tomorrowland version of the Oculus Rift, meaning not the VR system that Facebook just bought for a billion dollars, but the one that's going to emerge after they spend another billion developing the technology. But the larger point is that the playback device completes the picture. With a robust brain-computer interface, a chip capable of capturing experience, and a damn powerful playback device, the system is in place. Pretty soon, and for the first time in history, a living being will be able to experience the life of a dead one.

Not surprisingly, Cochrane takes a humanitarian view of all this work. He thinks in terms of preserving the wisdom of the ages, of the chance to interact with the future Einsteins, Sapphos, and Beethovens after their deaths. But he also acknowledges the risks. "I'm sure there will be problems," he says. "I may turn out to be a little like the guy who invented television. When they asked him what he thought television would be used for, the only thing he could think of was education. Now all we have to watch is crap."

How will we sort the potential Edisons from the basement tinkerers? Will we all eventually have our lives recorded for posterity? And forget about the big moral issues, what of the more prosaic possibilities? The brother who takes a peek into his sister's life and finds that she was a thief; the wife who discovers her husband's betrayal; and the thousands of other secrets we withhold from one another. They call it disruptive technology for a reason. There may be a dark side to our desire for this kind of "soul-to-soul" union. Sometimes the very things meant to bring us closer together can, in fact, drive us farther apart. Sometimes, what the future holds, well, there's really no telling.

Extreme States

THE BIOLOGY OF SPIRITUALITY

This is a story about both the science of mystical experience and a tectonic shift in our understanding of ourselves. Before this work had been done, telling a psychologist that you've had an out-of-body experience was enough to get you locked in a padded cell. Today, this phenomenon is understood as the product of regular biology.

This alone is shocking, but it also tells us something far more important: That we have misdiagnosed the upper range of human experience. Since the time of the ancient Greeks, we have believed in the hedonic principle—that humans want to avoid pain and increase pleasure. But the experiences described herein are far more potent and peculiar than pleasure. They hint at an entirely different realm of possibility, a whole new universe tucked inside ourselves, a universe we are just beginning to explore.

The other thing worth mentioning is the incredible bravery of the researchers involved. We don't think about it much today, but back when these efforts were getting going, delving into the "spiritual" was career suicide for scientists. And that's another testament to these men and women. In less than two decades, their work has been so successful that they turned the taboo into the topical and thus paved the way for all generations to follow.

1.

I was seventeen years old and terrified. The whole "let's go jump out of an airplane" concept had been dreamed up at a Friday night party, but now I was Saturday-morning sober and somehow still going skydiving. Making matters worse, this was in 1984. While tandem skydiving was invented in 1977, the concept had yet to make its way to the backwoods airfield in mid-Ohio where I wound up. So my first jump wasn't done with an instructor tethered to my back handling any difficulties we might encounter on the way down. Instead, I jumped alone, two thousand feet and falling, my only safety net an unwieldy old Army parachute dubbed a "round."

Thankfully, nobody expected me to pull my own ripcord. A static line, nothing fancier than a short rope, had been fixed between my ripcord and the floor of the airplane. If everything went according to plan, when I reached the end of my rope, the line would pull taut, and the tug would open the chute. It was just that getting to that point was a little more complicated.

As the plane zipped along at a hundred miles per hour, I had to clamber out a side door, ignore the vertiginous view, step onto a small metal rung, vise-grip the plane's wing with both hands, then lift one leg behind me, so that my body formed a giant T. From this awkward position, when my instructor gave the order, I had to jump. If things weren't bad enough already, the moment I leaped out of the plane — somehow — I also leaped out of my body.

It happened the second I let go of the wing. My body was already falling through space, but my *consciousness* was hovering about twenty feet away, just taking in the view.

During training, the instructor had explained that rounds opened, closed, then opened again in the first milliseconds of deployment. He mentioned that this happened too fast for the human eye to see and that I shouldn't worry about it. But I was a little worried. Not only was I floating outside my body, I was also watching the chute's open-close-open routine despite knowing that what I was watching was technically impossible to see.

While this was all going on, my body started to tip over, tilting into an upside-down sprawl that looked certain to produce serious backbreak when the chute finally caught. In what might best be described as a moment of extracorporeal clarity, I told myself to relax rather than risk whiplash. In the next instant, my chute caught. The jerk snapped my consciousness back into my body and everything returned to normal or as normal as can be expected under some pretty unusual circumstances.

Not for nothing, I never did get whiplash.

2.

Out-of-body journeys — like the one I had while skydiving — belong to a subset of not-so-garden-variety phenomena broadly called the *paranormal,* though the dictionary defines that word as "beyond the range of normal experience and scientific explanation," and, as it turns out, these experiences are neither. Despite serious skeptical misgiving, similar events have been reported in almost every country in the world. For centuries, mystics of all faiths, including the world's five major religions, have told tales of astral projection. Nor is this phenomenon reserved only for the spiritual. The annals of sport are packed with it as well. There are surfers who have been surprised to find themselves hovering above the waves and mountain climbers who have been surprised to find themselves suddenly possessing a bird's-eye view. Motorcyclists report floating above their bikes, watching themselves ride, and pilots report floating outside their airplanes, struggling to get back inside. In her essay "The Voice," Grace Butcher, who held the American track and field record for the 880 from 1958 to 1961, described her first major race:

> The starter gave us instructions, and the gun went off. I ran a few steps into a dimension I didn't know existed. Suddenly I seemed to be up in the rafters of the arena, looking down at my race far below. I could see the black framework of the high catwalks vaguely around me, the cables, the great spotlights, the blazing brilliance of the tiny track so far beneath me, and myself running in the midst of the others in my race that was clearly going on both with me and without me.

However, most out-of-body experiences don't take place within such extreme environments; rather, they transpire as part of normal lives. While different surveys have yielded different results, the research shows that one out of twenty of us have a story we can't quite explain, and those numbers go up substantially when you include the natural extension of the phenomenon: the near-death experience. While the rate of incidence for the near-death experience is slightly less than that for the out-of-body experience — a 1990 Gallup poll found thirty million Americans have had a near-death experience — if you combine these numbers, even the most conservative conclusion finds 10 percent of the planet's populace has shared in this adventure.

If you want to investigate this adventure, a good place to start is with Dr. Melvin Morse. In 1982, while working as a brain cancer researcher and finishing up his residency in pediatrics at Seattle's Children's Hospital, Morse made extra cash moonlighting for a helicopter-assisted EMT service. One afternoon, he got a call to fly out to Pocatello, Idaho, to perform CPR on eight-year-old Crystal Merzlock, who had spent a little too long at the bottom of a community swimming pool. When he arrived on the scene, Crystal had been without a heartbeat for nineteen minutes, her pupils already fixed and dilated, but Morse was good at his job. He got her heart restarted, climbed into the chopper, and headed home. Three days later, Crystal regained consciousness.

A few weeks passed. Morse was back at the hospital where Crystal was being treated, and they bumped into each other in the hallway. While they'd never met while Crystal was conscious, the girl still pointed at Morse, turned to her mother, and said, "That's the guy who put the tube in my nose at the swimming pool."

Morse was stunned. He didn't know what to do. "I had never heard of out-of-body experiences or near-death experiences. I stood there thinking: How was this possible? When I put that tube in her nose, she was brain-dead. How could she even have this memory?"

Morse decided to make a case study of Crystal's experience, which he published in the AMA's *American Journal of Diseases of Children.* For categorization purposes, he labeled the event a *fascinoma,* which is both medical slang for an abnormal pathology and a decent summary of the state of our knowledge at the time. But Morse was still curious. He didn't mind that his was the first published description of a near-death experience in a child; to him it seemed like an interesting first step into a longer research project.

He started by reviewing the literature, discovering that while out-of-body experiences are defined by a perceptual shift in consciousness, near-death experiences start with this shift and head on down that now-famous dark tunnel and into the light. Along the way, people report love, peace, warmth, welcome, the reassurance of dead friends, dead relatives, and the full gamut of religious figures. Occasionally, there's a whole life review, followed by a decision of the *should I stay or should I go* variety. Morse discovered that the near-death experience's classic explanation as delusion had been recently upgraded to a hallucination produced by a number of different factors, including fear, drugs, and hypoxia, a shortage of oxygen to the brain. But it was drugs that caught his eye. Morse knew that ketamine, used as an anesthetic during the Vietnam War, frequently produced out-of-body experiences. Other chemicals were also suspected triggers. Morse decided to study Halothane, another common anesthetic, believing his research might explain the frequent reports of near-death experiences trickling out of emergency rooms. "It's funny to think of it now," Morse told me, "but really I set out to do a long-term, large-scale debunking study."

Morse's 1994 research, commonly referred to as the Seattle Study, spanned a decade. He interviewed 160 children who died and were later revived while in intensive care at Seattle Children's Hospital. All of these children had been without pulse or breath for at least thirty seconds, some for as long as forty-five minutes. The average was ten to fifteen minutes. For a control group, he used hundreds of other children, also in intensive care, also on the brink of death, but whose pulse and breathing had not been interrupted for more than thirty seconds. That was the only difference. In every other category—age, sex, drugs administered, diseases suffered, and setting—the groups were the same. In setting, Morse not only included the intensive care unit itself, but also intimidating procedures such as the introduction of a breathing tube and mechanical ventilation. These are important additions, since fear has long been considered a trigger of out-of-body and near-death experiences and, as Morse later explained, might have been responsible for what happened to me while skydiving.

Morse graded his subject's experience according to a sixteen-point questionnaire designed by University of Virginia psychiatry professor Bruce Greyson that remains the benchmark for determining whether or not an anomalous experience should be considered a near-death experience. Using the Greyson Scale, Morse found that out of 26 children who died, 23 reported a classic near-death experience, while none of the other 131 children in his control group experienced anything of the kind. He later videotaped these children recalling these events and making crayon drawings of what they saw once outside their bodies. Many of these pictures included the standard fare: long tunnels, giant rainbows, dead relatives, deities of all sorts. But some also included pictures of the exact medical procedures performed, including elaborate details about doctors and nurses whose only contact with that child took place while that child was dead.

In the years since Morse did this work, other scientists have since duplicated his findings. Most recently, Pim van Lommel, a researcher at Rijnstate Hospital in Arnhem, conducted an eight-year study, involving 344 cardiac arrest patients who died and were later resuscitated. Out of that total, 282 had no memories, while 62 reported a classic near-death experience. Just as in Morse's study, van Lommel examined the patient's records for any factors traditionally used to explain near-death experiences — such as setting, drugs, or illness — and found no evidence of their influence. He too found death the only possible causal factor. He too found people with difficult-to-explain memories of events that happened while they were dead.

In other words, what Morse discovered and van Lommel verified is the same lesson I learned while skydiving: Out-of-body and near-death experiences are very real and very, very mysterious — but this latter fact, well, that's now starting to change.

3.

The first clues to the biological basis of these extreme states turned up in studies conducted in the late 1970s, when the Navy and Air Force introduced a new generation of fighter planes that generated tremendous g-forces that, in turn, were pulling too much blood out of pilots' brains and causing them to black out mid-flight. The problem, known as G-LOC, for gravity-induced loss of consciousness, was serious, and James Whinnery, a specialist in aerospace medicine, was the man charged with solving it.

Over a sixteen-year period, working with a massive centrifuge at Brooks Airforce Base in San Antonio, Texas, Whinnery spun over 500 fighter pilots into G-LOC. He wanted to figure out at what point tunnel vision occurred, how long it took pilots to lose consciousness under acceleration, how long they remained unconscious after that acceleration ceased, and how long they could be unconscious before brain damage started. Along the way, he discovered that G-LOC could be induced in 5.67 seconds, that the average blackout lasted 12 to 24 seconds, and that 40 of those pilots reported some sort of out-of-body experience while unconscious. Not knowing anything about out-of-body experiences, Whinnery called these episodes *dreamlets,* kept detailed records of their contents, and began perusing all the available literature on anomalous unconscious experiences. "I was reading about sudden-death episodes in cardiology," recounts Whinnery, "and it led me right into near-death experiences. I realized that a smaller percentage of my pilot's dreamlets, about 10 to 15 percent, were much closer in content to a classic near-death experience."

And then Whinnery went back over his data and realized there was a correlation: The longer the pilots were knocked out, the closer they were to brain death. And the closer they were to brain death, the more likely it was that an out-of-body experience would turn into a near-death experience. This was the first hard evidence for what had been long suspected: that the two states are not separate phenomena, but two points on a shared continuum.

Whinnery also found that if G-LOC was gradually induced it produced tunnel vision. "The progression went first to gray-out [loss of peripheral vision] and then to blackout," he says. "This makes a lot of sense. We know that the occipital lobe [the portion of the brain that controls vision] is a well-protected structure. Perhaps it continues to function when signals from the eyes are failing due to compromised blood flow." He also learned that upon waking up, his pilots reported a feeling of peace and serenity. In other words, Whinnery found that the pilot's transition from gray-out to blackout resembles floating peacefully down a dark tunnel, an experience much like the defining events of a classic near-death experience.

The simplest conclusion to draw from these studies is that, give or take some inexplicable memories, these phenomena are simply normal physical processes that occur during unusual circumstances. After all, once scientists set aside the traditional diagnosis of delusion as the source of these states and began looking for biological correlates, there were plenty of possibilities. Compression of the optic nerve could produce tunnel vision and neurochemicals like dopamine and endorphins could help explain the euphoria, while the neurochemical serotonin is known to produce vibrant hallucinations—but no one has directly tested these hypotheses.

What researchers have studied are the powerful after-effects of the near-death experience. Van Lommel conducted lengthy interviews and administered a battery of standard psychological tests to his cardiac arrest study group. The subset who had near-death experiences reported more self-awareness, more social awareness, and deeper religious feelings than the others. Van Lommel then repeated this process after a two-year interval and found the near-death group still had complete memories of the experience, while the other's recollections were strikingly less vivid. He also found that the near-deathers had an increased belief in an afterlife and a decreased fear of dying, while those without the experience showed the exact opposite effect. After eight years, he repeated the process and found those earlier effects significantly more pronounced. Compared to normal people, the near-death group was much more empathetic and emotionally vulnerable and often showed evidence of increased intuitive awareness. They still had little fear of death and held a strong belief in an afterlife.

In follow-up research done long after the Seattle Study, Morse too found similar long-term impacts. To confirm this finding, he also did a separate study involving elderly people who had a near-death experience in early childhood, but were now well into old age. "The results were the same for both groups," said Morse. "All of the people who had near-death experiences — no matter if it was ten years ago or fifty — were still absolutely convinced their lives had meaning and that there was a universal, unifying thread of love that provided that meaning. Matched against a control group, they scored much higher on life-attitude tests, significantly lower on fear-of-death tests, gave more money to charity, and took fewer medications. There's no other way to look at the data. These people were just transformed by the experience."

4.

In the mid-1990s, Melvin Morse's work caught the attention of Willoughby Britton, a clinical psychology doctoral candidate at the University of Arizona interested in post-traumatic stress disorder. Britton knew that most people who get up close and personal with death tend to have some form of PTSD, while people who had a near-death experience have none — meaning, people who have a near-death experience have an atypical response to life-threatening trauma.

Britton also knew about work done by legendary neurosurgeon and epilepsy expert Wilder Penfield in the 1950s. Penfield, one of the giants of modern neuroscience, discovered that stimulating the brain's right temporal lobe — located just above the ear — with a mild electric current, produced out-of-body experiences, heavenly music, vivid hallucinations, and the kind of panoramic memories associated with the life review portion of the near-death experience. This helped explain why right temporal lobe epilepsy was a condition long defined by its most prominent symptom: excessive religiosity. And given what Whinnery had found about hypoxia, it is possible that his pilot's out-of-body dreamlets were related to moments when blood flow to the right temporal lobe was seriously compromised.

Britton hypothesized that near-death experiencers might show the same altered brain firing patterns as right temporal lobe epileptics. The easiest way to determine this is to monitor brainwaves during sleep. So Britton recruited twenty-three people who had near-death experiences and twenty-three who had not. She then hooked these subjects up to an EEG and recorded everything that happened while they slept.

When the experiment was complete, Britton asked a University of Arizona epilepsy specialist to analyze the results. Three things distinguished the near-death group from normal people: They had unusual temporal lobe activity, needed far less sleep than controls, and went into REM sleep far later than controls. This was a startling finding.

When she examined the data, Britton found evidence that the near-death experience rewires the brain: 22 percent of her near-death group showed temporal lobe synchronization, the exact same kind of firing pattern associated with temporal lobe epilepsy and the mystical experiences it produces. "Twenty-two percent may not sound like a lot of anything," says Britton, "but it's actually incredibly abnormal, so much so that it's beyond the realm of chance."

More important was what the sleep data revealed. "The point at which someone goes into REM is a fantastic indicator of depressive tendencies," said Britton. "We've gotten very good at this kind of research. If you took 100 people and did a sleep study, we can look at the data and know, by looking at the time they entered REM, who's going to become depressed in the next year and who isn't."

Normal people enter REM at 90 minutes. Depressed people enter at 60 minutes or sooner. It works the same in the other direction. Happy people go into REM around 100 minutes. Britton found that the vast majority of her near-death group entered REM sleep at 110 minutes—a rating that is nearly off-the-charts for overall life-satisfaction and a neurophysiological correlate that supports the anecdotal evidence that these strange states are literally and completely transformative.

5.

Morse, van Lommel, and Britton are not the only researchers probing the transformative. In fact, just the opposite. Over the past fifteen years, as our brain-imaging technologies have continued to mature, a great number of scientists have begun studying the neurobiology of mystical experiences, be them out-of-body, near-death, or otherwise. Arguably, the most well-known of these researchers are University of Pennsylvania neuroscientist Andrew Newberg (he's now director of research at the Jefferson Myrna Brind Center of Integrative Medicine) and University of Pennsylvania neuropsychiatrist Eugene d'Aquili (now deceased).

In the late 1990s, Newberg and d'Aquili began trying to decode "cosmic unity," which is the sensation of becoming "one with everything" and the most celebrated of all mystical experiences. Unity shows up in nearly all of the world's wisdom traditions. In Tibetan Buddhism, for example, meditating monks reach a state of "absolute unitary being"—that is, a state where they feel one with the universe. In Catholicism, for nuns lost in ecstatic prayer, it's *unia mystica,* or oneness with God's love. So common, in fact, is this unitive experience that author Aldous Huxley dubbed it the "perennial philosophy," meaning it is one of the foundational cornerstones for all of our spiritual traditions.

To investigate this cornerstone, Newberg and d'Aquili put meditating Tibetan monks and praying Franciscan nuns into a single positron emission computed topography (SPECT) scanner and took pictures of their brains at the exact moments their subjects reported experiencing unity. It was the very first time anyone had tried to use next-generation brain imaging technology to capture the spiritual. It wouldn't be the last.

What the duo discovered was a marked decrease in activity in the right parietal lobe — which is a critical part of the brain's navigation system. The right parietal lobe is an area that helps the body move through space by helping us judge angles, curves, and distances. But to make these judgments, the right temporal lobe must also draw a boundary around "the self" — a border that allows us to know where our body ends and the rest of the world begins. (It is also worth pointing out that this border is flexible, which is why blind people claim to "feel" the sidewalk through the tips of their canes and tennis players "feel" the racket as an extension of their arm.)

The SPECT scans showed that intense concentration temporarily shuts down the information processing capabilities of the right parietal lobe. And to profound effect. Newberg explains: "Once we can no longer draw a line and say this is where the self ends and this is where the rest of the world begins, the brain concludes — it has to conclude — that at this particular moment you are one with everything."

This discovery marked a sea change. Before Newberg came along, telling a doctor that you felt one with everything was a pretty good way to end up in a locked psych ward. Afterward, it was the by-product of measurable biology. And that was only their first discovery.

The SPECT scans also showed that when the parietal lobes go quiet, portions of the right temporal lobe — the same portions that Wilder Penfield showed produced feelings of excessive religiosity, out-of-body experiences, and vivid hallucinations — become more active. They also found that activities often found in religious rituals — like rhythmic drumming and repetitive chanting — produce this same effect.

And all of this folds back on the work done by Morse, Britton, and van Lommel, helping explain some of the more puzzling out-of-body reports, like those of airplane pilots suddenly floating outside their planes. Those pilots were intensely focused on their instrumentation, much in the way that meditating monks are focused on mantras. Meanwhile, the sound of the engine spinning produces a repetitive, rhythmic drone, much like tribal drumming. If conditions were right, said Newberg, these two things should be enough to produce the exact kind of temporal lobe activity needed to trigger an out-of-body experience.

Another researcher probing this question is Michael Persinger, a neuroscientist with Laurentian University in Ontario, Canada. Using a specially designed helmet that produces weak, directed magnetic fields, Persinger applied these fields to the brains of over 900 volunteers, mostly college students. When he lit up their temporal lobes, these volunteers experienced the same sort of mystical phenomena common to right-temporal lobe epileptics, meditators, and — at least in my case — skydivers.

As a result of all this work, most scientists now feel that our brains are hardwired for mystical experience. This is not — as these researchers are quick to point out — proof for or against the existence of God. Instead, it's proof that these experiences are as real as any other, proof that there's biology beneath our spirituality.

Of course, as our imaging and measurement technologies continue to improve, we're going to get a much clearer picture of this biology. By itself, this is profound in its ramifications. Out-of-body experiences, near-death experiences, cosmic unity — these are all core mystical experiences at the heart of the world's major religious traditions; they are the very phenomena upon which all of our spirituality rests. Yet it's where this work leads that is truly startling.

Persinger's helmet proves that not only are these mystical experiences decodable — they're reproducible. Sure, today such phenomena are only accessible in the lab, but science always moves from ivory-tower research to commercial application. This means, at some point in the not-too-distant future, there are going to be consumer devices available — brain stimulators or immersive virtual reality googles or some combination of the two—that can provide us with direct access to the preternatural. So forget about the need to join a monastery or volunteer for a science experiment or, for that matter, go skydiving. Soon the experience of the numinous will be available via video game.

Amen.

Evolution's Next Stage

THE FUTURE OF EVOLUTION

There's a pretty good chance you know something about evolution. More importantly, there's a pretty good chance that the thing you know is how slowly it proceeds. It doesn't matter if you're talking about the "gradualism" of Charles Darwin or the "punctuated equilibrium" of Stephen Jay Gould (more on this in a moment), the point is the same: Evolution takes eons.

But not anymore. The changes we're talking about in this story aren't unfolding in millions of years; they're unfolding in a handful of decades. Moreover, these changes are far more radical than anything that came before. And none of these trends appear to be slowing down. In fact, just the opposite. Which means, as many are starting to suspect, the era of *Homo sapiens* is coming to a close. We have massively accelerated evolution and the results are soon to fracture our species. In short, we are no longer human beings, we are now human becomings—and that, my friends, is a whole new kettle of fish.

1.

In 1958, Harvard economists Alfred Conrad and John Meyer published a book about the financial profitability of slavery — which was too much for a University of Chicago economist named Robert Fogel to abide. While Fogel was white, his wife was African American. Very African American. "When I was teaching at Harvard," recounts Fogel, "she hung a sign outside the door to our house. It read: 'Don't be upset because you're not black like me — we're not all born lucky.'"

Not surprisingly, Fogel decided to prove Conrad and Meyer wrong.

He spent almost a decade on the problem. In his earlier work, Fogel had helped pioneer the field of cliometrics, sometimes called economic history, which is the application of rigorous statistical analysis to the study of history (this development earned him a Nobel Prize in 1993). Next, working alongside University of Rochester economist Stanley Engerman, Fogel began applying these methods to the study of slavery. As this enterprise required an understanding of caloric input and energy output, questions like *How much food did the average person consume in the Nineteenth century? How much work could be produced from that food?* and *How long did that person live?* became critically important. These questions led him deeper into the relationship between economics, physiology, and longevity, which is when the theory of evolution came into the picture.

To examine these relationships, Fogel needed data and metrics. For data, he used an NIH-maintained database of American Civil War veteran records, a physiological treasure trove containing things like height and weight at time of conscription, daily roll calls of the sick and injured, periodic postwar checkups, census data, and, often, death certificates. For metrics, he chose height and body mass, because of a steadily growing consensus among scientists that these factors were phenomenal predictors of mortality and morbidity. "Height," says UCLA economist Dora Costa, who cowrote papers on these ideas with Fogel, "turns out to be a fantastic health indicator. It's net for nutrition, infectious disease, sanitation, and demands placed on the body." (As a result, the United Nations now uses height as a way to monitor nutrition in developing countries.)

What all this information provided was a population-eye view of life in the nineteenth century, which is what Fogel needed to understand broad trends and reach startling conclusions. The first of those conclusions, which he and Engerman detailed in their now famous *Time on the Cross: An Economic Analysis of American Negro Slavery*, was that Conrad and Meyer were correct: slavery, while still morally repugnant, was neither as inefficient nor as unprofitable as most historians assumed.

"As it turns out," recounts Fogel, "most slaves, especially those on smaller plantations, were fed better and lived in better conditions than free men in the North. This meant they lived longer, healthier lives and thus produced more work. Certainly, it's an odious conclusion, but it's right there in the data."

And then things got even stranger.

Around 1988, Fogel began to notice another trend in the data: Over the past three hundred years, but predominantly in the past century, Americans have been growing taller. They have also been getting thicker, living longer, and growing richer. In 1850, for example, the average American male was 5′7″ and 146 lbs. By 1980, those numbers had jumped to 5′10″ and 174 lbs. And, as it turned out, it wasn't just Americans. Working with a team of economists, Fogel expanded this inquiry internationally, and the trends turned out to be global. "Over the past 300 years," he says, "humans have increased their average body size by over 50 percent, average longevity by more than 100 percent, and greatly improved the robustness and capacity of vital organ systems."

From an evolutionary perspective, three hundred years is an eye-blink. A sneeze. Not nearly enough time for these sorts of radical improvements. In fact, according to Darwin's theory of evolution, none of these developments should even be possible.

2.

To understand what should be possible, it helps to understand a little more about Darwin's theory. For starters, evolution is a search engine, but not a very good one. We're not talking Google. We might be talking Google drunk, blindfolded, on crutches, and with a frontal lobotomy. This is why the Nobel laureate Francis Jacob described evolution as a tinkerer, not an engineer. Engineers know where they're going — they have a plan, an aim, an end result in mind. Tinkerers are just fastening parts together, glomming this bit on to that in an exploration of functionality that is both goalless and relentless.

The realization that evolution's search engine proceeds blindly, thus gradually, came from Darwin. Before he came along, the assumption was that the process proceeded by huge leaps — which was the only way anyone could explain the sudden appearance of new species. Darwin saw things differently. He had been thinking long and hard about scarcity. He realized that because resources are often scarce, organisms are always in competition with one another. In this endless battle, those individuals who happen to possess some slight innate advantage will flourish, and pass along that advantage to their descendants. By this method, new species could be created — one imperfect change at a time. But this certainly wasn't going to happen quickly.

In fact, historically, massive geological shifts — like a meteor impact or an ice age — turn out to be the only way to speed up the process. What these shifts provide is a wedge that opens up novel ecological niches, new possibilities for the search engine of evolution to explore. This fits-and-starts hypothesis—what in 1972 evolutionary theorists Stephen Jay Gould and Niles Eldredge dubbed "punctuated equilibrium"—helps explain the sudden appearance of new species in the fossil record. But really, there's nothing all that sudden about it—according to Gould, those periods of punctuation span roughly 50,000 to 100,000 years.

The point is this: Natural selection is a plodder's game. It dithers. It wanders. Mildly beneficial mutations do not become radical steps forward overnight. Sure, one individual might be significantly taller or smarter or more long-lived than his peers, but no matter how beneficial the change, extremely long stretches of time are required for it to spread across an entire population. Those are the rules—or, at least until Robert Fogel came along—those were supposed to be the rules.

3.

Fogel spent the next two decades trying to figure out why humans were suddenly breaking those rules. He came to believe a steady stream of technological improvement—advances in food production, distribution, sanitation, public health, and medicine—facilitated our rapidly advancing evolutionary processes. "In the past hundred years," says Fogel, "humans have gained an unprecedented degree of control over their environment, a degree of control so great that it sets them apart not only from all other species, but from all previous generations of Homo sapiens."

Fogel's core idea, which he calls *techno-physio evolution* and explained most fully in his 2011 book *The Changing Body* (cowritten with Roderick Floud, Bernard Harris, and Sok Chul Hong), is fairly straightforward: "The health and nutrition of one generation contributes, through mothers and through infant and childhood experience, to the strength, health, and longevity of the next generation; at the same time, increased health and longevity enable the members of that next generation to work harder and longer and to create resources which can then, in their turn, be used to assist the next, and succeeding, generations to prosper."

These notions are not entirely new. Economists have known for almost a hundred years of a correlation between height, income, and longevity. What had not been properly explained was mechanism, or how this process worked. The idea that humans can take control of evolution's trajectory has been around since the 1970s, when polio vaccine discoverer Jonas Salk argued that humanity had entered a new era, which he dubbed "meta-biological evolution," where we have the potential to control and direct evolution (our own and that of other species). Moreover, the now well-established field of epigenetics has shown us that a myriad of factors beyond alterations in DNA can produce heritable change in an organism.

Fogel, though, goes farther by going faster. "It's a 'whole that is much greater than the sum of its parts' argument," he explains. "We're talking about an incredible synergy between technology and biology, about very simple improvements — pasteurization, a general reduction of pollutants, cleaning up our water supply — producing heritable effects across populations faster than ever before. Think about this: humans are a 200,000-year-old species. When we first emerged, our life span was twenty years. By the turn of the twentieth century, it had become forty-four years. We advanced by twenty-four years over the course of 200,000 years. But today, it's eighty years. These simple improvements doubled our longevity in a century."

University of Munich economist John Komlos explains further: "Evolution designed us to be quite plastic: Our size expands in good times and contracts in bad. As opposed to being hard-wired and unable to adapt to environmental conditions, this [flexibility] provided an evolutionary advantage. The gain in body mass that Fogel observed began in the 1920s — when people started working more sedentary jobs, driving automobiles, and listening to the radio — then started skyrocketing in the 1950s — with the introduction of television and fast food — and today has become an obesity epidemic. All in eighty years. We didn't know this much change was possible this quickly; we didn't know that extrinsic factors could make this kind of difference. Techno-physio evolution shows that economics has an impact at the cellular level — that it goes bone deep."

4.

Since Fogel first began this work, his ideas haven't stayed balkanized in economics. Everyone from cultural anthropologists to population geneticists have begun investigating the phenomenon. In a summary article published in February of 2010 in *Nature Review Genetics,* an international team of biologists argue that the interplay between genes and culture (with culture including things like economics and technology) has profoundly shaped evolution, especially when it comes to the speed of the process. "Gene-culture dynamics are typically faster, stronger, and operate over a broader range of conditions than conventional evolutionary dynamics," writes lead author Kevin Leland, a biologist from the University of St. Andrews in Scotland, "leading some practitioners to argue that gene-culture co-evolution [sometimes called dual inheritance theory] could be the dominant mode of human evolution."

In a very real sense, the process Leland calls gene-culture evolution and Fogel dubbed techno-physio evolution are just examples of punctuated equilibrium by a different name, with culture rather than catastrophe providing the new niches. The main difference is in frequency. Naturally occurring geologic events are historically rare occurrences. Technological progress, meanwhile, is ever-accelerating.

This is no small detail. In recent years, researchers have found that the same exponential growth rates underpinning computing (Moore's Law, for example) show up in all information-based technologies. Thus fields with a huge potential to drive techno-physio evolution — artificial intelligence, nanotechnology, biology, robotics, networks, sensors, etc. — are now advancing along exponential growth curves. Consider genomic sequencing, long touted as the "essential tool" needed to move medicine from standardized and reactive to personalized and preventative. In 1990, when the Human Genome Project was first announced, the cost of this tool was budgeted at $3 billion — about as far from personalized medicine as one can get. But by 2001, costs were down to $300 million. By 2010, they were below $5,000. In 2012, the $1,000 barrier had fallen. Within ten years, at the current rate of decline, a fully sequenced human genome will price out at less than $10. If standardized and reactive medicine managed to double human life span in a century, just imagine how far personalized and preventative medicine might extend that total.

Fogel's work documents how an increase in control over our external environment impacts our biology. But the fields that are now growing exponentially are cutting out the middleman, allowing us to take direct control over our internal environment. "Exponentially growing technology changes the evolutionary discussion," says molecular geneticist and Autodesk distinguished researcher Andrew Hessel, "because, if you follow those patterns out, you very quickly see that this is the century we take control over our genome. Just look at the technologies surrounding reproduction: fetal testing, genetic screening, pregnancy monitoring, genetic counseling. When I was a child, Down syndrome was a real problem. Today, roughly 90 percent of all fetuses with Down syndrome are aborted. Play these patterns forward and we aren't long from the day when we're engineering our children: choosing skin color, eye color, personality traits. How long after that until parents are saying: 'I bought you the best brain money can buy — now why don't you use it?'"

5.

Of course, this massive acceleration of natural selection raises additional questions — like how much does it take to create an entirely new species? Dartmouth neuroscientist Richard Granger, who works on brain evolution, doesn't think it will take much.

"Think about dogs," he says. "Used to be they all looked like wolves. Now they don't. In just a few thousand years of messing around with their genes, humans have created canine breeds that are completely physically incompatible — a Great Dane and a Chihuahua could not produce offspring without help. How much longer until they're genomically incompatible? There's nothing surprising here. When you start messing around with genes you get radiation [rapid, radical change]: It's true in dogs, and it's true in humans."

Think of it like this: When a subset of a population is isolated from their ancestry, as this subset rushes to fill new — competitor-free — niches, the result is rapid evolutionary change, or allopatric speciation. But the exponential changes occurring today are examples of what could be called *technopatric* speciation, a process that occurs when a species is technologically isolated from their ancestry. Either way, the results are the same: rapid radiation.

Right now, humans are the only hominid species on earth, but this wasn't always the case and, as these techno-physio trends continue to unfold, it seems unlikely to remain the case. Juan Enríquez, founding director of the Life Sciences Project at Harvard Business School, believes we've already fractured our species. "We're now no more than a generation or two away from the emergence of an entirely new kind of hominid," he says. "*Homo evolutus:* a hominid that takes direct and deliberate control over their own evolution and the evolution of other species."

The standard science fiction version of what happens after we take control of our evolution usually runs along eugenic lines — leading toward efforts to build a master race. But the situation is nowhere near that straightforward. Seemingly unambiguous genetic goals — like trying to make people more intelligent — not only involve millions of genes, raising the specter of easy error, but might involve conditional relationships. For instance, our intelligence might be tied to memory in ways we can't yet decode, so trying to improve one's ability might inadvertently impede the other.

Moreover, without some form of top-down control, there's little proof that human desires will be uniform enough to produce a master race. "Sure," says Hessel, "we may begin optimizing ourselves and engineering our children, but it's unlikely this will occur in a uniform way. We're still human. So we're going to engineer our children based on our egos, our creativity, our whims — this pretty much guarantees all sorts of wild varieties. It's highly improbable that all of these varieties will be able to interbreed successfully, not without the use of technology. That's when we really splinter the species; that's why *Homo evolutus* could easily end up the parent to a Cambrian explosion of subspecies — a radical explosion of entirely new breeds of humans."

Science is not always factually accurate, but it's usually directionally accurate. It is the result of torturous investigation, vociferous argument, and hard-won consensus. One of the best tests of veracity is when conclusions reached in multiple fields begin to strongly overlap. And that's exactly what's happening here. Fogel got the process started, but today, researchers from nearly a dozen different arenas have all lit onto the same conclusions. We have stepped on the gas of natural selection, turbo-boosted evolution, and are now speeding toward the end of an era — the era of *Homo sapiens*, which is, of course, the only era we have ever known.

In short, we started out *us*, but we're becoming *them*.

Vision Quest

THE WORLD'S FIRST ARTIFICIAL VISION IMPLANT

I spent over a year exploring the cutting edge of artificial vision research for this story. I had all my facts. I was set to start writing. Then my editor received a postcard in the mail from a mostly unknown and somewhat controversial vision researcher. Essentially, all it said was: "Hello, I'm William Dobelle, I've built an artificial vision brain implant. It's about to be installed in a human being, come check it out."

Neither of us knew what to think. Certainly, I didn't believe such a technology was possible. After a year spent delving into the field, no one I had met along the way was even close to a workable device, forget about one that could be installed in humans. But due diligence is due diligence, so I got on a plane.

Staggering doesn't come close to describing what I found when I landed. Day one: I met a blind man. Day three: He could see well enough to drive a car around a crowded parking lot.

According to the World Health Organization, there are 285 million visually impaired people on the planet—most of whom can be helped by this kind of innovation. But the crazier part is what comes next. Dobelle built an implant that restores normal vision, but devices capable of

augmented sight—eagle eyes or eyes that see colors outside of our visual spectrum or eyes that have microscopic
abilities—are not far behind. We are arguably less than a
decade away from talents lifted straight from the pages of
comic books. No, staggering doesn't even come close.

1.

I'm sitting across from a blind man — call him Patient Alpha — at a long table in a windowless conference room in New York. On one end of the table there's an old television and a VCR. On the other end are a couple of laptops. They're connected by wires to a pair of homemade signal processors housed in unadorned gunmetal gray boxes, each no bigger than a loaf of bread. In the corner stands a plastic ficus tree, and beyond that, against the far wall, a crowded bookshelf. Otherwise, the walls are white and bare. And when the world's first bionic eye is turned on, this is what Patient Alpha will see.

Our guinea pig is thirty-nine, strong and tall, with an angular jaw, large ears, and a rugged face. He looks hale, hearty, and healthy — except for the wires. They run from the laptops into the signal processors, then out again and across the table and up into the air, flanking his face like curtains before disappearing into holes drilled through his skull. Since his hair is dark and the wires are black, it's hard to see the actual points of entry. From a distance the wires look like long ponytails.

"Come on," says William Dobelle. "Take a good look."

From a few steps closer, I see that the wires plug into Patient Alpha's head like a pair of headphones plug into a stereo. The actual connection is metallic and circular, like a common washer. So seamless is the integration that the skin appears to simply stop being skin and start being steel.

"It's called a percutaneous pedestal," Dobelle tells me.

All I can do is stare. This man has computer jacks sunk into both sides of his skull.

On the far side of the pedestal, buried beneath hair and skin, is the wetware: a pair of brain implants. Each one is the size of a fat quarter, a platinum electrode array encased in biocompatible plastic.

Dobelle has designed a three-part system: a miniature video camera, a signal processor, and the brain implants. The camera, mounted on a pair of eyeglasses, captures the scene in front of the wearer. The processor translates the image into a series of signals that the brain can understand, then sends the information to the implant. The picture is fed into the brain, and, if everything goes according to plan, the brain will "see" the image.

But I'm getting ahead of myself. The camera's not here yet. Right now the laptops are taking its place. Two computer techs are using them to calibrate the implants.

One of the techs punches a button, and a millisecond later the patient rotates his head, right to left, as if surveying a crowded room.

"What do you see?" asks Dobelle.

"A medium-size phosphene, about five inches from my face," responds the patient.

"How about now?"

"That one's too bright."

"OK," says Dobelle. "We won't use that one again."

This goes on all morning, and it's nothing new. For almost fifty years, scientists have known that electrical stimulation of the visual cortex causes blind subjects to perceive small points of light known as phosphenes. The tests they're running aim to determine the "map" of the patient's phosphenes. When electrical current zaps into the brain, the lights don't appear only in one spot. They are spread out across space, in what artificial vision researchers call the "starry-night effect."

Dobelle is marshaling these dots like pixels on a screen. "We're building the patient's map, layer by layer," he explains. "The first layer was individual phosphenes. The next layer is multiples. We need to know where his phosphenes appear in relation to each other so a video feed can be translated in a way that makes sense to his mind."

Some phosphenes look like pinpricks or frozen raindrops. Others appear as odd shapes: floating bananas, fat pears, lightning squiggles. Of course, the use of the word *appear* is misleading, since the phosphenes appear only in the patient's mind. To the sighted, they are completely invisible.

Dobelle sits in a wheelchair beside the patient. His left leg was amputated a year ago after an ulcerated infection in his big toe spread out of control. Because being in a wheelchair makes it hard to dig into his pants pockets, he favors T-shirts — "the good kind" — with a chest pocket to carry his keys, a couple of pens, his wallet. His shirt is so weighed down that it sags from his neck, drooping cleavage-low. He has a patchy, unkempt gray beard. His forehead is high and wrinkled, and his glasses are thick and wide.

"Are we ready for multiple phosphenes?" asks one of the techs.

Dobelle nods his head.

So smoothly has the morning been going that while we're talking, the techs allow the patient to take control of the keyboard and begin stimulating his own brain. This isn't standard operating procedure, but with the excitement, the techs don't stop him and the doctor doesn't notice.

Suddenly, the color drains from the patient's face. His hand drops the keys. His fingers crimp and gnarl, turning the hand into a disfigured claw. The claw, as if tethered to balloons, rises slowly upward. His arm follows and suddenly whips backward, torso turning with it, snapping his spine into a terrible arch. Then his whole body wrenches like a mishandled marionette — shoulders tilting, neck craning, legs twittering. Within seconds his lips have turned blue and his deadened eyes roll back, revealing bone-white pupils, lids snapping up and down like hydraulic window shades. There's another warping convulsion, and spittle sails from his mouth. Since the doctor's in a wheelchair and the techs seem hypnotized, I rush over and grab him.

"Call 911!" one of the computer techs shouts.

But the doctor yells back: "No!"

"Lie him down," cries the other. "Get him some water!"

"No!"

My arms are under his, trying to steady the weight. His head snaps toward mine, and I take it on the chin with the force of a solid right cross. We're now close enough that I can count the wires going into his head. I can see a faint scar where a surgeon's saw cut a hole in his skull and removed a chunk of it like a plug from a drain. Finally, the techs move to action. They're up and struggling to unhook the patient from the seeing machine — but really, what can they do? It's in his brain. I'm pretty sure he's going to die in my arms.

2.

William Dobelle likes a good Wright Brothers story. Like how the first plane the Wright brothers built didn't have a steering mechanism, that it merely went up and down and straight. Or if you look at a plane these days you won't see their names on the side. Instead there's Boeing or Airbus, but even so, you know these makers are merely historical recipients of the Wright stuff, just as you know that your voting privileges are somehow owed to Thomas Jefferson. Of all the Wright Brothers stories, Dobelle likes the one about Lieutenant Tom Selfridge the best.

The Wright Brothers ran low on money. They built their airplane, but they needed more cash for further experimentation. A lieutenant from the US Army showed up for a demonstration, and after watching Orville pilot around for a little while he said, "That's great, now take me for a ride." So Orville strapped Selfridge into the passenger seat, took off, and promptly crashed. Crashed! The plane was wrecked, Orville was in the hospital for months, and Selfridge was killed — yet the brothers still managed to land a contract for a military flier.

The doctor treats this story like a talisman. Its moral — with great risk comes great reward—has been an inspiration for him during the past thirty years, since 1968, when he began working on an artificial vision system to restore sight to the blind. The moral was there in the 1970s, when he went under the hot knife of surgery and had his own eye slit open to test the feasibility of a retinal implant. It was there when he looked over the work that had been done on the visual cortex and realized the only way to create a visual neuroprosthesis was to slice through the skull and attach an implant to the human brain. It was there two years ago, when he decided to skirt the Food and Drug Administration by sending his patients to a surgeon in Lisbon, Portugal, because he knew there was little chance the US government was ever going to give him permission to experiment on humans in America.

There was one lab rat, however. In 1978, shortly before the FDA passed the last in a series of medical device amendments that would outlaw testing a visual neuroprosthesis on a human, Dobelle installed his prototype into the head of a genial, big-bellied, blind Irishman from Brooklyn named Jerry.

"When my grandkids meet a blind guy with a brain implant," says Jerry, explaining his participation in Dobelle's experiments, "I wanted them to be able to say, 'Let me tell you about my grandfather.'"

For years the prototype sat in Jerry's occipital lobe, largely unused. Back then Dobelle's concerns were infection and biocompatibility. When neither turned out to be a problem, he edged the research forward. Over the years, Jerry's visual field was mapped, but his implant never produced true "functional mobility."

Functional mobility is a bit of jargon defined as the ability to cross streets, take subways, and navigate buildings without aid of cane or dog. For the past forty years this has been the goal of artificial vision research. But Jerry's not there, instead he's caught halfway between sight and shadow.

When hooked up to a video camera, Jerry sees only shades of gray in a limited field of vision. He also sees at a very slow rate. It helps to think of film. Normal film whirls by at twenty-four frames per second — but Jerry sees at merely a fifth of that speed. The effect, Dobelle tells me, is a bit like looking at snapshots in a photo album through holes punched in a note card.

Patient Alpha, on the other hand, has the full upgrade: the Dobelle Institute Artificial Vision System for the Blind. Because the system has yet to be patented, the doctor is cagey about specifics. He won't say how many electrodes are inside the patient's head, though by my count the number is around 100. Other changes have been made as well. Instead of Jerry's one implant, the patient has two, one in each side of his head. Materials as well have been updated, and the power pack and signal processor made portable. But the biggest difference is that it took Dobelle twenty years to work Jerry up to any sort of vision. Patient Alpha, meanwhile, got out of surgery a month ago.

3.

William Dobelle was born in 1941 in Pittsfield, Massachusetts, the son of an orthopedic surgeon. Ask Dobelle how he got into this game and he'll say, "I've always done artificial organs; I've spent my whole life in the spare parts business. I just inherited it from my father. By age eight, I was doing real research."

Which sounds like hooey, until you check the records. He applied for his first patent, on an artificial hip improvement, at age thirteen. He was in college at fourteen and hooked on the challenge of artificial vision by eighteen. It was also at eighteen that he dropped out of Vanderbilt University to pursue independent research on visual physiology, supporting himself as a Porsche mechanic.

In 1960 he returned to school, earning an MS in biophysics from Johns Hopkins. This time he covered costs by selling scientific ephemera: iguana gall bladders and whale hearts that he collected in South America. He finished his PhD in physiology from the University of Utah and became the director of artificial organs at Columbia Presbyterian Medical Center. By 1984, he had a lab of his own.

Located in Hauppauge, New York, near the center of Long Island, Dobelle's lab sits inside one of the largest industrial parks in America. All around are the offices of high-tech whatevers — Aerostar, Gemini, Forest Labs, Nextech, Bystronic — housed in grim, squat warehouses accented only by trim lawns and odd awnings. Most of the buildings have them, these decorous afterthoughts: green shingles attached to aluminum siding, Spanish tile against cold stone. "We don't have an awning," notes Dobelle, proud of his austerity.

Walk inside and you'll see a carpet so thin it could be cement. The furniture in the front offices looks anonymous, wood-veneered, bought by the pound. Behind the offices is a larger workshop — the home to the breadwinners of the operation.

During his tenure as a spare parts man, Dobelle built hiccup suppressors and erection stimulators and pain inhibitors. Right now, there are 15,000 people running around the world with his inventory inside their bodies. The workshop is currently used to build lung, spinal cord, and deep-brain stimulators. Since he's never wanted to be beholden to anyone and thus never accepted venture capital, these devices pay the rent so Dobelle can pursue his real goal: artificial sight.

"It doesn't come cheap," says Dobelle, rolling himself into the workshop so I can get a look. We pass a machine shop — drill presses, lathes, saws of all varieties, tools hung on pegs and others left out among the dust and metal filings — then out onto an assembly room floor. In the center, separated from the rest by long sheets of heavy plastic, there's a clean room for delicate procedures. And against a far wall stands an ancient computer, weighing two tons, complete with a punch-paper tape input and a Teletype output. It measures ten feet wide and seven feet tall.

"What is that for?" I ask.

"That was the first artificial vision system, the one I built for Jerry. It's my past. Thirty-four years of work and $25 million."

4.

The cost has come down quite a bit. According to a printout Dobelle hands me, the price tag for curing blindness is now around
$115,000:

> **Visual Prosthesis System:** $100,000
>
> 1 miniature camera mounted on eyeglasses
> 1 frame grabber
> 1 microcomputer
> 1 stimulus generation module
> 2 implanted electrode arrays with percutaneous pedestals
> 3 sets of rechargeable batteries and 1 charger (customer is
>   responsible for replacement batteries as needed)
> 5-year full warranty (not including travel or freight)
> 5 years of annual follow-up examinations in Portugal (not
>   including travel), unlimited telephone consultation
>
> **Evaluation of patient:** $2,000 psychiatric evaluation/all
>   other testing
> **Hospital expenses:** $10,000
> **Miscellaneous expenses:** $5,000 airfare to Lisbon, hotel
>   and food for one week (2 people), miscellaneous (such
>   as taxis)

The first person ever to receive this bill was Patient Alpha. His
given name is Jens — pronounced *Yens*. Twenty-two years ago, at
age seventeen, while nailing down railroad ties, an errant splinter
took Jens's left eye. Then, three years later, this time fixing a snowmobile, a shiv of clutch metal broke free and took out his right.

Jens lives in rural Canada, where the winters are brutal. He
makes his living by selling firewood. Working alone, he splits
logs with the largest chain saw currently available on the market.
During the high season, he'll manhandle 12,000 pounds of wood

in a day. He helped his wife deliver six of his eight children at home, without a physician or midwife. Jens dismisses the whole hospital birthing process as rapacious big business.

Starting from scratch and without the aid of sight, Jens designed and built a solar-and wind-powered house and pulled his family off the grid. In his spare hours, he programs computers, tunes pianos, and gives the occasional concert. For a blind man to give a classical recital requires memorizing whole scores — a process that can take nearly five years. To cover his surgery, Jens gave quite a few recitals.

5.

Back in the lab, I'm still supporting Jens's weight. He's panting and jerking. Every pore on his body leaks sweat. His neck has gotten too slippery to hold, so I've jammed my right hand into his armpit. I can feel the throb of his axillary artery. His heart is beating. Thankfully, he's still alive.

Over the next five minutes, the gasping subsides. Respiration returns to normal. The full-body twitch stills to the occasional flutter. Soon the grim rigor of his hand relaxes, his fingers merely stretching now, as if reaching for the far notes on his piano.

Dobelle's glaring at the techs.

"What happened?" he demands.

"He was overstimulated."

"Yeah, I know that."

Beside him, Jens's head bobs once and then again. Slowly, motor control returns. He stretches his arms as if waking from a long sleep.

"What happened?" echoes Jens, his voice a low, percolating gurgle.

"You had a seizure," says Dobelle.

"I wha . . ."

"A seizure. Jerry never had one, but it was always a possibility."

"I wha . . ."

"You'll be fine," says Dobelle.

"For what I paid . . ."

"What?"

"For what I paid, I better be."

"OK," says Dobelle. "I think we're done for today."

6.

Later that night, Dobelle calls to explain. His voice is balmy, pre-ternaturally pacific. "My surgeon is the world's foremost expert on epilepsy. When someone's having a seizure, you don't lie them down or give them water — they could choke. I knew he would be OK."

And the next morning, when I walk into the lab, Jens is OK. He's back at the table, amid another round of testing. He doesn't remember much of the seizure, but he remembers seeing the phosphenes.

"It was wonderful," says Jens. "It is wonderful. After eighteen years in a dark jail, I finally got to look out the door into the sunlight."

"Are you ready for a little more?" asks Dobelle. In his hand is a pair of oversize tortoiseshell glasses. The left lens is dark, and affixed to the right is a miniature video camera: black, plastic, and less than 1-inch square. The wires that yesterday ran from the laptops are now plugged into the camera. It's time to see if Jens can see.

"Are you ready?" repeats Dobelle.

"I've been ready for twenty years."

Jens slides the glasses onto his face, and the techs power up the system. I am sitting across the table from him. As it turns out, when the world's first bionic eye is turned on, Jens sees me.

"Wow!" says Jens.

"Wow what?" I ask.

"I'm really using the part of my brain that's been doing dick-all for two decades."

"And that's only one implant," says Dobelle. "We still have to integrate the other side, and we haven't installed the edge-recognition software yet. The image is going to get better and better."

Jens turns away, and we clear all objects off the conference table. Dobelle picks up a telephone and puts it down on the far corner. Jens turns back around. The camera is sending data down the pipe and to the implant in his brain at one frame per second. So when he first scans the table his head swivels, robotic, and turtle-slow. It takes him nearly two minutes to find the phone — but he finds the phone. Then we do it again. Fifteen minutes later, Jens can pick up the receiver in less than thirty seconds. Within a half hour, it takes him less than ten.

They gradually work the frame speed up until there's nothing left to do but strap the signal processor and power pack to Jens's hips, like guns in their holsters. Then Jens heads out back, where he climbs inside a convertible Mustang. The top is down. The wind is in his hair. He fires up the ignition. Dobelle doesn't let him tour the freeways, but he has his way with the parking lot.

"The next version," Dobelle tells me, "may have enough resolution to use while driving in traffic." In fact, since this is only a simple camera we're talking about, one could imagine the addition of any number of superhuman optical features: night vision, X-ray vision, microscopic focus, long-range zoom. Forget the camera, even; there's no reason you couldn't jack directly into the Net. In the future, the disabled may prove more abled; we may all want their prostheses.

7.

Public discussion of electricity's effects on vision dates to 1751, when it was addressed by Benjamin Franklin following his celebrated kite-and-key experiment. Soon researchers were discussing the possibility of treating blindness through electrical stimulation, but despite some early advocates the idea did not catch on.

This is perhaps not surprising. The human eye occupies a weird place in history. For more than a century, creationists, staring down Darwin's evolutionary barrel, claimed sight as proof positive of God's existence. The eye was too complicated for anything as seemingly accidental as natural selection. By extension, curing blindness was the sole province of faith healers. "It used to be a religious miracle," says Tom Hoglund of the Foundation Fighting Blindness, "but now it's a scientific miracle."

On June 13 Dobelle addressed the annual meeting of the American Society of Artificial Internal Organs in New York. He told the stunned, packed house about eight patients of his who'd had the surgery, with Jens the first to have his implant turned on. Then he showed a tape of Jens driving. "I got the most applause," Dobelle told me, "but I don't think anyone really knew what they were seeing."

In fact, to most of the artificial vision community, Dobelle's breakthrough came out of the blue. For years he had been merely a footnote, known mainly for his early work in phosphene stimulation. People had heard of Jerry, but because the testing was done privately, outside of academia, many felt the work suspect.

Dobelle leads one of a dozen teams spread out over four continents racing ahead with all sorts of artificial vision systems. There are teams working on battery-powered retinal implants and solar-powered retinal implants, and teams growing ganglion cells on silicon chips, and teams working on optic-nerve stimulators. And there is Dick Normann, the former head of the University of Utah's department of bioengineering, who up until Dobelle's success was among the front-runners.

Like Dobelle, Normann is working on a visual neuroprosthesis. I was the first to tell him that the race was over: He lost.

"That's fantastic," Normann says.

"You're not even mad?"

"Fantastic, fantastic, fantastic"—and then he pauses—"if it works."

"What do you mean? I was there. I saw it work."

"But what do you mean by work? If a patient sees a point of light and it moves, is that sight? I need to know what the patient sees."

"OK. But what does it mean for your research?"

"Mean? It doesn't mean anything. We're going to keep going like we were going."

Normann also envisions a three-part system—implant, signal processor, camera—but with a critical difference. While Dobelle's implant rests on the surface of the visual cortex, Normann's would penetrate it.

Normann's implant is much smaller than Dobelle's—about the size of a nail's head and designed to be hammered into the cortex, sinking to the exact spot in the brain where normal visual information is received. According to Normann, the implant is so precise that each electrode can stimulate individual neurons.

"The reason this matters," he explains, "is that the cornerstone of artificial vision is the interaction between current and neurons. Because Dobelle's implant sits on the surface of the visual cortex, it requires a lot of current and lights up a whole bunch of neurons. Something in the 1- to 10-milliamp range. With that much juice, a lot can go wrong."

Tell me about it.

"With penetrating electrodes, we've got the current down to the 1- to 10-microamp range. That's a thousandfold difference." Lowering the amperage lowers the risk of seizure.

But that's not all. Decreasing the amount of current also allows an increase of resolution: "The lower the current, the more electrodes you can pack on an implant," explains Normann. "We're not there yet, but with my electrodes there's the chance of creating a contiguous phosphene field—that's exactly what you and I have—and that's just not possible with Dobelle's surface implant."

Which is the way things go when what was once a land of

mystics becomes a field for engineers. Just like every other new technology, like operating systems and web browsers, artificial vision is heading toward a standards war of its own.

Now that it's not faith healing, it's Beta versus VHS.

8.

To really try to understand what Jens sees, I head to USC in Los Angeles, where Mark Humayun has his lab. Like the competition, Humayun uses eyeglass-mounted video cameras and signal processors to generate an image, but unlike Normann's and Dobelle's neuroprostheses, his implant sits atop the retina. It's designed to take the place of damaged rods and cones by jump-starting the still-healthy ones and then using the eye's own signal processing components — the ganglion cells and optic nerve — to send visual information to the brain.

"It's a limited approach, aimed at a limited number of pathologies, but it has its advantages," says Humayun. "We thought it was a better idea to operate on a blind eye than on a normal brain."

Humayun's Retinal Prosthesis Lab runs out of USC's Doheny Eye Institute. The room is small and square. Piles of electronic gear sit atop counters of maroon plastic — the same hue that off-sets the bright yellow on Trojan football jerseys. Lab-coated technicians hunch over computers, barely registering my arrival.

James Weiland, an assistant professor at the institute, helps me into an elaborate headdress: Wraparound goggles cover my eyes, and black, light-blocking cloth hangs down over my ears. Plastic straps secure a miniature camera to the middle of my forehead, and wires run down my back and to a laptop computer to my left. The camera moves where my eyes move and then projects that image onto the "screen" of the goggles. The device, called a Glasstron and built by Sony, turns my normal eyesight into a pixelated version of itself.

With the power shut off, the view is complete darkness. Weiland flips a switch and asks me what I see.

"Vague gray shapes. Big dots. Blurry edges."

"Can you see the door? Could you walk to the door?"

"Yeah, I could, if you want me to trip over things and fall down."

"That's a five-by-five display. Hold on," says Weiland. "I'm going to up your pixel count to thirty-two by thirty-two."

It's Weiland's belief that a 32-by-32 array, 1,024 pixels, should satisfy most vision needs. This is probably ten times the count on Dobelle's implant and much closer to Normann's design.

Beside me I can hear Weiland futzing with the computer. There's a sudden wash of light, like viewing the *Star Wars* jump to hyperspace through a waterfall.

"Can you see now?"

"Not really."

"Give it a minute, let yourself adjust."

"OK, I've got blobs and edges and motion."

Suddenly, things become clearer. What moments ago was attack of the Jell-O creatures has become doorways and faces.

"What happened?" I ask. "Did you up the resolution again?"

"No," says Weiland, "that's your brain learning to see."

It's a weird feeling, watching my brain reorganize itself, but that's exactly what's happening. Beside me the fuzzy edge of the counter becomes a strong line, and then the computer atop it snaps into place.

I take one last glance around. Weiland is still not visible. Then there is a subtle shift in color. A drizzle of gray firms up, and I can see the white plane of his forehead offset by the darkness of his hair.

I look around: door, desk, computer, person.

So this is what a miracle looks like.

PART TWO

THE FUTURE OUT THERE

Reengineering the Everglades

THE WORLD'S FIRST TERRAFORMING PROJECT

Certainly, science and technology are transforming our internal environment – our bodies, our biology, our brains – but what about the external environment, what about our impact on the world at large?

As of late, there has been much talk about this impact. From an environmental perspective, we have not played well with others. Melting icecaps, dying species, poisoned landscapes – the list goes on and on. To combat such decline, researchers have begun using big words – mega-engineering, terraforming, hydroforming – to discuss having an even bigger impact. No longer are we simply tinkering with ecology; now we're transforming ecosystems.

The story told in this chapter is one example: an attempt to rebuild the Everglades, the world's largest saw-grass prairie, once a free-flowing wonder, now a devastated mess. This effort is the largest and most expensive public works project ever undertaken. It also marks our first attempt at terraforming, our once sci-fi term for the sculpting of worlds, and both a testament to the incredible scale at which our species can now play and, perhaps, the incredible hubris it takes to play at this scale.

1.

The Everglades are dying. Nearly half of their 4 million acres have been swallowed up by sprawl and sugarcane. Almost 70 plant and animal species that reside there hover on the brink of extinction. The wading bird populations — egrets and herons and spoonbills and the like — have declined a staggering 90 percent. The saw grass prairies, for which the region is famous, have grown smaller with each passing year, and the once legendary game fish populations aren't doing much better. Among the few fish that do remain, scientists have detected enough mercury in their fatty tissue to open a thermometer factory.

In truth, this degradation is nothing new. The Everglades have been suffering since 1850, when Florida's first settlers began draining the swamp. But it was a later effort to fix the state's weather that really spelled ecosystem doom. The state has only two seasons: wet and dry. The wet season produces floods; the dry, drought. This bad-news cycle ran unchecked until the 1920s, when a pair of back-to-back hurricanes created a deluge that killed 2,500 people. Public outcry moved the government into action. The Army Corps of Engineers, the world's greatest earth-movers, were called in to do a top-to-bottom liquid redesign of the entire state. The "4 Ds" was the Corps's unofficial motto: Dike it, dam it, divert it, drain it. Over the next 50 years, they cut 1,800 miles of canals between Lake Okeechobee and the Florida Bay and installed 300 floodgates and 16 major pump stations to manage the water.

The Corps captured the Everglades. By taming the flood-and-drought cycle, the engineers made Florida's Atlantic Coast safe for development and its midlands safe for agriculture. But like most wild things, this ecosystem had trouble with captivity. What once had been one of the world's largest contiguous wetlands was jigsawed into 16 parts — separate and isolated and not faring well. By 1990, it was clear that the Everglades were facing more than the loss of native species. The underlying hydrology was out of whack; the whole deal was fading fast.

To combat environmental disaster, President Clinton, in his last year in office, signed the Comprehensive Everglades Restoration Plan (CERP) into law. It's the largest, most complicated, and — with a cost of $8 billion — most expensive ecological restoration project ever attempted. Former secretary of the interior Bruce Babbitt, who helped usher the measure through Congress, contends that future historians will rank the Everglades Plan as one of the most important pieces of environmental law ever passed. Maybe the most important. But unlike, say, the Clean Air Act, which merely limits the release of pollutants, CERP is a massive engineering project on a scale that is literally out of this world.

Scientists and engineers and politicians are still dithering with the details, but everyone agrees upon one fact: You can't just "go back to nature." Florida's population has grown exponentially over the past hundred years and, in many places, there's no nature to go back to. Instead, you have to bulldoze this land back to its original ecological function, Roto-Rooter the planet's plumbing, rethink and redesign and rebuild it. The plan calls for rechanneling a major river, transforming Florida's natural aquifer into a hundred-billion-gallon freshwater storage tank, and developing a new type of filtration system that meets the toughest water-quality standards on earth.

Celestial dreamers studying Mars have coined a catchall for this sort of mega-engineering: *terraforming*. Down here in South Florida, where all that separates dry land from wet sea is a bit of limestone and landfill, there's a new word in play: *hydroforming*. But whatever the terminology, the idea of rebuilding ecosystems from scratch has always been the stuff of science fiction — a way of preparing a distant and environmentally hostile planet for human colonization. Terraforming or, in this case, hydroforming, was never meant to be a game played here on Earth.

Then dire ecological necessity changed the game.

2.

Lou Toth is the chief scientist in charge of river restoration for the South Florida Water Management District and my guide to the hydroforming. The tour starts sixty-five miles east of Tampa, on a boat, on the Kissimmee, the great feeder river of the Everglades. The water is dark, the day hot. Off in the distance, cattle egrets perch in oak trees, and nearer to the shore are great blue herons, their wings spread wide in flight. It's quite a vista, enough to make one believe this is pristine nature, untouched by man, undisturbed by civilization. Nothing could be further from the truth.

In 1962, working on flood control instructions from Congress, the Army Corps set out to tether the Kissimmee. It yanked out a ruler, drew a straight line down the middle of the state, and got out shovels. By 1971, two-thirds of the floodplain was drained, and one-third of the river was filled in with dirt. The river's languid S-curves were replaced by one monster ditch: 56 miles long, 300 feet wide, and 30 feet deep.

"Before the Corps came along," says Toth, "this river was beautiful. It had some of the best fishing in the world, it was a treasure. Afterward, it was a muddy mess."

Creating that muddy mess was also expensive, costing taxpayers $30 million at the time. But that's nothing compared to the price of reversing devastation. Simply restoring the Kissimmee — forget about the Everglades proper — will run taxpayers $500 million. It's the cost of playing at scale. Eighty-five thousand acres will be returned to the river; 22 miles of canal will be backfilled; 2 major dams will be removed; 9 miles of river will be redug; and the original water flow of Lake Kissimmee will be reestablished. The goal? Restoring 40 square miles of river and floodplain without the loss of flood control.

To maintain control, the Kissimmee will never be entirely free. The river's upper and lower thirds will remain dammed and channeled, but the middle — those 40 square miles — will flow unhindered. If everything stays on schedule, the Kissimmee Restoration project will finish around the end of the decade.

Until then, there's merely this pilot project, the 14-mile stretch of river that we are now floating down. Known prosaically as "phase one," this portion of the reconstruction project started in June 1999 and was completed in February 2001. Phase one was a trial run on a mad scale: 614 miles of canal were backfilled and 13 miles of meanders reconnected. Toth, himself, dynamited Control Structure S-65B — one of six dams built on the Kissimmee. In time-lapse photography of the explosion, you can watch water gushing forth and farmlands disappearing and the works of man undone.

And the undoing is working. Toth points to the broadleaf plants that cover the landscape. "A few years ago," he says, "you could have counted their numbers individually; not so anymore. Now, it's whole fields of them, stretching miles from river to tree line."

A couple hours later, after we've floated most of those 14 miles, we leave the river and head over to the Riverwoods Field Laboratory, the research station from which Kissimmee restoration is carefully monitored. The lab is not much in the way of buildings: a rambling shack, a few computers, posters of wading birds on the walls. Out front, the porch gives way to a dirt field, with a butterfly garden tucked in one corner and a few pickups scattered around the yard.

"When we're done," says Toth, pointing from the porch, "all this will be gone, turned back into wetlands. Restoration here is pretty low-tech — mostly dynamite and ditch digging — but I'll tell you something: If this low-tech approach doesn't work here, the high-tech stuff they've got planned for the rest of the ecosystem doesn't stand a chance."

3.

That high-tech stuff made its debut in Octave Béliard's 1910 novel, *The Journey of a Parisian in the 21st Century*, wherein the author proposes terraforming the moon — giving it an atmosphere and vegetation and turning it into a sanctuary for endangered species and a possible human colonization site. The idea reappeared in a 1927 essay by famed evolutionary biologist J.B.S. Haldane, popped up in a 1930 novel by Olaf Stapledon, then entered the mainstream psyche in 1950, when Robert A. Heinlein published *Farmer in the Sky*. With his mathematical approach to the transformation of the Jovian moon Ganymede, Heinlein added a much more rigorous slant to the mega-engineering of ecosystems, plucking the notion out of the realm of pure fantasy and placing it squarely in the world of future science.

Here on Earth, that high-tech approach debuted in central Florida, at the spot where the Kissimmee river flows into Lake Okeechobee — a body of water so large it produces its own weather systems and so domesticated it hardly deserves to be called a lake. All of Lake Okeechobee's 730 square miles are penned in by an earthen levee, a massive cage some 143 miles long and 20 feet tall. Built to reduce flooding and provide optimal growing conditions for the sugarcane plantations that hug the lake's lower banks, the levee dumps water into 5 massive drainage canals — 4 dug east to the Atlantic and one west to the Gulf of Mexico. Altogether, these canals send 1.7 billion gallons of freshwater out to tide each day.

Those 1.7 billion gallons are the key to the entire restoration project. While the penning in of Lake Okeechobee has provided flood protection, not enough water is reaching the Everglades.

The entire ecosystem is dying of thirst. Thus, saving the Everglades requires saving those 1.7 billion gallons. "The idea is to bring this water back to the ecosystem," says Rick Nevulis, senior water-storage hydrologist for the project. "We have to store it in the wet season for when we need it during the dry. Everything else comes second. To make that happen, we need water impoundments, and we need wells."

Water impoundments are man-made lakes. CERP calls for a total of 180,000 combined lake acres—split between 10 to 20 sites—designed to capture nearly 500 billion gallons of water. But that's only 60 percent of the water storage that the hydrologists need. It's a conundrum, alright. They can't build more reservoirs without displacing people or farmland and thus risking the ire of Florida's politically powerful real estate and sugarcane lobbies. They can't dig the reservoirs deeper than 8 feet because the state sits on the country's most porous limestone—hit that and the water would simply drain away. The only real solution is to store excess water deep underground, in wells.

I see my first well at the eastern edge of the Arthur R. Marshall Loxahatchee National Wildlife Refuge, 20 miles west of Boca Raton, in a small clearing the size of a suburban backyard. At the center of the clearing, bordered by a smattering of weeds, there's a skinny green pipe sticking out of the ground. This is the high-tech approach.

"It doesn't look like much," says Nevulis. "But it can store a whole lot of water."

He's not kidding. This well is designed to pump 5 million gallons of water a day—or roughly what it would take to fill 100 Olympic swimming pools—down a thousand feet of pipe and into the rocky bowels of the Floridan aquifer. Normally, the aquifer is filled with seawater, but when freshwater is injected, it pushes back the brackish water. The pressure works such that very little mingling occurs. And—with 333 wells called for in the final plan—it better work.

At the height of the wet season, when all of these 333 wells are operating at maximum capacity, some 1.6 billion gallons of water will be pumped into the ground every day. Hundreds of billions of gallons — enough to submerge all of Washington, D.C., in more than 20 feet of water — will be stored underground over the six-month wet season, then released in the dry months, effectively transforming the Floridan aquifer into the world's largest water tank.

Of course, there are issues. "This kind of volume creates tons of unanswered questions," says Nevulis. "We're doing calculations to determine the effects of the added pressure. Will pumping year in and year out fracture the matrix? We just don't know."

And that's just the first of the unknowns. There are also chemical and biological dangers associated with moving this much liquid around. Fecal contaminants in the groundwater could spread through the whole aquifer, essentially rendering it useless and much of Florida uninhabitable. Mercury in the surface water — the same industrial toxin contaminating the fish — reacts with the sulfates in the ground to create the far more poisonous methyl mercury, and again threatens the entire ecosystem. This list goes on.

To put this in different terms, the only other time terraforming has been attempted at scale — and a much smaller scale than is being tried here — was in the early 1990s, when the 3.4 acre dome in the desert known as Biosphere 2, the Arizona-based "Earth systems research facility," was created to see if we could actually engineer ecosystems. Unfortunately, Biosphere 2 suffered an onslaught of unintended consequences — wildly fluctuating CO_2 levels, massive fish die-offs, a cockroach and ant population explosion, to name but a few — and while the lessons learned were myriad, the moral was straightforward: Playing God ain't easy.

But, at least here in Florida, the upside is considerable. Drought has plagued this state for much of the past decade, with water rationing now the law of the land. "One thing's for sure," says Nevulis. "If we can solve these problems and get these wells to work, no one around here is going to go thirsty for a very long time."

4.

As you leave Lake Okeechobee and head south, the sheer scale of the Corps's original engineering project becomes clear. One hundred and fifty years ago, this entire landscape was swamp. Today, it's sugarcane. Four hundred and fifty thousand acres of sugarcane to be exact. And that acreage is the next challenge the Everglades Restoration Project must face.

Sugarcane farmers use phosphorus as fertilizer—but not without consequences. When introduced into the Everglades, the chemical produces a drastic rise in exotic green algae, which kills off the native blue-green variety and enables cattails— traditionally found here in small numbers—to outcompete the saw grass. As cattail density thickens, sunlight can no longer penetrate the canopy, and the blue-green algae below begins to die. Without algae, the invertebrates go hungry and the small fish that feed on them and then the larger ones that feed on them, and so on up the food chain, until the wading birds themselves either starve or head elsewhere for a meal.

This is a complicated problem. To combat it, the restoration plan calls for one of the largest and most complicated water-quality treatment facilities ever devised. To create a buffer between the phosphorus-using farmers and the phosphorus-hating Everglades, scientists have designed six Stormwater Treatment Areas that sprawl over 41,000 acres. These areas are phosphorus-eating wetlands, giant septic swimming pools big enough to float an oil tanker. Farmland runoff will be diverted through these treatment areas before being released into the Everglades with the ambitious goal of reducing phosphorus levels from their current 200 parts-per-billion down to 10 ppb—scientists' best guess of the early Everglades' phosphorus levels.

"Ten ppb is the toughest phosphorus goal anywhere on the planet," says Jana Newman, the senior scientist working on the treatment areas. "It's on the threshold of what's even possible to detect. We're trying everything from green technologies to chemical technologies, but there's a cost factor here. When phosphorus is depleted, it gets more and more difficult to remove; down around 10 ppb, it takes 400 pounds of chemicals to remove one pound of phosphorus."

The Storage Treatment Area known as 1 West is the proving ground. It's a swampy rat's maze. Water enters through a giant pump station and travels along 18 miles of levees, concrete spillways, and culverts that push it into five man-made chunks of marshland, or cells. Each cell is stocked with a carefully selected mixture of cattails, submerged aquatic vegetation, floating plants, and algae. As water passes into the cells, the plants suck up the phosphorus, die off, and fall to the bottom, where they're entombed in heavy peat. When the water exits, its phosphorus count is measured again. So far, 12 ppb is the lowest concentration achieved, but that number came during a drought in which the flow rate was exceptionally low.

As mentioned, playing God ain't easy.

5.

One of the main difficulties with trying to save an ecosystem is how little we really know about ecosystems themselves — a lesson driven home to me when I go out for a nighttime tour of the Everglades. I had joined a couple of field biologists, Laura Brandt and Frank Mazzoti, for a boat trip into the Loxahatchee Refuge, long after the park is closed. My goal was to experience this landscape as it once was, empty of man, full of saw grass and water. Their goal was to count alligators.

Alligators are the keystone predator in the Everglades — meaning it is their health that determines the health of the entire ecosystem. The goal tonight is just simple science. We shine flash-lights over the water, looking for the telltale glimmer of alligator eye-shine — the refractory glow their eyes give off at night (this is also why we're traveling in the dark, as you can't see eye-shine in daylight). Once a gator is sighted, we pull alongside, notate loca-tion with a GPS, and take rough size measurements as a way of determining age: newborn, juvenile, adult, senior citizen. "It may seem basic," says Brandt, "but no one has ever done this research before. We want to save the Everglades, but really we know so little about them. The reason we're doing this survey is to make sure that the things we want to save are really being saved."

Our boat weaves through head-high saw grass tangles. It's a tough old plant, evolved to withstand a tough environment. The tops of the shafts form spears, and tiny, sharp teeth run up both sides of the blade. Unsuspecting tourists have been known to gash their palms while copping a feel. The early explorers told tales of men lost for months in this maze.

Motoring on, we start to see the tree islands, places where, over hundreds of years, the sediment level has risen and seeds have blown in and taken hold. The islands are teardrop-shaped, symmetrically aligned so that the fat end faces north and the taper faces south, pointing out the water's otherwise impercep-tible flow.

At one point, we spy a marsh rabbit swimming from tree island to tree island. A few days later, when I'm back at Water Management headquarters, I mention the rabbit to one of the top scientists working the project. He looks at me like I'm crazy.

"An aquatic rabbit?"

"Yeah."

"Aquatic?"

"It looked like it was doing the breaststroke."

"No shit," he says. "I had no idea there was such a thing. We really don't know much about the Everglades — that's the real challenge."

6.

Few people understand the challenge better than Jerry Lorenz, a marine ecologist with the National Audubon Society who studies spoonbills in the Florida Keys. "In the sixties," he says, "when the system started to break down, we had no idea what was going wrong, let alone how to fix it."

But over the past thirty years, ecology has morphed from a fuzzy, soft art into a rigorous statistical science. What started out as fragmented crisis management — an endangered species here, an oil spill there — has become a unified systems-based theory. But it's a very new theory.

"Realistically," continues Lorenz, "ecosystem ecology itself is quite young. What we have in South Florida right now is a bunch of separate ecosystems. If you want to save the whole thing by piecing them back together — what's called landscape ecology — then you're dealing with an entirely new field. Ten years ago, the whole philosophical underpinning that's driving this restoration project didn't even exist."

I am riding next to Lorenz as he pilots a small boat across the Florida Bay. He wears jungle fatigues, a bandanna to cover his head, and has a long ponytail trickling out the back. We slide inland, up a feeder river, one of the many that connect freshwater to saltwater. In seconds, dense canopy blots out the daylight. Lorenz hardly notices: He's too busy shouting about spoonbills over the engine.

"You know, people say that this project is about restoring the hydrology of the Everglades. Yet, down here, at the end of the pipe, you can get the hydrology perfect for 360 days a year, but if you fuck it up for five days, then Florida Bay takes it on the chin. If you get a surprise storm and the farmers start bitching about excess water in their fields and that water gets dumped at the wrong time, say during breeding season, then the spoonbills are screwed. All the modelers and engineers deal in averages. They'll tell you five days is a blip on the radar, that it's inconsequential. Well, it's not inconsequential if you're a spoonbill in heat."

Thus, much in the same way that Brandt and Mazzoti are collecting alligator data, Lorenz is collecting spoonbill data. The results of all this research is sent to the computer modeling department at the Water District offices, where scientists are doing their best to fight against that five-day blip, among other catastrophes.

It's another massive undertaking. The database being built doesn't just contain facts about the Everglades present, it's a treasure trove of the entire natural history of the area. There are botanical tidbits gleaned from eighteenth-century survey records, expedition accounts and agricultural deeds, interwoven with thirty years of hydrological data, including information about evaporation, canal flow, levee seepage, and water quality. There are disaster patterns from fires and tropical storms, topographic facts, population numbers, and all levels of biotic minutia: everything from the mating habits of aquatic insects to statistics on the Florida panther.

The model tells the engineers in the field what to do — which dam to blow up, how much water to store — but the model's predictions could be wrong. Thus, the only way to change the Everglades is to change it slowly, carefully, monitoring each step and being prepared to unstep at any moment. In other words, just as ecology gave way to engineering in an attempt to dismantle the past, ecology must once again become engineering to reassemble the future.

But even that past is a mystery. No one really knows what the Everglades used to be — sure, there's the random fact scooped out of the muck of soil deposits, yet there's no groundwater table for the Mesozoic era, no aerial photographs from the Dark Ages. This is the largest eco-engineering project ever undertaken, our greatest effort to undo the damage we have done. Yet the scientists and engineers are hydroforming blind, as their actual goal exists only in imagination.

Lorenz and I are punching out into the Florida Bay, with nothing but empty ocean stretching out to a far horizon. I spin around and look back toward the land, but we've moved too far away to gain any perspective. I see neither mangroves nor saw grass prairies nor behemoth lakes nor meandering rivers. There's only the thin edge of the continent: a green line over the shimmer of water.

"It's just seems too damn big to fix," I say.

"Yeah," says Lorenz, "yet the plan is tiny compared to what it represents. The Everglades aren't the planet's only endangered ecosystem. The whole world is watching—if we fail here, then people aren't even going to want to try elsewhere."

Buckaroo Banzai

It was 2004. Hollywood, California. I was sitting in my apartment in the late afternoon, writing the initial pages of what would eventually become my second book, when the doorbell rang. It was Dezso Molnar, the aerospace engineer we met in the Preface (when he worked with Craig Breedlove in the attempt to drive a car through the sound barrier). In the years since, Dezso and I had become friends, but — back then — we hadn't seen each other in a little while.

He walked into my apartment with an armful of schematics and a smile on his face. "I solved it," was the first thing he said.

"Solved what?"

"The flying car."

Then he unrolled the schematics.

Now, sure, this was not the first time in history someone told their buddy that they'd figured out how to build a flying car. After all, when it comes to our science fiction dreams, what's dreamier than a flying car? But here's the thing: Dezso's flying car — which, albeit, is actually a flying motorcycle — really flies.

At a personal level, nothing is more emblematic of the radical change being described in this book than that conversation. It was my "Welcome to Tomorrowland" moment — not just a paradigm shift, but a paradigm shift in my freaking living room.

1.

The Calfee Design Factory is 10,000 square feet, a few stories high, and perched on the edge of a lonely bluff in La Selva Beach, California. Below the bluff, the Pacific rumbles and moans. Above it, in the factory, on most days, they build bicycles — technically some of the very best in the world. Today is not most days.

Today is October 20, 2005. An afternoon of dark skies and light rain. A man named Dezso (pronounced *Dezh-ur*) Molnar is braving the elements, pushing a strange, three-wheeled contraption out of the warehouse and onto a 2,000-foot runway. A few years back, when Molnar started hunting for a place to build this contraption, he had three key needs. The first was isolation. What he wanted to build in his skunk works was the kind of project that attracted all sorts of unwanted attention. Calfee's warehouse fit the bill. It sits on 379 acres of private land and sees few visitors. His second need was expertise. Molnar's contraption had to be light — very light. Calfee's bicycles are made from carbon fiber. They weigh about 12 lbs. The engineers who work here understand light. Molnar's last requirement was a straight stretch of pavement. It didn't have to be a runway, but — considering the true nature of Molnar's invention — it was a fitting touch.

The true nature of Molnar's invention is hard to discern at a glance. The machine looks like some Mad Max version of a recumbent bicycle, only with training wheels, a giant steel roll cage, and a 68-inch, three-bladed propeller strapped to the back end. Today is the very first day Molnar is going to fire up that propeller and see if it can push his machine down the road. He's hoping for speeds about fifty mph — because, at least according to Molnar's calculations, that's about what it should take to get his flying motorcycle off the ground.

2.

The flying car, the flying motorcycle, the stuff of dreams — of very old dreams. Aviation pioneer Glenn Curtiss invented the first flying car back in 1917: a forty-foot-long tri-winged beast made from aluminum. The beast never did fly, but it did manage to hop. That hop was enough, inspiring almost a century of innovation. Next came Waldo Waterman's 1937 winged Studebaker — dead because of lack of funding. A bad crash destroyed the 1947 ConvAirCar. The Aerocar, perhaps the most famous of all roadable aircraft, went through six iterations before the oil crisis of the 1970s killed off production plans. Since then, there have been dozens of other attempts; a few have flown, most have not. Today, the two most widely known versions are Paul Moller's M400 Skycar and the Terrafugia Transition. Both of these vehicles are currently for sale; neither of them have actually been delivered to a customer. And that's really the issue. Out of the 104 roadable aircraft (80 of which have patents on file), none have seen mass production.

There are, of course, good reasons for this. While the upside of a flying car is easy to imagine — no traffic jams, shorter commutes, another excuse to quote *Blade Runner* — the downsides are considerable. Cost and noise, for starters (at $196,000, the Terrafugia has already been branded a rich man's toy, to say nothing of Moller's $3.5 million reserve price).

Safety and ease-of-use are bigger stumbling blocks. As with anything that flies, the consequences of pilot error can be severe. Add in the possibility of bad weather and it's no surprise that the safest pilots are the ones with the most practice and the best knowledge of their airplane, twin requirements that further put the flying car out of reach of the average citizen. Moreover, right now, most small planes require constant (and expensive) upkeep. They also tend to be gas-guzzlers. Flying cars, especially if they become everyman tools, can be neither. And this list doesn't include the bevy of concerns that arrive when one wants to create a street-legal aircraft.

Until about eight years ago, Molnar never intended to get into the street-legal aircraft business, but, considering the nature of his pedigree, perhaps it was inevitable. Molnar flew hot-air balloons as a teenager, then paid his way through college by flying planes in the Air Force and moonlighting at Truax Engineering, where Robert Truax had a Navy contract for building a replacement vehicle for the space shuttle (this was right after the *Challenger* crash). They built a workable rocket, but funding issues shut down the effort. Afterwards, Molnar spent a few years playing music in bands, building robots with the performance art outfit Survival Research Labs, and designing DIY vehicles like his buzz-bomb jet-powered go-cart. He next signed on as a crew chief for Craig Breedlove's attempt to drive a jet car through the sound barrier. When that project ran its course, Molnar jumped back into music, and that's where he might have stayed had it not been for London's 2004 heatwave.

"In 2004, I was in the UK shooting a music video. It was hot and fun until I got back to Los Angeles, where it was foggy and dew was dripping from the walls in my house. I called a friend and suggested we drive out to Palm Springs, just to warm up. But it was the middle of the day and my friend worked downtown, and the traffic there was bumper-to-bumper. We were trapped. We couldn't leave."

But that's when Molnar got curious about the kind of vehicle that could leave. A vehicle unencumbered by traffic on the ground because, well, his vehicle wasn't going to travel on the ground. More important, Molnar wasn't interested in fairy tales — he was interested in practicality. A flying car capable of vertical takeoff was the most obvious solution, but the only thing that could take off vertically was a helicopter, and those were both expensive and difficult to pilot. But what if he threw that requirement out the window. There are 14,000 airports in America — 30 in the LA area alone. What if you could depart from those airports — which typically sit in less congested areas so getting there isn't as much of an issue — and land in a congested area? There are dozens of parking garages in downtown LA. What if you could land atop one of those?

Then Molnar remembered an advertisement from his childhood for a gyrocopter, a type of "rotorcraft" invented in 1923 by Spanish engineer Juan de la Cierva. Gyrocopters use an unpowered rotor for lift (like a helicopter) and an engine-powered propeller for thrust (like a small plane) and have the distinct advantage of being able to land at very slow speeds (to maximize pilot safety), and in extremely small spaces (like the roof of a parking garage). Even better, gyroplanes are cheap — kits start at a thousand bucks — and easy to fly. A sport pilot's license is required: roughly twenty hours of practice time. There was one small issue, however: Gyroplanes had a bad habit of crashing.

"The problem," says Molnar, "is that the most popular gyroplane on the market was designed without a horizontal stabilizer, which is what keeps a plane's nose from pitching up or down. People kept getting killed because of it, and too often it was considered pilot error. The gyroplane was originally designed to create a safe wing that would not stall, but the perceived option of removing the horizontal stabilizer was a design error. If you put the stabilizer back on, the result is potentially one of the world's safest aircraft — and one that can land in less than twenty feet."

Molnar's stabilizer solved only part of the problem. He could land in a congested area, but he still had to evade traffic on his way out. "I took a very realistic approach to this question. Since vertical takeoff is too limiting, and no one's going to build a long runway in places like downtown Los Angeles, then flying away isn't the solution. You need to be able to drive. This is where the motorcycle comes in: If you drive away on a motorcycle you can split lanes. It's the fastest way to get away from traffic, and it's legal in twenty-five countries."

What makes the motorcycle even more interesting is the engine. Motorcycle engines are cheap (a new one costs around $2,000, versus $36,000 for most aircraft engines), powerful, durable, quiet, get great gas mileage, and—their best feature—are standardized. "Because these engines always have to fit between the driver's legs," says Molnar, "manufacturers devote tremendous time and energy into making them within these limits, while simultaneously making them increasingly more powerful. They're constantly getting better, and you can get them fixed at any roadside shop. It's a perfect solution."

All of these ideas came together in the vehicle Molnar wheeled onto the tarmac that October afternoon. And the test drive went exactly according to plan. The one-cylinder engine and propeller generated more than enough wind to push the vehicle past the 50 mph mark. A series of road tests confirmed that it could master the freeways (the two-wheeled bike did 90 mph no problem; the newer tri-wheeled configuration goes 160 mph and handles like a sports car). Because of his engine choice, Molnar also evaded a problem that plagued both Moller and Terrafugia—his vehicle passed a smog test. The bike was street legal. Now, it was time to see if it could fly.

3.

First flight took place in Texas in 2005, with video of the event available all over the Internet. Again, everything went according to plan. The crew logged four hours of flight time without a mishap, so Molnar started thinking about production.

Originally, his plan was to sell single-seat models, constructed from kits. But while he waited for his patent to clear (it did, in 2011), his backers wanted to explore upscale markets—which meant two seats, room for cargo, and all kinds of doodads. So Molnar and his partners spent a couple years working on that design, simultaneously trying to convince the FAA that gyroplanes could be engineered safe enough to be sold as turn-key light sport aircraft. But the FAA wouldn't budge, so Molnar went back to his roots.

"I decided," he says, "that this had to be a DIY project. The FAA won't allow a ready-made gyroplane, but tens of thousands of aircraft that are now flying are homebuilt, and the FAA regulations allow gyroplanes that are built from kits. Plain and simple, I had a machine that could fly and drive, but if it was going to help launch the flying car revolution, then DIY'ers will need to assemble their own to push it forward."

Unlike traditional kit airplanes, which often take five years to assemble in a hangar, Molnar believes his design could be snapped together in a garage in less than four weeks. But, before the kit is available, there is still work to do. "The machine has been invented, driven, flown, and patented, but it hasn't been engineered for production, or optimized." Right now, for example, because the process is not yet streamlined, it takes about ten minutes to re-position the rotor blades and wheels to go from driving to flying. But this is where Molnar's business plan deviates further from most flying carmakers. Instead of trying to drum up the necessary financing for mass production, Molnar wants to establish a gyrocycle racing league populated entirely by kit builders.

"Sure, it's not a huge market like toothpaste, but this is not a machine for grandmothers picking up groceries. It's for skydivers and guys who ride Ninjas. And that's exactly what I want. These people live for adventure, they know they're on the cutting edge, and consider what happens if we're successful: Suddenly the chuckle factor is gone from the flying car discussion. In its place, you get all the optimization and engineering that results from any race program, and nobody streamlines better than a racing pit crew."

4.

What is the true size of the flying car market? Nobody really knows. There are estimates that put it in the high billions, but usually those best guesses are reserved for vehicles capable of vertical takeoff and landing. "The Zee-Aero is one of those," says Molnar, citing another recent entrant in the space. The brain-child of NASA aerospace engineer Ilan Kroo, the Zee-Aero has a canard wing design and eight propellers for lift. In photos released online, it appears to be a very sexy machine. "The Zee-Aero would be great," continues Molnar. "It'd be the real-deal commuter model. But right now it's only theoretical. And even if they did get it into production, it would cost millions of dollars."

Molnar, on the other hand, has built a machine that can fly high enough to clear tall mountains and drive fast enough to give Formula One racers a run for their money. And it's here today. Molnar, in fact, is about to take it on a cross-country trip. A few years from now, you'll be able to assemble one from a kit and do the same. It is both the stuff of very old dreams and the very first flying vehicle that's actually available to the masses. So get your *Blade Runner* quotes ready.

Meltdown or Mother Lode

THE POSSIBILITIES OF NUCLEAR ENERGY

Nuclear fusion, the energy released when two atoms collide, is gods' fire, both the fuel that powers the stars and the all-star light in "Let there be light." Nuclear fission, meanwhile, is the energy released when an atom is subdivided. It is our attempt to steal fire from the gods, and a story so muddled that there are arguably none left among us with an unbiased opinion about it.

The problems with these opinions are growing: overpopulation, global warming, resource scarcity, to name but a few. Many smart scientists claim that nuclear energy is the only way through these crises. Plenty disagree. But lost in all this fuss is a four-decade revolution in the science of gods' fire — call it Prometheus 2.0 — that promises a next wave of nuclear power: cleaner, safer, and less vulnerable to terrorist attack or natural disaster. This wave is startling in its implications, arguably the most exciting shift in energy since we replaced blubber with steam. But the story is complicated and controversial, and to truly understand this radical next, we first must decipher the bewildering past. In this, it helps to start at the beginning.

1.

First there was the atom.

The idea of the fundamental particle came from India, dating to sixth-century BCE Hindu philosopher Kanada, but it was the Greek thinker Democritus who gave us the word, taking *atom* from *atomos*, Greek for "indivisible." This concept of an indivisible particle, a fundamental building block for all of nature, had staying power, holding fast for nearly two thousand years — then crumbling within thirty.

Things got wobbly in the late 1890s, when, in short succession, researchers discovered X-rays, radioactivity, and, finally, the first radioactive elements. Then, in 1905, Albert Einstein's Special Theory of Relativity proposed that a large amount of energy could be stored in a very small amount of matter. Twenty-seven years later, Ernest Walton and John Cockcroft verified this suspicion and proved Democritus wrong. Turns out, the atom is divisible.

In 1935, Enrico Fermi and Leó Szilárd leveraged this knowledge to build the Chicago Pile-1, the world's first nuclear reactor. It went — and you've got to love this word — "critical" on December 2, 1942. In 1951, an experiment in Idaho, dubbed EBR-I, became the first reactor to produce electricity. EBR-I melted down in 1955 — also another first — though not many people outside of Idaho noticed. Instead, Eisenhower's "Atoms for Peace" speech and US Atomic Energy Commission Chairman Lewis Strauss's promise of electricity "too cheap to meter" had us dazzled. The nuclear age was upon us.

Calder Hall, in England, started pumping out an annual 50 megawatts and the world had its first commercial nuclear power station. The following year, the US got reactors in Pennsylvania and California, and not coincidentally the Price-Anderson Act passed, limiting the financial risk of nuclear-plant owners in the event of a catastrophe. Historians feel that the industry really arrived on November 9, 1965, when a blackout left the Northeastern United States without electricity for twelve hours. Add in the brownouts of the early 1970s and it's no surprise that 1973 was a banner year for the industry: Forty-one new plants ordered, and no end in sight.

But then, an end in sight. "China Syndrome" is shorthand hyperbole for what happens when an American nuclear reactor melts down — it melts straight through to China. The disaster movie of the same name came out on March 16, 1979, twelve days before "Unit 2" at Pennsylvania's Three Mile Island partially melted down. It wasn't a winning combination.

Not long after, when *Mad Magazine*'s Alfred E. Newman posed in front of Three Mile Island's cooling towers with the caption, "Yes, me worry," he spoke for much of the country. In 1984, a *Forbes* cover story called the nuclear industry "the largest managerial disaster in business history." In 1986, Ukraine's Chernobyl became a bigger disaster and, as Allan Winkler points out in his book, *Life Under A Cloud*, "Some Americans masked their concerns with black humor: 'What's the weather report from Kiev? Overcast and 10,000 degrees.'"

Popular wisdom holds that Three Mile Island slowed the industry, while Chernobyl ground it to a halt, but nuclear experts feel that cost overruns were a much worse problem. In the end, it didn't matter. Dozens of new plants were cancelled. One became a coal factory. In America, no new plants have been ordered in over thirty years. As far as most are concerned, that was the end of the story.

2.

This might have stayed the end of that story except, in the early 2000s, we started hearing other tales. Global warming, peak oil, resource wars — the list goes on. And it's this list that's put the nuclear option back on the table, a process well summarized by Peter Schwartz and Spencer Reiss in a recent *Wired* article: "Burning hydrocarbons is a luxury that a planet with six billion energy-hungry souls can't afford. There is only one sane, practical alternative: nuclear power."

Many feel the same. Both the previous Bush administration and the current Obama administration back the nuclear option, as do an increasing number of serious environmentalists like Whole Earth Catalog founder Stewart Brand, Gaia theorist James Lovelock, and eco-author Bill McKibben. Congress as well. In 2007, they gave the nuclear industry $18.5 billion in loan guarantees for up to 80 percent of the cost of new units. Since then, US power companies have submitted applications for 30 new plants. Worldwide, there are 31 new plants under construction and even more promised. China alone has plans for 26. All of this, the experts say, might signal the end of our energy woes or the end of the world — no one is quite sure which.

Among the stakes in this debate are deep-seated fears about nuclear safety and security, and the boatload of regulations meant to allay those fears. Since the cost of licensing a new reactor in America is roughly $1 billion, as Heritage Foundation nuclear energy analyst Jack Spenser explains: "Those regulations amount to an industry killer."

This discussion is still ongoing, but some believe misdirected. "When most people argue about nuclear energy," says energy expert and author Tom Blees, "they're arguing about Three Mile Island and 1970s technology — which is about when the US nuclear industry ground to a halt. But research didn't die off, just new construction. We're two generations beyond that earlier tech and the changes have been massive."

In light of all this, the better question might be: What do we mean by safe and secure?

3.

We use a lot of energy. A *lot* of energy. Thus, if you want to talk safety and security, you have to start with the options available. Can solar and wind even satisfy our needs? Can green techs ever handle base load demands? Will better energy storage systems soon come online? Hard to say. As a result of this uncertainty, most experts frame the discussion as coal versus nukes. "Nukes win every time," says retired Argonne National Laboratory nuclear physicist, George Stanford. "Fifty-six people died outright at Chernobyl. We could have three or four of those a year and not do the damage coal does."

New York Times journalist and author of *Power to Save the World: The Truth About Nuclear Power* Gwyneth Cravens explains further: "If an American got all his or her lifetime electricity solely from nuclear power, that person's share of waste would fit into one soda can. If an American got all his or her electricity from coal, that person's waste would weigh 68.5 tons and fit into six 12-ton railroad cars. And their share of carbon dioxide coal emissions would come to 77 tons." Nukes, meanwhile, have virtually no carbon footprint.

Coal is also a serious pollutant, containing arsenic, mercury, lead, and a host of radioactive materials — uranium, thorium, and radium at levels 100 to 400 times the level of nuclear plants — yet remains exempt from hazardous-waste regulations. 24,000 people die coal-related deaths in the US each year. In China, it's 400,000. "Worldwide," says Cravens, "nuclear power is responsible for the fewest deaths of all large-scale energy production."

Settling this debate may take some time — and since time is the one luxury both sides agree we don't have — there are heated arguments about the best way forward. Greens feel that any energy dollar not directed toward renewables is a dollar wasted, while the pro-nuke camp thinks the same about new reactors. But still, even if we do move forward with new reactors, there are a bevy of economic concerns to address.

"The first 75 reactors in the US had $100 billion in cost over-runs," says Jim Riccio, a nuclear spokesman for Greenpeace. "The nuclear industry has received over $100 billion in government subsidies [that's roughly $13 billion a plant, or, actually, the cost of a new plant] and still can't find a way to make money." The industry counters by arguing that every new business goes through growing pains and the 103 reactors currently operating in the US all do so at 90 percent capacity — up from 60 percent in the days of Three Mile Island. But this doesn't seem to impress would-be backers. In a recent article on the topic, *Time* pointed out: "The red-hot renewable industry — including wind and solar — last year attracted $71 billion in private investment, the nuclear industry attracted nothing," then quoted energy expert and chairman of the Rocky Mountain Institute Amory Lovins on the subject: "Wall Street has spoken — nuclear power isn't worth it."

Obviously, a carbon tax or more government handouts could change this picture, though the National Resource Defense Council computed that we would have to tax carbon at $40–$60 per ton for nuclear power to be competitive. That said, these numbers are based on a ten-year timetable for nuclear plants construction at a cost of $6–10 billion per gigawatt. General Electric just completed two nuclear plants in Japan; the first was done in thirty-six months, the second in thirty-nine. Both came in with a final cost of $1.4 billion per GW.

Still, cost is not the only factor. Environmental unpredictability is a bigger concern. How long until the oil runs out? How long until our supplies of natural gas are gone? Do we have five years to stabilize the climate or do we have fifty? Because, if we only have five, forget the economics, there's simply no way to build enough new nuclear power plants in time. But even if we have fifty, when it comes to nukes, is the risk worth the reward?

In trying to answer this question, Princeton's Robert Socolow and Stephen Pacala, codirectors of the Carbon Mitigation Initiative, have created the concept of "stabilization wedges." These are the 25-billion-ton "wedges" that must be cut from predicted emissions in the next fifty years to avoid doubling atmospheric carbon dioxide to pre–Industrial Revolution levels.

They explore fifteen different approaches, from wind power to transportation efficiency to reducing deforestation. Nuclear power is also on the list. They point out that fission currently produces, with zero carbon emissions, 17 percent of the world's electricity, and that doubling this number could cut emissions by one wedge (out of seven total) if the resulting power is used to displace coal. But, because of concerns over waste and proliferation, they argue that nukes are the only technology out of their fifteen that we might want to skip. However, another question remains: Which nuclear technologies do we want to skip?

4.

When scientists talk about nuclear reactors, they denote them by generation. Generation I reactors were the ones built in the 1950s and 60s. Generation II began in the 1970s, and comprise all the reactors currently supplying power in the US — predominantly light-water thermal reactors that burn a combination of 3 percent *fissile* Uranium-235 (U-235) and 97 percent *fertile* U-238.

The difference is stability. All reactors work by bombarding heavy metals with neutrons. When a neutron hits U-235, the nuclei split — thus fissile — releasing both energy and a few more neutrons. U-238 is fertile because sometimes it splits, but occasionally it absorbs that neutron and transmutates into plutonium (P-239), which, when it later fissions, produces even more energy.

These days, the fuel cycle for reactors lasts three years. By the end of it, less than 1 percent U-235 remains, and more than half the power generated comes from splitting plutonium. The results are a three-part waste product. About 5 percent of which is composed of lighter elements that remain radioactive for around 300 years (this has been called the "true ash from the nuclear fire"). Another 94 percent is uranium, not all that different from the version we mine from the ground. But the remaining 1 percent is a blend of plutonium elements, augmented by americium, and this is the stuff that stays "hot" for tens of thousands of years and requires secure storage sites like Yucca Mountain to protect.

For this reason, in 1976, the UK Royal Commission on Environmental Pollution declared it "morally wrong" to make a major commitment to nuclear power without demonstrating a way to safely isolate radioactive waste. Attitudes haven't changed much. But waste is not all that it's been made out to be. "All the spent fuel from power plants and other sources since the beginning of nuclear power in the US fifty years ago is so small in volume that it could fit in a Walmart stacked to a depth of nine feet," says Cravens. "All the spent fuel generated in the annual operation of a single reactor would fit in the bed of a standard pickup truck."

To deal with this detritus, many suggest that the right way to go is to follow France's lead and recycle our spent fuel. America (and Sweden, Finland, Canada, Spain, and South Africa) utilize an "open, once-through fuel cycle," in which nuclear fuel is processed only once. But the French take that resulting plutonium, purify and oxidize it, then mix the results with fresh uranium to make MOX—essentially fresh fuel—and restart the whole cycle. This is known as the Plutonium Uranium Extraction (PUREX) process. America was firmly committed to this path as well, but in 1976 India developed nuclear weapons from a version of reprocessing technology and a lot of people got very scared, including then President Jimmy Carter.

By executive order, Carter cancelled development of any domestic reprocessing in 1977. His goal was to set a nonproliferation example for the world, which the world pretty much ignored. So Reagan lifted the ban in 1981, but didn't provide money to restart research. Nothing resumed until 1999 when the Department of Energy finally reversed their policy and signed on with a business consortium to build a reprocessing plant in South Carolina. Who knows when it'll be open. Until then, there are 55,000 tons of nuclear waste in storage in the US.

Since the PUREX process—by separating the plutonium—raises proliferation concerns, perhaps this form of reprocessing isn't the best solution. But the other problem is inefficiency. When uranium finishes a once-through process, only 5 percent of its potential energy is used. When reprocessing plutonium, that ticks up to 6 percent. This still leaves 94 percent of that fuel's potential energy and, since uranium is neither an infinite resource nor environmentally friendly to mine, we would do well to tap these remains.

And this is where newer technology comes into play.

5.

Generation III reactors are one example of a newer technology. These are streamlined light-water reactors with significantly better safety systems. They are also built modularly, allowing them to be manufactured in factories and keeping costs significantly down. There are currently two Generation III reactors deployed in the world and two more under construction. But it's really the generation after Generation III that has people so excited.

Conventional nuclear reactors are called "thermal" reactors, because the speed of the neutrons flying around within them has been slowed down to produce thermal energy. This happens

by using a "moderator" — usually water (thus the light-water reactors). Fast reactors, which are what we're talking about with
Generation IV, don't have moderators, thus the neutrons bounce
around at a much faster rate, allowing more energy to be extracted from fuel.

Also, because water slows down neutrons, fast reactors use
liquid metal — mostly sodium — as a coolant. The advantage here
is that water-cooled systems need to run at very high pressure, so
a small leak can quickly become a large problem. Liquid-metal
systems run at atmospheric pressure and don't have that trouble;
instead, they have other concerns.

Liquid sodium is not the most stable of substances. Expose it to
water or air and the result is fire. The reason most people haven't
heard about this technology is because early iterations did catch
fire. The EBR-I that melted down in Idaho was an experimental
fast reactor, as was Japan's prototype Monju reactor, which burst
into flames in 1995 and has remained shut down ever since. Other
iterations suffered a similar fate. In 2008, Thomas Cochrane, a
nuclear scientist with the National Resources Defense Council,
testified before the House of Representatives on this technology:

> Despite decades of research costing many tens of billions of
> dollars, the effort to develop fast breeder reactors has been a
> failure in the United States, France, United Kingdom, Ger-
> many, Italy, Japan, and the Soviet Union . . . After investing
> tens of billions and decades of effort in fast breeder R&D,
> Congress should ask itself why there is only one commer-
> cial-size fast reactor operating in the world today — one out
> of approximately 440 reactors. NRDC knows why. Fast reac-
> tors are uneconomical and unreliable.

Yet there's still more to the story. The original nuclear dream
was to take spent fuel from thermal reactors and use it to power
fast reactors. These were then called "breeders," as they bred
more plutonium than they consumed. "In the early days," says
Cravens, "before we discovered the uranium on the Colorado

Plateau, there was a real concern that we would run out. Breeders were the solution to that problem."

Work began on that solution with the EBR-I in 1951 and progressed into the EBR-II in 1964. "Sure, EBR-I partially melted down," says Dave Rossin, former president of the American Nuclear Society and Assistant Secretary of Energy under Reagan, "but this was in the day when being intelligent was still allowed. People studied what went wrong and made changes and the result was EBR-II, which started up in 1964 and ran perfectly until the 1980s. Unfortunately, by then, anything called a 'breeder' was frowned upon in Washington and the project was shut down for political reasons."

In 1984, trying to avoid that fate, scientists at Argonne National Laboratory renamed their breeder reactor the Integral Fast Reactor (IFR). By 1992, the IFR designs were complete, but then Bill Clinton decided to save money by shutting down any nuclear projects he deemed unnecessary. "It's a crime," says former Argonne nuclear physicist George Stanford. "We set out to build a reactor that addresses all the nuclear concerns: safety, efficiency, proliferation, and waste. It worked perfectly. IFR solves all our problems. And it's just sitting on a shelf."

Among the problems "solved" by IFR is safety. Liquid metal fuel expands when heated. As the metal expands, its density decreases. This changes the geometric trajectory of the neutrons bouncing around inside and the laws of physics don't allow it to sustain a chain reaction. "It can't melt down," says Stanford. "We know this for certain because in public demonstrations using the EBR-II, Argonne duplicated the exact conditions that led to both the Three Mile Island and Chernobyl disasters and nothing happened." This is known as "passive safety" and every Generation IV reactor works this way.

Proliferation is another problem solved. An IFR reactor is built so that whatever fuel enters always leaves as electricity. What's actually inside the reactor — if terrorists, say, seize a facility—is far too hot to handle, so the main result of such an attempt would be dead terrorists. And the waste is only a fraction of what's produced by thermal reactors (a 1000-MW thermal reactor produces slightly more than 25 tons of spent fuel annually; a fast reactor generating the same power produces one ton). Moreover, this waste doesn't contain weapons-usable material, only stays "hot" for several hundred years, and remains as an inert solid—essentially stored as glass bricks—so even if the containment facility were to breach, it can't leach into the ground water.

All of this explains why, in 2002, the US Department of Energy organized the most comprehensive study of nuclear design options ever conducted, asking over 250 scientists to rank nineteen existing nuclear options based on twenty-seven criteria. IFR came in at number one. For this reason, Columbia University professor and head of NASA's Goddard Institute, James Hansen—often credited with being the first person to sound the alarm bells about global warming—put IFR on his top-five list of things we need to do to stave off climate disaster. Both China and India jumpstarted IFR programs (China's first fast reactor started producing electricity in 2011). "The truth of the matter," says Tom Blees, "is once most anti-nuke people hear about IFR, they tend to switch sides pretty quickly."

6.

Beyond IFR, there are two remaining new nuclear technologies that have people's attention: Liquid Fluoride Thorium Reactors (LFTR, pronounced *lifter*) and Small Scale Nuclear Reactors (SMRs). We'll take them one at a time.

LFTR began its life as a solution to a peculiar 1940s Air Force question: Can we use nuclear power to fly a bomber indefinitely? The basic answer was yes, but intercontinental ballistic missiles turned out to be a better way to fight the Cold War. Before that happened, research on the project was spread among a number of different centers, though Oak Ridge National Laboratory took the lead throughout the 1960s, even building a prototype LFTR reactor that went critical in 1954 and ran for 100 hours nonstop before being shut down.

After that program was cancelled, the idea never quite went away. A small cadre of Oak Ridge scientists kept it alive. Lately, the cadre has been expanding, primarily because LFTR has some significant benefits over other nuclear technologies — mainly the fact that it runs on thorium.

Thorium is a mildly radioactive element found in significantly greater quantities than uranium. As there are growing concerns about our dwindling uranium supply — some experts predict we could run out of our main nuclear fuel within 100 years — this is good news. More important, thorium provides more bang for our buck. In a standard thermal reactor, it takes 250 tons of uranium to create a gigawatt-year of electricity. LFTR requires only one ton of thorium to produce the same output. And less fuel makes for less waste. A lot less. Thorium creates less than 1 percent of the waste of a standard light-water reactor, and most of that "waste" isn't waste — rather a collection of valuable elements like rhodium.

Finally, LFTR allows for continuous refueling, meaning the reactor never stops operating, which makes it both incredibly efficient and a lousy target for terrorists intent on theft of nuclear materials. This level of safety and efficiency could lead to assembly-line production, making thorium reactors the Model T of nuclear designs. "To stop global warming," says Kirk Sorenson, chief technologist for the Energy from Thorium Foundation, "we need thousands of new reactors worldwide; currently we have hundreds. It took three years from when they invented the fluoride reactor until they built the first one. That was fifty years ago, and we know a lot more about how to do it now."

It's for this reason that a number of countries now have serious thorium programs underway. India, which has abundant thorium reserves, plans to generate 25 percent of their electricity from the element. China, meanwhile, is being even more aggressive. Asia's giant has a dedicated team of 750 researchers working the problem and plans to have its first thorium reactor up and running by late 2015. In the US, TerraPower, founded by former Microsoft chief technology officer Nathan Myhrvold, with backing from Bill Gates, is working on a "traveling wave reactor" — often described as "the world's most passive fast breeder reactor" — that will be able to run on both thorium and uranium and is due, in prototype form, by 2020.

The final technology worth considering are Small Scale Nuclear Reactors (SMRs) — or so-called "backyard nukes." These mini-nukes generate between 45 and 300 megawatts of power (compared to 500 megawatts for the smallest thermal reactor now on the market), are built modularly (and, at roughly $1 billion per, relatively cheaply), then sealed completely at the factory, shipped via rail, and arrive at their destination "plug and play." Once installed, they're designed to run for years without maintenance. A number of familiar faces (like Toshiba and Lawrence Livermore Laboratories) and several nuclear newcomers (like New Mexico–based Hyperion Power Generation and Oregon-based NuScale Power) have gone into this area because SMRs are believed to fill a niche.

In places where water shortages are a problem, SMRs could be used to run desalination plants; in places too remote for other options, SMRs could be the best alternative to trucking in barrels of diesel. Much interest is centered around providing power for remote mining operations (like extracting oil from tar sands, which currently uses more oil than it produces), backing up intermittently plagued solar or wind facilities, or even — in the very long term — serving as hydrogen generators.

All that said, as a pilot project of sorts, Toshiba has spent five years trying to give their SMR—known as the 4S for "super safe, small, and simple"—to the remote town of Galena, Alaska. But, as Greenpeace's Jim Riccio points out: "How good do you think the technology really is if they can't even give it away?" Along similar lines, the Nuclear Regulatory Commission has said it's unwilling to review SMR applications until each of the companies involved has found a domestic utility partner and, so far at least, none have.

While in office, President Barack Obama has been supportive of nuclear energy, but he also called the Nuclear Regulatory Commission a "moribund agency that needs to be revamped and has become a captive of the industries it regulates." This doesn't bode well for new nuclear technologies since they all must be approved by the Commission before deployment. And if Obama plans on revamping an agency that already claims to be severely understaffed, then once again we run into the wall of time.

Which raises the final question worth asking—what does all this excitement really mean? Not much as yet. In fact, despite recent and significant forward progress, because of the devastation that occurred when an earthquake, then a tsunami, struck Japan's Fukushima Daiichi Nuclear Power Plant, many countries are revamping their nuclear plans. Japan itself has shut down forty-eight of its plants. Germany halted its efforts to become a leader in nuclear power. Once again, the experts are predicting the end of the industry.

Yet a few key facts are often left out of the post-Fukushima debate. First, nuclear development hasn't completely stalled. As of September 2014, there are sixty-seven new plants under construction and more on the way. China continues to ramp up production and Saudi Arabia just announced plans to become a major player, wanting to draw 15 percent of its total energy from nuclear by 2034. More importantly, if the reactors inside the Daiichi plant had been Generation IV, their passive safety design would have ensured that all of this mess could have been avoided. Instead of tragedy dominating the news, we could have been having discussions about the safety and efficiency of new nuclear designs. Either way, whether it's a new nukes revolution or a Manhattan-style project to bring renewables up to speed, everyone agrees that if something doesn't happen soon, we may very well be designing our future technologies in the dark.

Space Diving

THE FUTURE OF SPORT

In the first section of this book, *The Future In Here,* we looked at the ways science and technology are impacting you and me. In *Part Two: The Future Out There,* we've been examining the inverse, the ways science and technology are impacting the world at large. In this chapter, we're going to look at the point at which these trends intersect: the future of sport.

If you scratch under the surface of sport, you'll pretty quickly encounter the burgeoning science of play. Over the past few decades, a topic that was once dismissed as mostly unimportant is now considered a critical biological process, a developmental necessity that allows us to learn fundamental social and survival skills, stimulate creativity and innovation, and test the limits of our own potential. Sport, meanwhile, is the cultural manifestation of play, the place where—in the guise of a game—we collectively explore the limits of human potential, penciling the outlines of future possibilities.

That's what makes this story so compelling. It's technically the tale of skydiver Felix Baumgartner's attempt to break a world record, except that the record he's set his sights on is actually an off-world record—it is a demonstration that our urge to play, interwoven with our need to push limits, has actually left the planet. In short, we have just added an entirely new level of meaning to the phrase "We got next."

1.

The balloon is a marvel, ghostly silver, as thin as a dry-cleaning bag. Partially inflated at the Roswell, New Mexico, launch site, it looks like an amoeba dressed in haute couture. In the lower atmosphere, at full height, it rises a majestic fifty-five stories. In the stratosphere, pancaked by pressure, it stretches wider than a football field. And it's the stratosphere where skydiver Felix Baumgartner is heading.

The date is October 14, 2012. The plan is for Baumgartner to ride that balloon higher than anyone has ridden before — some twenty-four miles above the Earth. To make this possible, he wears a one-of-a kind pressure suit designed to buffer temperatures as low as 70 degrees below zero and wind speeds more than 700 miles per hour. His ultimate goal: "space-diving" out of the balloon, falling back to Earth, and becoming the first human being to bareback the sound barrier — exceeding Mach 1 without aid of an engine or protection from a craft.

Conceived in 2005, the Red Bull Stratos Project, as this space dive is known, began as a joint venture between the energy drink company and Baumgartner, an Austrian skydiver. The big idea is to "transcend human limits which have existed for fifty years" — that is, since Air Force pilot Joe Kittinger plunged nineteen miles out of a balloon as a test procedure for "extreme high-altitude" bailouts. The big question was: Could an energy drink company and an action sports hero accomplish what a half century of government-backed space programs could not?

But it's not the only question. The space dive also raises queries about the future of action sports. Over the past few decades, extreme athletes have pushed progression farther and faster than ever before. In this evolutionary eye-blink, more "impossible" feats have been accomplished than at any other point in human history. Thus, despite the fanfare, the most incredible thing about Stratos might be the fact that it's actually the next logical step.

Still, it's no small step. The technological issues are myriad, the list of catastrophic unknowns even longer. No one has any idea whether the human body can go supersonic. Will the shock waves tear Baumgartner's body apart? Will the suit breach? Even bigger are the athletic hurdles. Normally, skydiving is sensation rich: an exceptionally wide field of view and a full complement of air friction. But Baumgartner's face mask narrows vision to a slit and the suit puts four layers of thick protection between skin and sky. Instead of reacting to the air itself, flying the suit requires reacting to far subtler clues — sort of like playing a video game with a delay built in.

More alarming, in the nonexistent atmosphere of the strato-sphere, falling objects have a tendency to spin — and keep spin-ning. If Baumgartner can't regain control, as he once told report-ers: "At a certain rpm there's only one way for the blood to leave your body, and that's through your eyeballs."

Under such duress, redundancy is security, so when the bal-loon reaches its top altitude, Mission Control runs through a forty-item checklist: "Item 26, move seat to rear of capsule; item 27, lift legs onto the door threshold." When the list is complete, Baumgartner stands outside the capsule, on a tiny exterior step. He takes a moment to take in the view then says a few words: "Sometimes you have to go up really high to understand how small you really are." Next he salutes; next he leaps.

It takes him 30 seconds to reach 600 miles per hour, less than a minute to shatter 700. He just became the first human being to go supersonic. This is also when he started spinning. At mis-sion control, where they're watching the entire dive on monitors, everyone holds their breath. Some begin praying. But somehow, miraculously, Baumgartner gets everything back under control.

He pulls out of the spin and locks into delta position: feet down, head up, and heading home.

In total, his freefall lasts 4 minutes and 19 seconds; his complete air time lasts approximately 10 minutes; his top speed reaches 833.9 miles-per-hour — Mach 1.24. Baumgartner also takes over the records for the highest manned balloon flight and the highest altitude jump and, with 8 million watching the broadcast live on YouTube, the highest numbers of concurrent viewers.

Perhaps more interesting than these records is the deeper why. On the Stratos website there's a short list of potential applications for the knowledge gained from Baumgartner's jump: "Passenger/ crew exit from space; developing protocols for exposure to high-altitude and high-acceleration environments; exploring the effects of supersonic acceleration and deceleration on the human body; and testing the latest innovations in parachute systems." In plainer language, experts have said that if the passengers on the space shuttle *Challenger* had been equipped with Baumgartner's suit they might have lived through their midair crack up.

Along just these lines, some six months after Baumgartner's jump, Virgin Galactic's *SpaceShipTwo* powered up its engines for the first time. *SpaceShipOne,* you might remember, was the craft that won the Ansari XPRIZE in 2004. This original XPRIZE was a demonstration project, both proof that a private company could produce an affordable, reusable spaceship and the necessary first step in opening the space frontier. The idea behind *SpaceShipTwo* is the next step: tourism — taking paying customers on suborbital cruises.

This is why Baumgartner's jump is critical. We're going to space. That's what's next. Within a few years, human beings will be routinely visiting low-Earth orbit. In fact, Bigelow Aerospace, another private space company, is now developing an inflatable space hotel that's scheduled for 2017 deployment. With these developments around the corner, having basic space evacuation procedures in place — including a supersonic-capable space suit — just seems to make sense.

But if you want to really talk about the adjacent possible: The combination of Baumgartner's success and the birth of the space tourism industry means that space diving could be the next extreme sport frontier. It sounds silly, of course, but it wasn't too long ago that surfing a 100-foot wave or free-soloing Half Dome — two "impossible" feats lately accomplished — were equally ludicrous. Plus, consider the space-diving upside. Imagine giving athletes 25 miles of fall time to work with. Talk about pushing the limits of kinesthetic possibility. Despite the acrobatics involved, formation skydiving never really took off — but 25 miles is enough fall time for a team to pull off an entire aerial opera. Space ballet anyone?

Consider, in 2003, Shane McConkey paradigm-shifted skiing when he invented the ski-BASE (that is, ski an amazing line that ends in huge cliff, ski off the cliff, then deploy a parachute). Baumgartner touched down in the desert, but sooner or later isn't someone going to try to land on a ski slope? How long then until we turn the space dive into the first stage of a double ski-BASE? How long until it gets stranger than that? In other words, while Baumgartner's triumph seems the apex of achievement, the truth might even be stranger: The space dive was merely the beginning.

Building a Better Mosquito

THE WORLD'S FIRST GENETICALLY ENGINEERED CREATURE

Over the course of this book, we've discussed a number of topics that could be considered "miracles," in the biblical sense of the word. In this chapter, we are investigating two more: the curing of disease and the creation of life, and both at the same time.

Taken together, these feats are among our oldest dreams. They are ideas that comprise our myths and legends, ideas that have been with us for so long that they seem woven into the fundamental fabric of our being, ideas that combine into what might be called our "aspirational genome."

But aspirational no more. 3.5 million years ago, life emerged on this planet from the primordial soup; 3.5 million years later, we have duplicated this miracle and then some. Call it hubris, call it the opening of Pandora's box, call it what you will—but that's the point. Call it something. Put a name on it. Over time, the miraculous always becomes the mundane, so before that happens, label this moment. Preserve it, so that later, when recall becomes dim, we can remember just how far we've come.

1.

In 77 CE, Pliny the Elder published his *Natural History*, an imaginative, thirty-seven-volume attempt to catalog the entire contents of the world. From Pliny, we learn that the artichoke is one of the earth's great monstrosities; that rubbing mouse poo on bald spots can increase hair growth; and, on islands off the coast of Germany, there lives a tribe of people whose ears are so large they cover their bodies. It is also in *Natural History* that we first hear of a mixture of arsenic, sulfur, caustic soda, and olive oil being used to protect crops against pestilence. This last bit of information might seem trifling compared to the more mythic elements in Pliny's compendium, but it is the first written record of an insecticide and, for reasons that will soon become clear, an entry that seems especially prescient.

Right now, the threat posed by mosquito-borne illnesses — malaria, dengue fever, yellow fever, West Nile virus — is growing at alarming rates. In America, where many of these ailments haven't been seen in over fifty years, the danger is especially menacing. Asian tiger mosquitos, a carrier of yellow fever, encephalitis and other diseases, have been seen as far north as Chicago. In Key West, Florida, researchers have identified a unique strain of dengue fever — meaning the virus was not recently imported by an unsuspecting tourist but rather has been around long enough to become genetically distinct.

In an attempt to fight back, scientists are now heading down a radically new road and breeding a radically new breed of mosquito — the world's first genetically altered insect destined to be released into the wild. Better or worse, we're crossing a line. Which means that the mosquito we're about to release is a hybrid descendent of two of Pliny's mythic lineages — both a fantastical creature and a pesticide — and both at once.

2.

The modern war against insect-borne disease dates back to 1897, when British scientist Ronald Ross discovered that malaria was spread by mosquitoes. He was also the first to propose reducing or eliminating the world's mosquito population as a way of controlling the disease. But it wasn't until early WWII forays into chemical warfare — leading to the discovery of insecticides ferocious enough to take on the insects — that his idea became truly possible.

Since that point, the fight against mosquito-vectored ailments has been a chemical battle. Scientists developed drugs that were useful against these diseases and insecticides that were useful against the mosquitoes that transmitted these diseases. For a time, it looked like we were winning this fight. Unfortunately, in the past thirty years, the rules have changed. Mother Nature interceded and evolution occurred. We're now fighting insects that are resistant to our pesticides and diseases that are resistant to our drugs.

A number of these diseases are considered the deadliest on earth. Today, principally in Africa and Asia, dengue fever annually infects more than 50 million people and kills 500,000. Malaria infects about 400 million and kills more than a million — most of them kids. More disturbingly, the combination of pesticide and drug immunities, along with the rise of global transportation and climate change, has resulted in mosquito-vectored ailments appearing in places where they have not been seen before. In 2003, in the US, dengue fever appeared for the second time in Hawaii and the first time in the Gulf states, and the following summer there were 4,000 reported cases of West Nile and 300 deaths. Malaria has so far failed to make serious inroads into the

country, but in the slightly purple words of the Malaria Foundation International, "a plague is coming back, and we have only
ourselves to blame."

To address these concerns, during the past fifteen years, scientists have been trying to move beyond the chemical paradigm
and toward a genetic one. The dream has been to build a *transgenic mosquito,* a genetically modified insect unable to transmit
illness. This new insect would then be introduced in the wild,
thus supplanting disease carriers with a harmless imposter.
Seven teams, both in America and in Europe, have been working
on the project — and that work is heading for prime time.

It is now possible to walk into any number of molecular biology labs and peer through a microscope at a mosquito unlike
any other in history. The magnified insect shows a feature not
found in the wild: a pair of bright, fluorescent green eyes — the
telltale sign of successful genetic modification. These eyes are
proof that one of the most scientifically advanced cures for disease ever conceived is feasible. They are also proof that, if we
are not exceptionally careful, we could do irreparable damage
to our ecosystems or, worse, create new, more devastating ailments currently unknown to science. One thing is certain: The
bioengineered mosquito hangs precariously off the cutting edge
of genetic research — how we proceed matters plenty.

3.

Before we can talk about how to proceed, it's helpful to understand how we got here — a story that starts with the relationship
between malaria and mosquitoes. Of the 2,500 kinds of mosquitoes in the world, no more than a tiny minority evolved to
feed on humans. But evolve they did. And as these mosquitoes
were learning to live off humans, malaria — the most prolific of
mosquito-borne diseases — was learning to live off both.

Most mammals and quite a few birds are susceptible to the

disease. Up to now, all of the transgenic research has been done with malaria's avian or rodent varieties, but the parasite spreads the same in every species. Transmission begins when a hungry female mosquito (only the female feeds on blood) drinks her dinner from an infected animal, along the way ingesting the malaria parasite. In a few days, the parasite travels into the mosquito's mid-gut, where it develops sexually reproductive cells that mate and mature and release thousands of malaria sporozoites. In turn, these cells make their way into the mosquito's circulatory system, eventually taking up residence in their salivary gland. The whole cycle takes about ten days. Afterward, the next time that mosquito bites into something, malaria goes along for the ride.

This malarial life cycle was mostly understood by the early portion of the twentieth century, but our attempt to remake insects into allies in the war against insects dates to the 1930s and work done by the late Barbara McClintock. In 1983, McClintock won a Nobel Prize in medicine for her discovery of short chains of DNA called "transposable elements" or, more commonly, "jumping genes." A jumping gene is so named because the proteins it encodes can splice open a chromosome, jump inside, and then sew the whole deal back together again. This discovery makes it possible to piggyback other, more helpful DNA — such as DNA that would be useful in the fight against malaria — on a jumping gene and use this gene to insert the mutation into a foreign genome.

At least that was the theory. It took a half century for theory to become practice. But, in 1981, biologist Gerald Rubin discovered a jumping gene in the fruit fly *Drosophilia melanogaster.* He named it "P." A year later, working with embryologist Allan Spradling, Rubin used P as a Trojan horse to build the world's first genetically modified insect. "It was a huge accomplishment," says Peter Atkinson, an entomologist at the University of California, Riverside and one of the scientists leading the quest for transgenic mosquitos. "They took a gene that gives eyes a reddish color, attached it to P, and then inserted the whole thing into a fruit fly. That fly's offspring were born with reddish eyes, and their offspring as well. The trait was stable and heritable."

Unfortunately, being able to manipulate fruit flies, while scientifically exciting, was not real-world important. Fruit flies neither carry disease nor pollinate crops and, other than being research tools, have little economic or social impact on our lives. Still, there was hope that P would be found in other insects and, once found, would be useful in manipulating genes in the fight against insect-borne diseases. "The eighties were pretty much a wild goose chase down this road," recounts Atkinson. "Entomologists thought P was going to be this great breakthrough, but all that got published were negative results."

By the early 1990s, it was pretty clear that P was finished. Scientists began looking for other jumping genes, Atkinson among them. In 1996–97, working with University of Maryland molecular geneticist David O'Brochta, he found one in houseflies — dubbed Hermes, for the speedy Greek messenger. The hope was that Hermes would be workable in a way that P wasn't, and, the following year, hope was vindicated: Anthony James, an insect geneticist at the University of California, Irvine, used the gene to modify a mosquito that transmits yellow fever.

But this was only the beginning of the battle.

Fruit flies are the workhorse of modern genetics. As such, we have a long list of fruit fly traits that have been identified and cultivated in the lab. Eye color, for example. In their work with fruit flies, Spradling and Rubin had only to look for a change in eye color — what's called a genetic marker — to see if their experiments were successful. But no such marker existed in mosquitos. Thus, the only way to figure out if a jumping gene had done its job was to breed potential transgenics by the boatload, dissect the results, and use a microscope to see if the inserted DNA had taken hold. For the long-haul work of fighting malaria, this process was too arduous to be economically viable. Plus, dissection killed the mosquito being studied, which — even if she did contain the inserted DNA — put a serious damper on her future breeding abilities.

In the late 1980s, to get over these hurdles, scientists began looking for an easily identifiable genetic marker that could be attached to jumping genes. In the early 1990s, researchers at Columbia University began experimenting with a Puget Sound jellyfish that glowed fluorescent green when exposed to UV light. Turns out, the protein that created the glow could be inserted into other species without killing them. Then, in 2000, Peter Atkinson attached this Day-Glo protein to Hermes, and suddenly the use of genetically altered mosquitoes to fight mosquito-borne ailments became a much more viable proposition.

A few years later, with Atkinson's Day-Glo marker guiding the work, Johns Hopkins geneticist Marcelo Jacobs-Lorena found a small peptide that binds to receptors in the mosquito's gut — the same spot where the malaria parasite normally attaches itself. He next engineered a gene that expressed this peptide and inserted it into mosquitos. In these new transgenics, with vulnerable receptor sites blocked by the peptide, the parasite dies before it can reproduce and infect anything else. It was a major breakthrough. Jacobs-Lorena had turned a mosquito into an insecticide.

Unfortunately, that insecticide can still adapt — and that leads to an entirely different set of problems.

4.

One of the main lessons learned in the pesticide wars of the last century was that mosquitoes and malaria are both nimble mutants. Therefore, while everyone acknowledges Jacobs-Lorena's achievement, everyone knows it's not enough to win the war. "In order to ensure success," notes Anthony James, "we need to build a transgenic mosquito that kills malarial parasites in a number of different ways — it's the only way to stay a few steps ahead of evolution."

This work is also under way. For example, Jacobs-Lorena blocks the receptor that the parasite binds to inside the insect's mid-gut, but James has found a way to block the parasite's ability to bind to a mosquito's salivary glands. Meanwhile, at the University of California, Riverside, Alexander Raikhel has taken a very different approach — he's figured out how to boost a mosquito's immune system so it turns on every time there's a chance the insect can get malaria — thus killing the disease before it has the ability to spread.

Yet, even if we can outfox evolution and find a way to completely kill malaria in the lab, researchers still need to make this work in the real world. The transgenics that Jacobs-Lorena has created have the same life span and produce the same number of offspring as normal mosquitoes. "This means," he says, "that in laboratory conditions there's no fitness cost to building mosquitoes with an immunity to malaria. But there could be a fitness cost in the wild, and to really control the disease, we have to find a way to make our transgenic insects have more offspring than wild mosquitoes."

This isn't the only issue. Another problem is that we still need to make the switch from mosquitoes that carry animal malaria to mosquitoes that carry human malaria — a feat not as easy as it sounds. Not only are the mosquitoes that carry human malaria much harder to breed in captivity, there are also key differences between animal models and human models. The same gene that blocks malaria in mice, for example, does not work in humans, although Jacobs-Lorena believes he's found a different gene to accomplish this task.

But once that task is accomplished, containment becomes an even greater concern. As there's no way to build transgenics with a human form of malaria immunity without first breeding insects with the human form of malaria, much of this work has been moved to Level-3 biocontainment facilities — the kind that come with electronic passkeys, multiple airlocks, and drainage systems that dump waste water into a heating chamber that boils off any remnant of disease.

And this Fort Knox approach better work. Escaped mosquitos could easily lead to disease outbreaks, but more alarming is the fact that jumping genes not only hop around genomes — they also hop from species to species. An escaped transgenic could inter-breed with wild populations and produce something that we've never seen before — something even more deadly than what we have today.

And even if unintentional escape can be prevented, eventually we're going to have to release these transgenics into the wild (a Key West pilot project is already heading down this road). The downside here is that we know very little about how mosqui-toes live in the wild. We don't completely understand how they breed — meaning everything from how they select certain mates to why they choose to lay their eggs in one puddle rather than another. Nor do we know how seasons affect population size or how wide a territory certain populations inhabit or, critically, how and why genes travel through given populations. Thus, what we really don't know is the full list of dangers involved in tinker-ing with this balance.

Mosquito-borne ailments are among the most devastating and successful diseases on earth. The chemical paradigm of the last century produced a disease immune to our drugs and an in-sect immune to our pesticides. Could we produce a Frankenstein mosquito carrying super-malaria? "There's just no way to know exactly what will happen in ten thousand generations of mosqui-toes," says Atkinson. But it looks like we are about to find out.

So here we are, some two thousand years post-Pliny. A line has been crossed and another is about to fall, and the next time someone sets out to catalog the entire contents of the world, they will need to create a whole new mythic category: The very first man-made creature to venture into the wild.

The Great Galactic Gold Rush

THE BIRTH OF THE ASTEROID
MINING INDUSTRY

The first time I met XPRIZE founder Peter Diamandis — the story that opens this book — he told me about the possibilities of asteroid mining, arguing that the very first trillionaire on Earth was going to be the person who figured out how to mine the sky. It was, without question, one of the zaniest things anyone had said to me. For a science writer, asteroid mining sat somewhere between "cold fusion" and "cloak of invisibility" on the list of things not likely to happen anytime soon.

But Peter also argued that without asteroid mining — that is, without an economic driver powering space exploration — our species would never really get off our planet. In this, it was hard to disagree. Thus, in the aftermath of that conversation, asteroid mining became one of those technologies I decided to track.

The story you're about to read is the result of that effort. It marks the first time asteroid mining appeared not in the pages of science fiction (or in a magazine dedicated to future forward ideas), but in a mainstream publication with a general readership. This is a big deal. Next time you open up a magazine, know that for every article you see, there are five more that ended up on the cutting-room floor. And one of the easiest ways for an article to get cut is for the subject matter to seem too outlandish. The fact that as-teroid mining made it through this editorial process tells you much about the state of the industry, which is to say that the economic engine that will unlock the solar system seems to have finally arrived. Very soon, we will no longer be a one-planet species.

1.

Brother Guy Consolmagno is fifty-eight years old, with a thick beard, round glasses, and a scholarly manner. In public, he favors the black robes of his Jesuit order, though his garb may be somewhat misleading. While Consolmagno is certainly a man of the cloth, most of his life has been focused on the details of God's creation rather than the deity itself. With a PhD in planetary science, Consolmagno's held teaching positions at both Harvard and MIT and is considered one of the world's leading experts on the evolution of the solar system.

This expertise has served him well within the Society of Jesus. These days, Brother Guy, as he prefers, is a Vatican astronomer. To many, especially those who remember that Galileo was severely punished for his heliocentric heresy, the fact that the Vatican now employs professional star watchers seems peculiar — an issue well-summarized by former Comedy Central host Stephen Colbert: "I don't understand why the Church is suddenly all 'ground control to Cardinal Tom.'" Brother Guy told Colbert that the Vatican supported astronomy because "It's a good way to know there's more important things in the universe than what's for lunch."

And this very well may be the case, but lately the list of things the Vatican considers more important than lunch has taken a turn for the unusual. Not too long ago, for example, the Church brought together top scientists and major religious leaders to explore the possibility of alien life in the universe and what that possibility means for Jesus. CNN dubbed the event "E.T. phone Rome," but, truthfully, this topic was nowhere near as future forward as the one Brother Guy turned his attention to in 2008.

That year, in "The Ethics of Exploration," a speech given at the Manreza Symposium in Hungary, Brother Guy got serious about asteroid mining, which, as it sounds, is the act of using rocket ships to chase down giant, floating space rocks, land on their surface, then mine them for minerals and ores. The fact that a Vatican astronomer was speaking about this topic was odd enough, but Brother Guy's concerns that day were less about the possibility of asteroid mining ever occurring and more about the ethical consequences that would result. "On the one hand," he said, "it's great. You've taken all of this dirty industry off the surface of the Earth. On the other hand, you've put a whole lot of people out of work. If you've got a robot doing the mining, why not another robot doing the manufacturing? And now you've just put all of China out of work. What are the ethical implications of this kind of major shift?"

And Brother Guy is correct — it would be a major shift. Asteroids are rocky, celestial bodies that orbit the sun. Their sizes range from large pebbles to small planets, with plenty in between. The main belt has over 40,000 asteroids larger than a kilometer in diameter, and this is the critical part: Most are thick with ore. Jeffrey Kargel, a planetary geologist from the University of Arizona, recently calculated that FE90, a typical Apollo-class asteroid, contains some \$50 billion worth of metal, including some 41,000 kilograms of gold, or double what Fort Knox held at its operational height. So forget about merely putting China out of work — dumping this much lucre on the market could, well, end the market.

And here's the strangest part — all of this could happen much sooner than you might expect.

In the fifty years since *Vostok 1*, the first ever manned spaceflight, asteroid mining has gone from a perennial pipedream of the *Star Trek* Forever crowd to a serious enough proposition that a Vatican astronomer felt the need to address ethical concerns in public. In fact, in April 2012 — and with backing from the likes of

Google cofounder Larry Page, Google executive chairman Eric Schmidt, and Virgin founder Sir Richard Branson — Peter Diamandis, creator of the XPRIZE, alongside Eric Anderson, CEO of Space Adventures Ltd. (the private space tourism company that flew Stephen Hawking into zero-G and sent billionaire Dennis Tito to the International Space Station), announced Planetary Resources Inc. (PRI), a newly formed asteroid mining company. This time, it was Comedy Central host Jon Stewart who summed things up nicely: "Space pioneers going to mine motherfucking asteroids for precious materials! *BOOM! BOOM!* YES! Stu-Beef is all in. Do you know how rarely the news in 2012 looks and sounds like you thought news would look and sound in 2012?"

2.

No one's entirely sure where the concept of mining asteroids originated, though the great Russian rocket scientist Konstantin Tsiolkovsky — who pioneered steering thrusters, multistage chemical rockets, space suits, space stations, artificial gravity, airlocks, and, really, most of the technologies in use off-world today — wrote about the idea in the early twentieth century. From there, it orbited the space community for a decade, making a mainstream debut in a 1932 publication of Paul Simak's short story "Asteroids of Gold" — wherein the brothers Vernon and Vince Drake earn their keep as space miners. By the early 1940s, asteroid mining had become a sci-fi mainstay. Concurrently, a Libertarian ethos began to infuse these tales. Miners, usually known as "rock rats," were seen as frontiersmen, asteroids as the new Wild West. This theme progressed until the 1970s and 1980s, wherein asteroid mining came to be seen as an anti-environmental, hard-right fairy tale: Don't worry about using up all the resources here on Earth because we can always go into space and get more. Outside of the space community, mostly, this is where things still stand, but inside the community, in the past few decades, a tectonic shift has occurred: Asteroid mining has gone from science fiction to science fact.

What really bridged that gap was a trilogy of recent space missions. The first of those was the Near Earth Asteroid Rendezvous Shoemaker, launched by NASA in February of 1996. NEAR Shoemaker became the first unmanned spacecraft to prove that we could actually catch up to an asteroid — which is no simple trick.

In our solar system, the vast majority of asteroids are found around fifty-six million miles away, hurtling through the gap between Jupiter and Mars. Despite the degree of difficulty involved in catching something that moves at 15.5 miles per second, in 2000 NEAR Shoemaker combined a well-crafted hibernation period (to conserve energy) with an Earth swing-by gravity assist and two carefully controlled thruster burns to catch the second-largest near-Earth asteroid, Eros 433, in midstride.

Shoemaker spent a year orbiting and studying Eros, which is less interesting to would-be space miners than the fact that NASA ended the mission in 2001, by landing the probe on the asteroid's surface. In 1999, the agency went a step further, launching Stardust — a ship that traveled three billion miles to rendezvous with the comet Wild 2 — a meeting that took place at the dizzy speed of 33 miles per second. Even better, once Stardust caught up to Wild 2, it used a specially designed air filter to take samples of comet dust, then turned around, traveled another billion miles, and brought those samples back to Earth in 2006.

Since any successful asteroid mining mission is going to require not only getting to an asteroid but landing on it, digging in, and then coming back home, by far the most impressive mission to date was Japan's Hayabusa probe. In September 2005, Hayabusa chased down asteroid Itokawa and spent a month analyzing its shape, spin, topography, color, composition, density, and history before landing on the surface in November 2005. There it used a robotic arm to scrape the surface and gather a few samples.

On June 13, 2010, Hayabusa returned to Earth, making a parachute landing in the South Australian outback. The spaceship burned up in the atmosphere, but a heat-shielded return capsule brought the samples back intact. The first half of those have now been analyzed (confirming, in fact, that they did come from Itokawa) and show roughly the same chemical makeup contained in meteors already found here on Earth — which makes Itokawa rich in exactly the kinds of minerals we want to mine.

"That scrape of the surface confirmed we're capable of asteroid mining," says Brother Guy. "That's one of the main differences between drilling for minerals here on Earth and on asteroids. The Earth has been chemically processed, so our mineral wealth is only found in certain regions, and many of those regions are very deep underground. Asteroids, though, are homogenous. What's on the surface is what's below the surface. You don't have to dig, you can scrape — and that's exactly what Hayabusa did."

University of Arizona professor of planetary science Erik Asphaug believes the final piece in the puzzle came with the mapping all of the near-Earth asteroids — an ongoing international effort to avert planetary disaster. This effort began in the 1970s, when scientists figured out that an asteroid with a diameter of ten kilometers killed off the dinosaurs. By the early 1990s, they'd realized a one-kilometer-diameter rock could jeopardize the survival of the human race, and, even more alarmingly, rocks of that size impact the Earth once every 500,000 years. Which is when most everyone in the space field decided it might be good to figure out where all those rocks were lurking and what exactly were their intentions.

Thus began the great asteroid hunt of the aughts. In the past decade, using a wide variety of telescopes, researchers have located 90 percent of the large near-Earth asteroids — those over one kilometer in diameter — and 10 percent of the smaller ones. In terms of planetary safety, we've discovered no species-ending impacts in our near future, but there have been other gains as well. "All of this mapping can be used for asteroid mining," says Asphaug. "Sure, we're trying to save the world from a catastrophic event, but along the way we've drawn up a pretty good prospector's map of our solar system."

During this same time, there's also been a philosophical shift surrounding the idea. Brother Guy believes its roots are generational: "So many of us now in the science field got started by reading science fiction. Our view of how the universe could work really was shaped by writers like Robert Heinlein. Once we got old enough and educated enough to be in a position to check the reality of the numbers behind science fictional ideas, we were able to see which ones were really possible and to ask ourselves how to make those dreams into reality."

XPRIZE founder Peter Diamandis agrees, but also feels the discovery of deep-sea oil deposits were equally critical. "Asteroid mining is about working robotically in a very far away, very harsh, and extreme environment. Well, the first deep oil deposit was found by Shell in the 1970s — beneath five thousand feet of water and another ten thousand feet of rock. That's a very far away, harsh, and extreme environment. At the time Shell found the oil, no one alive knew how to drill at those depths. We didn't have the necessary robotics, and we didn't have the AI systems to drive those robotics. But oil was precious enough that Shell placed [and won] a multibillion-dollar bet. This means that today, right now, we have companies willing and able to place multibillion dollars bets [a typical deep-sea platform runs between five and fifty billion] on high-risk, robotically-run, resource extraction missions — which is asteroid mining to a tee."

"You need to examine the facts," says Eric Anderson, "No laws of physics need to be reconfigured to mine an asteroid. There are no technology gaps. Truthfully, building a North Sea oil platform is a lot harder."

And, suddenly, Houston, we have proof of concept.

3.

So what will this concept look like in our lifetime? Already, Planetary Resources has raised over $1.5 million to help launch the ARKYD 100 space telescope, which is specifically designed to hunt for near-Earth asteroid mining prospects. There's also President Obama's announcement that he wants to land astronauts on an asteroid by 2025. Teams at Johnson Space Center in Houston and the Jet Propulsion Laboratory in Pasadena are hard at work on this goal, so a government-sponsored first step is not out of the question. Others believe that big energy companies — the same ones who built North Sea oil platforms — will have, by then, staked claims on near-Earth asteroids. Jeffrey Kargel compares the short-term future of asteroid exploitation to the early exploration of North America, starting with the Lewis and Clark expedition in 1803. "That expedition was followed by decades of military expeditions, geologic surveys, and infrastructure development. Major exploitation of the West's mineral riches began in 1848 and helped power American industrialization over the succeeding century. With asteroid mining we also may face a period of several decades where the world's space agencies will support asteroid, lunar, and Martian resource exploration while key infrastructure is improved. Profitable commercial development of extraterrestrial resources may begin midcentury and fundamentally shape Earth's economy before this century is out."

The reason asteroid mining will reshape the global economy comes down to the numbers. In his Manreza lecture, Brother Guy examined the value of a typical S-class asteroid (S for stony, thus only 10 percent metal). By his calculations, an S-class asteroid contains about one billion metric tons of iron, or as much as is currently mined on Earth each year. The total value of this haul sits in the high, high trillions. And that's only one type of asteroid. There are also M-class asteroids, with M standing for mostly metallic.

While iron is the most abundant metal found in asteroids, they also contain nickel, gold, cobalt, and perhaps the biggest find: all of the platinum-group metals. "In human history," says Eric Anderson, "all the platinum that's been mined on Earth would fit in a tractor trailer. But platinum has excellent technological properties. It's a great conductor. But at two thousand dollars an ounce, we really can't build new industries around it."

Getting the necessary platinum for the creation of new industries is a tantalizing possibility, but more practical concerns will likely drive early mining missions. Fuel cells are a necessity if we're going to fight global warming, but we need platinum to run them. If all five hundred million vehicles on the road today suddenly had fuel cells, then our entire supply of platinum would be exhausted in fifteen years. Meanwhile, iridium, used for LCDs and flat-screen TVs, and tantalum, used in cell phones, are both abundant in space but in short supply on Earth. The same holds for phosphorus — needed for fertilizer — and gallium, hafnium, and zinc — all needed for electronics. "The Earth," says Diamandis, "is a tiny crumb in a supermarket of resources. I've said for a long time, the very first trillionaire on Earth will be the person who figures out how to mine an asteroid and open up that supermarket."

But gold in 'dem hills isn't the only thing fueling our space rock fire. In the past few years, for reasons ranging from "because it's what's next" to "because it's the only way to guarantee the survival of the species," NASA has firmly committed itself to establishing off-world colonies. While colonizing either the Moon or Mars seems the next logical step, most feel that we should learn to crawl before we walk. "Visiting an asteroid is a fantastic stepping stone to Mars," says Derek Sears, professor of space and planetary science at the University of Arkansas. "You can test out the hardware and the human behavior."

Human behavior is key. A trip to Mars will take three years. Space flight is extremely punishing, both physically and mentally, so no one has any idea how humans would fare over that duration. But an asteroid, one that's passing close to the Earth, is a few month's voyage, which makes them a very good place to learn to crawl.

Even more important to our off-world plans is water. "Most aerospace engineers feel," continues Sears, "that water is the real key to off-world colonies. Carrying water out of a gravity well is extremely expensive. But there is a whole class of asteroids that are 25 percent water. We call them mudballs. So a rocket ship could stop off at an asteroid on the way to a space colony and tank up on water. There's no cost. Just warm up a chunk and off you go."

Nor is this where possibilities end. As far out as asteroid mining or Mars's colonies might still seem, there's much more in the works. University of Arizona emeritus professor John Lewis, in his now classic *Mining the Sky,* points out that as we get better at the technology, we could also learn to mine gas giants like Jupiter for their massive quantities of helium-3. "What would you do with our 10 tons of helium-3 when we get back to Earth?" writes Lewis. "The market value for helium-3 is set by the amount of energy that it can produce in a helium-3/deuterium fusion reactor. That has a cash value of $160,000,000,000 . . . That means helium-3 is worth 1,000 times its weight in gold or platinum. Here is surely the most valuable raw material in the solar system, well worth the cost of transportation back to Earth!"

So how far are we from launch? Eric Anderson thinks we're five to ten years away from our first asteroid mining mission, and a great many people in the private space sector agree. NASA believes things will go the other way round: First we'll have manned missions to asteroids, next we'll have robotic ones, but, as Anderson also says, "NASA doesn't like to fail in public, so their scientists tend to be fairly conservative. A year before Burt Rutan won the XPRIZE, if you asked them if a private company could send a ship to space, they would have said it was impossible."

And once we're actually mining asteroids, well, look out. "This is a truly disruptive technology," says Brother Guy. "Certainly, in the long run — whether you're talking about wealth creation or the taking of mining, one of the most environmentally damaging industries, off-world — everyone is better off. Frankly, in the long run, the upside is so big it's almost utopian. But in the short run, there will most definitely be some consequences."

PART THREE

THE FUTURE UNCERTAIN

The Psychedelic Renaissance

THE RADICAL WORLD OF
PSYCHEDELIC MEDICINE

In my other job as the cofounder and director of research for the Flow Genome Project (flowgenomeproject.com), I have spent the past fifteen years studying the intersection of altered states of consciousness and ultimate human performance. As a result, I have also kept a close eye on research in nearby areas, and that includes the science of psychedelics.

Few topics hold as much promise as this science, though it is safe to say that most people don't share this opinion. Not many "technologies" have drawn as much ire as these drugs. Yet, as this story makes clear, society's longstanding hostility is finally starting to abate. For the first time, we are starting to see these substances for what they really are: Both an amazing window into the outer ranges of human experience and a treatment for some of our most intractable conditions.

What's more, these chemicals give us deep insight into philosophical questions of enormous importance—how the brain constructs reality; the relationship between mind, brain, and body; and the neurobiological correlates for belief, meaning, and transformative experience. To put this differently, psychedelics are among our oldest disruptive technologies—literally pre-dating our species—yet their potency and potential, then as now, remains as mind-bending as ever.

Yet the real point of this story is compassion. Discussions of future technology often omit this element. Sure, they may talk about the "human factor"—how a certain tech will cure disease or end poverty or some other glistening proclamation—but that is empathy at a distance, not compassion on the ground. This story is an exception. It peeks into a controversial future that already exists, that already impacts the lives of real people with real problems. It expands the meaning of compassion. It is an honest look at the real human factor: fragile, brave, and—as is often the case—in need of a miracle.

1.

The room where they wait is a long rectangle. The floor is covered in thick green carpeting, so everyone calls it the "green room." One wall of the green room is covered in books, the other three in paintings. There are marble fireplaces and a high ceiling. In the center of that ceiling sits an old floral medallion — once the anchor point for a massive Victorian chandelier. The chandelier is long gone, but the medallion remains. When Mara Howell lies in bed, she looks straight up at it. The flowers are braided into a wreath, and maybe it's all that Victorian ornamentation distorting the image, or maybe the design was intentional, but either way, the result looks less botanical than celestial. The flowers look like angels. A hovering swirl of angels. And Mara hopes, like everybody in the green room hopes, that they are angels of mercy.

Marilyn Howell, Mara's mother, and Lindsay Corliss, Mara's close friend, are also waiting in the green room. Lindsay is nervously tidying up. Marilyn is just nervous. She stands beside her daughter and beneath the angels, but can't stay still. Instead, she walks to the window and glances into the street again. It is late morning and early summer, and the trees are full of leaves and the sky is free of clouds and none of these things are making Marilyn feel any better. Even the angels no longer make her feel better. For her, these days, the passing of spring is far too metaphoric. The season of hope and renewal is ending. Maybe the angels have lost their power. Maybe they never had any to begin with. She glances out at the street again and wonders — where the hell is Allan?

Marilyn doesn't know much about Allan — though she knows he's late and she knows that's not his real name. Allan is an underground therapist of sorts and the work he does, what he calls his "crimes of compassion," remains very much illegal. It took Marilyn some serious effort to even drum up his phone number. Then there were the meetings. On the first meeting, Marilyn had several hundred questions, but Allan had several hundred answers. His knowledge was impressive, as was his willingness to take great risks for perfect strangers. Marilyn liked him immediately — which was a good thing, because there were no other options.

Mara was thirty-two when diagnosed with colon cancer. That was a little over a year ago and an unusual diagnosis. The disease typically strikes the elderly — in 2001–2002, the median age was seventy-one. On top of that, Mara is, to all who know her, "vibrant." She rarely drinks, does no drugs, eats right, sleeps well, is ridiculously optimistic, always battles her weight but gets plenty of exercise. A month before her first major surgery, she'd been in Honduras gathering data on fish populations and earning a master's certification in scuba diving.

Another word often used to describe Mara is "tough." She taught school in Oakland, California, for starters, but the story everyone likes best is the one from back when she was nineteen and trekking through the Kenyan bush on a National Outdoor Leadership School training program. Their team leader got gored by a buffalo, suffering broken ribs and a gaping chest wound. Mara was the only one in the group with first aid training, so she stayed with him — stayed alone in the bush — while everyone else went for help. She banged pots together to keep away lions, used clean socks to stanch the chest wound. Her story now appears in the NOLS first aid manual as an example of "Best-Case Performance in an Emergency Situation." And when it comes to cancer survival, these days, young, vibrant, tough, healthy, and optimistic is also the stuff of best-case performances in an emergency situation. Unfortunately, Mara remains the exception to that rule.

In the past year, Mara has tried all the traditional drugs and all the alternative therapies. Wow, has she tried all the alternative therapies. Massage, macrobiotics, Chinese herbs, Tibetan herbs, acupuncture, acupressure, the Feldenkrais method, chiropractic realignment, the power of prayer. At a Catholic Mass in Boston the priest read from the pulpit: "Blessed Virgin Mary, please intercede to heal Mara Howell." Jews at the Aquarian Minyon in Berkeley chanted "*Mi Sheberakh Avoteinu*," while Buddhists in Hollywood tried "*Nam-Myyoho-Rebge-Kyo.*" Twice, Mara went to Brazil to meet the famed faith healer John of God. Purportedly, John of God has healed over 15 million people. Maybe as many as 45 million. But he couldn't heal Mara. Nor could he ease her pain.

Mara falls into another anomalous category—alongside 2 percent of the populace—whose pain cannot be controlled by current medications. Pain is usually measured on a scale from zero to ten, with zero being "no pain" and ten being "worst pain imaginable." Despite a dozen different meds, morphine, methadone, the works, Mara's pain rarely dips below a five. It is often up around an eight—which is when most of us would be screaming.

About five weeks ago, it got so bad that Mara was forced to leave her apartment in Oakland for the home where she grew up. So the green room, which was really the front room in Marilyn's Boston home, was converted into a sick ward. It was after a hospital bed had been installed beneath that floral medallion that Marilyn decided it was time for a chat.

A few months back, she'd heard rumor of Allan and the particular work he does, but broaching the subject with her daughter was not easy. The treatment is not only radical, not only illegal, but also geared toward helping patients confront what's politely called "end-of-life anxiety," and known to most as mortal terror. Mara's reaction was immediately hostile. "I'm not interested in discussing end-of-life issues," she snapped. "Who told you about this? How could they be so insensitive?" Then she thought it through. She knew she needed a miracle, and this treatment, unlike all the others, had a peculiar history of spiritual transformation—that is, she also knew, if it didn't kill her first.

The second meeting Marilyn had with Allan was more difficult than the first. Allan is an underground psychedelic therapist. Psychedelic therapy is built on the 1960s idea that psychedelics—

drugs like LSD and psilocybin (the "magic" in magic mushrooms) that are known to radically alter cognition and perception — also have the ability to produce profound insight at lower doses, and cathartic life-changing experiences at higher doses. Psychedelic therapists not only administer these drugs, but act as guides throughout the journey. While psychedelics are generally considered neither habit-forming nor physically harmful, there are exceptions to that rule. And this is why that second meeting between Allan and Marilyn was more difficult than the first — because that was the meeting they discussed risk.

The drug Allan's considering for the first session is MDMA, known on the street as Ecstasy, and a latecomer to the psychedelic tool kit. First discovered by Merck in 1912, MDMA didn't hit the therapeutic world until the middle 1970s when pharmacologist Alexander Shulgin, then teaching at the University of California, San Francisco, heard from his students that it helped one of them get over a stutter. Shulgin dosed himself, reporting "altered states of consciousness with emotional and sexual overtones." He also noticed the drug "opened people up, both to other people and to inner thoughts," and decided its primary benefit was mental. Others agreed. Ecstasy was criminalized in 1984, but not before it had been introduced to thousands of therapists.

Because Allan and Marilyn don't want to compromise Mara's palliative care, the MDMA will have to be administered on top of all her other medications, and this is where the danger lies. Researchers describe Ecstasy not as a psychedelic, but rather as an *empathodelic* — "psychedelic" means *mind-manifesting*, while "empathodelic" means *empathy-manifesting* — but chemically it's an amphetamine. Because amphetamines increase heart rate and blood pressure, and Mara is already suffering palpitations, there's a chance of inducing a heart attack. Peril of neurotoxicity is another concern. A third problem is diminishing her emotional and physical reserves — it would not be hard to trigger a slide from which there would be no return. But the greatest threat is ignorance. Mara would be on nine of the world's strongest drugs simultaneously, and nobody really knows the effects of that potent cocktail. Allan decided to consult outside doctors. It's dicey, they said, but doable. Marilyn and Allan decided on a low starter dose. Mara agreed to roll those dice. That was two days ago.

Today, the doorbell rings. Allan and that starter dose have arrived. Mara's excited. Lindsay is hopeful. Marilyn thinks she might throw up. Her mind won't stop racing. *This starter dose is just a best guess, right? Can I even trust Allan?* But Allan is buoyant, gloriously optimistic, not patronizing or pitying like the other therapists Mara has met. His demeanor calms everyone. As he walks into the room, Allan takes the pills from his pocket and holds them up.

"We are going to have an adventure," he says.

And he is not lying.

At 11:15 a.m., Mara swallows 110 mgs of pharmacologically pure MDMA, lies down in bed, and looks at the angels on the ceiling. Marilyn follows her daughter's upward gaze. She too spots the medallion, and utters one final prayer.

"Please be angels of mercy," she says. "Please, please, please."

2.

While the work Allan does remains illegal and underground, that is now starting to change. We are teetering on the threshold of a major psychedelic renaissance. For the first time in forty years, and without resistance from the law, in countries all over the world and cities all over America, some of the most infamous substances in history are again being put to the test. Scientists in Israel, Jordan, and Canada are looking at the therapeutic potential of MDMA. In Brazil, Germany, and Spain researchers have begun untangling ayahuasca, a plant that contains DMT — arguably the most potent hallucinogen on earth. In Switzerland, it's LSD as a treatment for the anxiety produced by life-threatening illness. In Mexico and Canada, it's ibogaine (another powerful plant-derived psychedelic) for opiate addiction. In Russia, it's ketamine (a tranquilizer known to produce dissociative states) for heroin addiction. Here at home, scientists at the Johns Hopkins University have concluded a long-term psilocybin study that examined the purported "mystical experiences" people have while hallucinating. At UCLA, they've already completed an end-of-life anxiety psilocybin study, while teams at NYU and Johns Hopkins are beginning ones of their own. At the University of Arizona, it's psilocybin as a treatment for obsessive-compulsive disorder. At Harvard, having finished up neurotoxicity studies on both MDMA and peyote, researchers are about to get underway with LSD for cluster headaches and MDMA for end-of-life anxiety. Down in South Carolina, working with combat veterans returning from Iraq and Afghanistan among other trauma victims, researchers already completed one study of MDMA as a treatment for post-traumatic stress disorder (PTSD) and are about to begin another.

Moreover, the majority of scientists involved feel their work is no longer governmentally frowned upon nor the easiest way never to get tenure. Roland Griffiths, a Johns Hopkins professor of psychiatry and neuroscience and a psychedelic researcher himself, says, "I think institutional resistance to this research was much stronger than governmental policy. For three decades, just proposing a psychedelic study was an academic career-ender — the electric third rail for any serious scientist. But that's just no longer true."

"The difference," says Rick Doblin, "is we're getting it right this time." And Doblin would know. As a Harvard PhD and the founder of the Multidisciplinary Association for Psychedelic Studies (MAPS) — a nonprofit drug company whose goal is the eventual manufacture of psychedelics — Doblin sits at the forefront of this new movement. For the past twenty-five years, he's worked to get governments all over the world to reconsider their stance on these drugs, to get psychedelics back into the laboratory, and, perhaps most critically, to help design experiments rigorous enough that even the most adamant of opponents would be forced into reconsidering their position.

What Doblin means by "getting it right" is not just a reference to experimental execution; it's also to overall attitude. "We lost this battle the first time around because of arrogance," he says. "Tim Leary wanted LSD to bring down the establishment. Terrance McKenna said 'psychedelics are inherently opposed to culture.' That was the arrogance. Theirs was an entirely romantic notion, but also isolationist and uncomfortably superior. I'm trying to reverse that trend. I want to mainstream psychedelic medicine. My motto is: Tune in, turn on, and go to the bake sale."

Doblin isn't kidding. On the day I meet him, just after getting breakfast at the local bagel shop, we're walking back to his house. He lives in Belmont, Massachusetts, a town so idyllically quaint that neighboring Cambridge—home of Harvard and MIT— seems I. M. Pei modern by comparison. Belmont is tree-lined and plaid-friendly, one of the last places one would describe as revolutionary. But looks can be deceiving. A woman stops Doblin not far from the bagel shop. She's in her late forties, well-dressed, the poster child of an overprotective suburban mother.

"Rick," she shouts from down the block, "did you see that great special on LSD on the History Channel the other night?"

What follows is a ten-minute discussion about the current state of psychedelic affairs. The woman knows much about this work and seems entirely in favor of it. When she leaves, Doblin tells me he belongs to one of the most popular temples in town.

"And that," he says with a smile, "was the rabbi's wife."

"The who?"

"I don't ever hide what I do. It's a small community. Everybody knows everybody's business. Most people are really supportive."

Doblin believes the support he gets is the best kind. "It's based on knowledge, compassion, and social justice," he says. "OCD and end-of-life anxiety—these are very difficult conditions to cure—but the research clearly shows that psychedelics can help with both. We've got vets coming back from Iraq with intractable post-traumatic stress syndrome. The government doesn't know what to do for these people. But MDMA-assisted psychotherapy works for them as well. Cluster headaches are also called 'suicide headaches' for the level of pain they produce and their frequency of occurrence. They're another incurable. But treating them with LSD looks really promising right now."

Doblin raises a hand and sweeps it around the neighborhood.

"People around here know all this. Belmont is a small part of the future I'm working toward. This may be the only town in America where's it's not usual to find people discussing the benefits of psychedelic therapy at a PTA meeting."

3.

Mara grits her teeth and stares at the angels. It's been over an hour since she took Ecstasy, and all that's happened since hasn't been pleasant. Her pain level has risen. Her noon dose of methadone didn't help. It's now 1:00 p.m. Everyone in the green room begins to discuss options. At 110 mgs, Mara's starter pill is 15 mgs shy of the standard therapeutic dose. In most studies, patients are given an initial hit of 125 mgs and 75 mgs an hour later. Allan believes that doubling that starter would be safe. Mara doesn't want to give up so soon. She swallows another 110 mgs of MDMA and asks, "Is spiritual transformation ever easy?"

The reason Mara believes psychedelics can produce spiritual transformation has little do with her own story and everything to do with her mother's. Marilyn had been born with the congenital deformity *pectus excavatum,* a dent in the center of her chest, roughly the size of a golf ball. Her organs were pushed to one side, her rib cage jutted out. In her early thirties, Marilyn met psychotherapist and pioneer of mind-body medicine Ron Kurtz. He opined that the dent was the result of trapped childhood emotion. Release the emotion, he said, and the dent goes away.

Marilyn tried everything to release the emotion, and then

she tried LSD therapy. Her session also took place in the green room, also beneath the angels. She had a blindfold across her face and a "sitter" — the technical term for someone who stays sober and guides the trip (a scaled-down version of the job Allan now does) — by her side. A half hour after taking the drug and much to her surprise, Marilyn felt her brain split in two — and she began to wail. Primal screams came pouring out. Eventually the screams softened to chants and for the next four hours, Marilyn made spontaneous repetitions of the sound *aaaaah* — though, in those moments, calling her "Marilyn" might be something of a misnomer. "I no longer perceived any boundaries separating me from my surroundings. I was sound and love and peace. Every emotion I had ever felt seemed insignificant by comparison. At that moment I knew what was meant by mystical experience, by transcendence. For me, it had nothing to do with faith or religion or belief in God. I had *experienced* God."

And when she was done, the dent in her chest was almost gone. Her rib cage flattened, her organs shifted toward traditional spots. Marilyn had gone on a twelve-hour mental trip and come back a physically different person. And when Mara agreed to try psychedelic therapy, her hope wasn't just for emotional release. What Marilyn experienced is known as spontaneous healing and classified, at least in the Judeo-Western traditions, as a miracle. This was why Mara dropped that second pill; this was the kind of miracle she was after.

For similar reasons, on a small side table in the green room, Lindsay has arranged a display of gifts from Mara's former students: a twinkle of votive candles, a sea bed of crystals, carved stones, colorful beads, all encircling a bronze statue of Ganesh, the elephant-headed god of wisdom and transcendence in the Hindu canon. Ganesh carries a bronze umbrella. An hour after Mara takes her second pill, the afternoon sun begins to slant through the windows. Sunlight dapples across the wall and spotlights the umbrella. Ganesh glows gold. Maybe it's a sign, maybe it's the drugs, but for the first time in a year, Mara's pain is gone.

Paul Winter is on the stereo. Mara closes her eyes and floats off with the music. Lindsay sees peace on her friend's face for the first time in, well, she doesn't remember how long. Marilyn glances back at the angels on the ceiling.

"Thank you," she says, "thank you, thank you, thank you."

An hour later, the MDMA's effects are fading. Mara doesn't think she needs Allan's help any longer.

"That was great," she says. "I think I'm ready to go deeper next time."

Everybody hugs everybody and Allan walks out the front door. Mara watches him go, the sight of sunlight giving her an idea. It's been over a month since she's been outside and now wants to go for a walk. She and Lindsay cross the street and sit down on an iron bench in a small park, under the shade of a towering oak. They talk boys and first sexual experiences and Lindsay's upcoming wedding. Mara doesn't feel sick. She just feels like herself—a feeling she was not sure she would ever have again. Lindsay has something of a contact high. She's been having personal problems. Now she opens up, and what everyone involved will soon call the best part of the day arrives: Mara starts giving Lindsay personal advice.

"It meant so much to her," Lindsay says later, "to be helpful, to feel useful, to get to be normal again."

Two hours pass and they head back inside the house. Mara has an appetite for the first time in weeks. She eats a large meal, takes her pain meds, and feels a slight jolt—either a wave of anxiety or her heart skipping a beat. She begins to sweat. Nausea comes next. And then pain. Marilyn helps her upstairs to the bath. Warm water doesn't help. More methadone doesn't help. Mara's palpitations return; her tics and twitches arrive next. Now her body feels like a marionette, some madman pulling the strings.

A bad night passes. In the early morning, Lindsay heads to the airport. She lives in Oakland and has to fly back home to get married. Mara can barely say good-bye. Ten minutes later, Marilyn checks Mara's heart rate again—which is when she decides to take her daughter to the emergency room. When they leave the house, both of them wonder: Will Mara come home again?

4.

We now suspect that humans learned about psychedelics the same way we learned about most early medicines — from copying animal behavior. There's plenty to copy. Everywhere scientists have looked, they've found animals who love to party. Bees stoned on orchid nectar; goats gobbling magic mushrooms; birds chomping marijuana seeds; rats on opium; also mice, lizards, flies, spiders, and cockroaches on opium; felines crazy for catnip; cows loco for loco grass; moths preferring the incredibly hallucinogenic datura flower; mandrills taking the even stronger iboga root. So prevalent is this behavior that researchers now believe, as UCLA psychopharmacologist Ronald Siegel wrote in his 1989 book *Intoxication: The Universal Drive for Mind-Altering Substances:* "The pursuit of intoxication with drugs is a primary motivational force in the behavior of organisms."

And, just like us, animals are known to take specific drugs for specific purposes. Among the Navajo, the bear is revered for teaching them about osha, a root effective against stomach pains and bacterial infections. Wild carrot, as we learned from birds, repels mites. Horses in pain will hunt for willow stems, because that's where aspirin comes from. The zoological use of hallucinogens is no different. Herbivores may have first ingested these psychoactives when the threat of starvation gave them no other choice, but later on sought them out for different rewards.

The same is true for humans. For millennia, psychedelics sat at the center of most spiritual traditions. For example, the Eleusinian Mysteries of the Greeks — arguably the most famous initiation rite in history — required drinking *kykeon:* a grainy beverage containing the rye ergot from which LSD was later derived. The Aztecs prayed to Teonanácatl, literally "god mushroom," while the sacred Hindu text, the Rig Veda, contains 120 verses devoted to the rootless, leafless (aka a mushroom) plant *soma,* including 8.48.1-15: "We have drunk Soma; we have become immortal; we have gone to the light; we have found the Gods."

All of which is to say: One of the least-understood facts about psychedelics is how well understood these drugs actually are. Ralph Metzner, psychologist and pioneering LSD explorer, explains: "Anthropologists now know that by the time our modern inquiry into psychedelics began, humanity had already accumulated an encyclopedia's worth of knowledge on the subject."

The modern inquiry into psychedelics dates to 1874, when philosopher Benjamin Paul Blood produced a short pamphlet on the effects of nitrous oxide. Blood's writings inspired Harvard psychologist William James into a trial-and-error investigation of his own, later summarizing his conclusions in an 1882 essay: "The keynote of the experience is the tremendously exciting sense of an intense metaphysical illumination." In 1887, Parke-Davis and Company began distributing peyote to anyone who was curious. Many were curious. By the turn of the century, mescaline—the psychoactive inside of peyote—had been synthesized, jump-starting three decades of phenomenological investigations into what author Hunter S. Thompson called "*ZANG,*" as in: "Good mescaline comes on slow. The first hour is all waiting, then about halfway through the second hour you start cursing the creep who burned you because nothing is happening . . . and then *ZANG!*"

Then, in 1938, Albert Hofmann, a Swiss chemist working for Sandoz Pharmaceuticals, went looking for a new way to boost circulation and ended up synthesizing LSD. Sandoz began distributing LSD free of charge to scientists around the world, listing two possible uses in the accompanying literature. LSD had potential as a psychotomimetic—a drug that mimics psychosis, thus giving researchers a better way to understand the schizoid state—and, perhaps, as a therapeutic tool.

By the middle of the 1950s, not long after Aldous Huxley told

the world about mescaline in *The Doors of Perception,* University
of California at Irvine psychiatrist Oscar Janiger — appropriately
nicknamed "Oz" — was giving acid to celebrities like Cary Grant
and Jack Nicholson in the hopes of learning more about creativity. Around the same time, Humphry Osmond — the British
psychiatrist who coined the term *psychedelic* — suggested LSD
might be used to treat alcoholism. His idea was later backed up
experimentally, with the most famous example being the 1962
Saskatchewan Study, wherein Canadian scientists found that 65
percent of their research group stopped drinking for a year and
a half (the duration of the study) after one LSD experience. Says
NYU's Stephen Ross: "Addiction was the number one reason
psychedelics were administered during this period. Thousands
of people were involved. All the research showed the same thing:
Afterward, addicts tended toward abstinence. Sometimes sobri-
ety lasted weeks, sometimes months." Addiction remains one of
the top public health concerns in America, but despite such tantalizing potential, most of this research has been buried for forty
years.

Most date the start of that burial to 1960, when Harvard psychologist Timothy Leary traveled to Mexico to try magic mushrooms for the first time, later saying he learned more about the
brain "in the five hours after taking these mushrooms . . . than . . .
in the preceding fifteen years of doing research in psychology."
Over the next few years, Leary began conducting research on
psychedelics, first at Harvard and, after he was thrown out, at
an estate on the East Coast. Along the way, he dosed hundreds,
maybe thousands, including Ken Kesey and the rest of the Merry
Pranksters. The fire that was the sixties had been lit — which
is what most remember from this period. But psychedelic research didn't go away. By the time that party was over — LSD was
banned in 1968, psilocybin soon after, though most point to the
1970 Controlled Substance Act (and the resulting exportation of
US drug policy to the rest of the world) as the real end — there
had been dozens of books written, six major conferences, and

more than 1,000 papers published about research conducted on over 40,000 patients.

"Nixon shut it all down," says Doblin. "He called Leary 'the most dangerous man in America.' That's what we remember. But all this work was the beginning of modern brain science: the serotonin revolution, our first real picture of the subconscious, potential cures for some of the most serious conditions in the world. It's kind of incredible most people don't know this."

5.

Marilyn takes Mara to Brigham and Women's Hospital in Boston. By the time she checks in, most of her symptoms have subsided. The initial ER examination report reads: "awake, alert, and in no obvious distress." But still, tests come back with problems, and she ends up staying two weeks. When she's finally discharged, now fourteen pounds lighter and on fifteen different meds, the first thing she wants to do is take more Ecstasy.

Her mother isn't so sure, though she understands the logic. "Some of this is Mara's search for a miracle, but mostly it's about the pain . . . On MDMA, she didn't hurt, she could move, she got to be herself."

Again Marilyn consults with Allan. Together they try to back-track the crisis. Mara's symptoms could have been triggered by MDMA, but they both feel methadone a more likely culprit. Lindsay believes she measured wrong and the dose she'd given Mara after returning from the park—immediately after which Mara's bad symptoms arrived—was really an overdose. Mara is taking significantly less methadone, which seems a good sign, but is also on twice as many meds as before. Allan consults with outside doctors. The main issue is Lovenox, an anticoagulant. MDMA increases blood pressure, and combining it with Lovenox increases the chance of a hemorrhage. They think stopping Lovenox the night before the session should cure that problem, but there's another concern: Mara still wanted to go deeper, meaning a stronger dose of MDMA. Could it kill her? No one knows for sure.

In her master's thesis on outdoor adventure education, Mara wrote: "Risk is an essential element in adventure programming . . . To shelter youth from reality, with all its dangers and uncertainties, is to deny them real life." And she practices what she preaches.

A week after checking out of the hospital, as June sweeps into July, at 10:45 a.m., Mara drops 140 mgs of MDMA, adding a booster pill of another 55 mgs about an hour later.

"Buy the ticket," said Hunter S. Thompson, "take the ride."

6.

Rick Doblin is fifty-six years old, with a strong, stocky frame, curly brown hair, a wide forehead, and a face creased with laugh lines. His demeanor is mostly high school guidance counselor, though his stories are often Burning Man. He was born Jewish, in Oak Park, Illinois, and raised, he says, "under the shadow of the Holocaust." This produced a teenager who eschewed sports and girls for books about civil disobedience. At fourteen, he had already devoted his life to social justice. By sixteen, he'd decided to become a draft resister, meaning he would always have a criminal record and "couldn't be a lawyer or a doctor or do most of the things a good Jewish boy was supposed to do."

Instead, Doblin enrolled in the New College in Florida. He was then seventeen years old. "I had yet to speak to a girl," he says. "I thought the Beatles wrote silly love songs." To this day, he's never drunk alcohol or coffee or smoked a cigarette or tasted a fizzy drink, but back then it was 1971 and Doblin believed the hype. "Acid scared me," he says. "I was sure one hit made you crazy." Then he got to the New College and discovered a nudist colony at the campus pool and psychedelic dance parties going on all night and, well, it didn't take him long to get over that fear.

"LSD was an eye-opener," he says, laughing. "When I was younger, like everything else, I took my bar mitzvah very seriously. I had all these questions about religion that I wanted answered. I expected a spiritually transformative experience. When it didn't happen, I got really pissed off at God. A decade later I did psychedelics for the first time and all I could think was: LSD is what my bar mitzvah should have been like. This was what I wanted."

Doblin was instantly obsessed. There were more trips and more research. He stumbled across John Lilly's *Programming and Metaprogramming in the Human Biocomputer* — Lilly's attempt to map the mind while on acid and inside an isolation tank — and Stanislav Grof's *Realms of the Unconscious: Observations from LSD Research* (Grof was one of the main LSD researchers during the 1950s and 1960s). "Psychedelics were exactly what I was looking for," Doblin says. "Here was a scientific way of bringing together spirituality, therapy, and values. You could journey deep into the psyche and come back with important moral lessons free from prejudice. Talk about a tool for social justice. I thought then, and think now, psychedelics, used properly, are a powerful antidote to Hitler. "

Antidote or not, Doblin was too late for that trip. "The drug war had shut everything down. Researchers were moving onto dreaming, meditation, fasting, chanting, holotrophic breathwork — ways to alter your consciousness without drugs. And it wasn't the establishment's fault; it was our fault, the counterculture's fault. We had it in our grasp and lost it." So Doblin dropped out of college, took more drugs, raised a wolf as a pet, underwent intensive primal scream therapy, underwent plenty of other therapies, learned to build houses for grounding purposes — whatever he could do really to distract himself from the fact that psychedelic research was the only thing he wanted to pursue.

In 1982, he caught a break. MDMA had just arrived on the scene, and Doblin was enthralled. "It was a great tool to liberate inner love, to promote self-acceptance and deep honesty. I knew immediately it had amazing therapeutic potential, but it was already being sold in bars. Too many people were doing it. Obviously, a government crackdown was coming. But I knew that if we could get out ahead of that, this was our chance to make up for all that arrogance, this was our chance to do something different."

The DEA's MDMA crackdown began in early 1984, but Doblin was ready for them. He'd met Laura Huxley, the widow of Aldous, and through her a psychedelic community he never knew existed. "It was then I realized psychedelic researchers hadn't disappeared, they had merely gone underground." He used these newfound connections to initiate a number of serious research studies and, in the hopes of winning the PR battle, began sending MDMA to the world's spiritual leaders. About a dozen of them tried it. In a 1985 story, "The Ecstasy Debate," *Newsweek* quoted famed Roman Catholic theologian, Brother David Steindl-Rast, about his experience: "A monk spends his whole life cultivating this same awakened attitude [MDMA] gives you."

One of the studies Doblin was then trying to get the government to approve involved one subject: his own grandmother. She was dying at the time, suffering unipolar depression along the way. He wanted to try treating her with MDMA, but his parents refused to let him break the law. "Here was this very sick old woman who desperately needed help," recalls Doblin. "We had a drug that could help her — a drug that thousands of other people had already taken safely — and a law that prohibited it."

In 1986, Doblin started The Multidisciplinary Association for Psychedelic Studies (MAPS) and — in an attempt to keep Ecstasy legally available to doctors — helped sue the government. He lost that battle. In 1988, the DEA added MDMA to Schedule I, alongside heroin and PCP and other drugs "with high potential for abuse" and "no currently accepted medical use in treatment in the United States." This meant that if Doblin wanted to reverse that decision he had to convince the FDA that MDMA was both safe and medically useful.

Doblin finished college and decided to go to graduate school to pursue his passion. But this was 1988, and no graduate schools were interested in letting him study psychedelic research. "I realized the politics were in the way of the science," he says, "so I decided to study the politics." He enrolled in Harvard's Kennedy School of Public Policy, eventually getting his PhD, but before that happened, in 1989, the FDA made an internal decision that forever changed the fate of psychedelic research. "They underwent a sea change," says Doblin. "They decided to depoliticize their work and strictly review drugs based on scientific merit."

"Rick figured out the secret," says Mark Kleinman, director of the drug policy analysis program at UCLA and, before he switched universities, one of Doblin's professors at Harvard. "He discovered that the FDA was going to play it straight." And for the first time in two decades, psychedelic research was no longer a pipe dream — suddenly it was in the pipeline.

7.

Mara's second MDMA experience goes deeper than her first. She talks about her issues with intimacy, her fear of losing control, her dread of betrayal. She begins to speak about her recent refusal of medical updates. "I could find out, but I don't want to be defined in those terms — as a lost cause. Whatever happens, cancer gave me an opportunity to seek God."

But the MDMA does not help her find God. By early evening, the drug is wearing off. Allan will be out of town for a few weeks, so more work is temporarily on hold — but Mara's disease is not. By the end of July, her dose of Dilaudid has increased thirtyfold. She is then two months away from the date the doctors told her not to expect to live past. Allan and his psychedelics still seem like her only hope, but MDMA isn't getting the job done. Mara wants to switch to stronger stuff.

Again, there is discussion. Allan has LSD, but feels that the kind of breakthrough Mara desires requires a breakdown of her emotional defenses — which could trigger a greater fear of death.

Mara has rarely spoken of that fear, though she once told Lindsay her concern wasn't dying. "I'm an only child," she'd said. "I'm terrified of leaving my parents. I'm terrified about what will happen to them if I die." Even so, for their next session, Allan feels mushrooms are the better idea, and his opinion wins out.

While there remains quite a bit scientists don't know about the medical uses for psilocybin, one surer thing is its efficacy in treating end-of-life anxiety. Freud believed "existential anxiety" a primary motivational force in humans. In 1973, Ernest Becker won the Pulitzer Prize for arguing that its flipside, which he called the "denial of death," is the reason for all our behavior — the reason we created society in the first place. A long line of scientists have also pointed out that there's only one cure to end-of-life anxiety: Attach the finite self to an infinite other. This, they believe, is one of the biological purposes of religion — a way to ease our fear of death. It may also explain why psychedelics can ease the human condition. Psychedelics are known to produce a mystical experience known as unity. Exactly as it sounds, unity is the undeniable feeling of being one with everything. And if you're one with everything, death becomes irrelevant.

Mara drops mushrooms for the first time on a muggy day in early August. An hour passes. Two hours pass. Maybe they've given her too mild a dose, maybe it's her own emotional resistance, but not much is happening. Mara wants more mushrooms, but Allan has a different suggestion. He's also brought along marijuana, which can enhance the effects of psilocybin. Mara decides to try it, but can't tolerate hot smoke in her feeble lungs. So Marilyn becomes her daughter's "water pipe." She takes sips of cold water, breathes marijuana smoke into her mouth, then puts her lips onto Mara's and blows. Suddenly, for the first time since their last MDMA session, Mara's pain is gone.

"There is some pain," she says, "but I don't feel so uptight about it. It's there, but it's not me."

Then Allan asks about her disease.

"There's a snake in my house," is her chilling response.

The rest of the session passes without incident. Mara is disappointed. She wants more, wants to try LSD, but Allan has to go back out of town. Mara will have to wait until he gets back for that session. The waiting is difficult. There is, after all, a snake in her house.

8.

It took ten years for Doblin and his associates to convince the government that Ecstasy might have therapeutic potential. That victory came in 1992 when the FDA approved the first basic safety and efficacy study in humans. At roughly the same time, Doblin had more ambitious plans. He'd teamed up with Michael Mithoefer, a psychiatrist with a specialty in trauma and an interest in psychedelic therapy, to explore a still radical idea. "Therapists had already figured out that MDMA helps people confront traumatic memories — memories with a deep component of fear and anxiety — and get past them. Michael already had experience with PTSD, and PTSD is exactly that kind of problem. It seemed like a perfect fit."

To help prove he was right, Doblin wrote the first paper to appear in the scientific literature about MDMA and PTSD. It ran in the *Journal of Psychoactive Drugs* in April 2002. That was also the year Mithoefer received permission to begin his formal study — which is how he met John Thompson (not his real name).

Thompson, forty, now lives in Missouri, but in his younger days was an Army Ranger. During Gulf War II, he was on patrol, chasing insurgents in Iraq, when an IED blew up beneath him. He broke his back and both of his feet and suffered traumatic head injury. "I've been in fights," he says. "I've been shot before, but the trauma of getting blown up — it's a soul shaker."

Almost immediately, Thompson developed PTSD. He had nightmares every night. Every piece of trash on the road was enough to set off an episode. After about a year, with no respite,

Thompson was searching the Internet for cures and found a link on the MAPS website to upcoming studies, including Mithoefer's PTSD trial. "I'd never done MDMA before," says Thompson. "I smoked a little pot when I was younger, and when I was in my early twenties tried acid once. At the time, I was already a Ranger, already a well-trained, hardened killer, but on LSD I thought I was a disciple of Christ — that was pretty unusual."

Mithoefer's study was nothing but intensive. Patients were given lengthy pretrial counseling. This was followed by three eight-hour MDMA sessions, each with two therapists present (most psychedelic therapy involves two therapists, one male, one female). Between sessions, for integration purposes, there was daily phone contact and a weekly in-person meeting.

"Almost immediately," Thompson says, "I was shocked by the access I had to my memory. I started recalling parts of the experience that I didn't remember. I really went deep. It was completely cathartic. The next day [after just one session], the nightmares were gone. I was glowing and extroverted — for the first time since getting blown up. MDMA gave me back my life. I hesitate to use the word 'miracle,' but I'd definitely call it a 'sacred molecule.'"

And Thompson wasn't the only subject to find relief. Mithoefer's patient population included war veterans, crime victims, and child abuse victims. While he has yet to publish his data, it has already been presented at conferences, so he will say, "With MDMA (instead of placebo) we had a very clear reduction of PTSD — well into statistical significance. And it's been a year or more after the last MDMA session — in some cases up to five years — so the effects appear to last. I think the treatment holds a lot of promise."

Doblin will go further. "Eighty-five percent of our patients saw their PTSD vanish. It took twenty-two years to get this study done, but if that's all MAPS ever does, it's enough."

Thompson, though, goes the furthest. "I think MDMA is a gift to mankind. I think every vet, when they leave the service, should go through MDMA therapy. I think it should be part of the formal discharge process."

9.

It is late August. The phone rings. Allan is back in town, has a free afternoon and quite a cocktail in mind. The next day Mara, Marilyn, and Allan are again assembled in the green room. Allan has brought LSD, MDMA, and marijuana. LSD is one of the most powerful mind-altering substances ever discovered, and the fear is still a bad trip increasing Mara's anxiety. But Allan explains that "when MDMA combines with LSD, it can soften the experience, smooth out the overwhelming visuals, and help maintain a train of thought." He also says that marijuana deepens the trip, allowing them to use a lower dose of the psychedelic. Mara is game. At 4:20 p.m. she swallows 300 micrograms of LSD.

By 6:00 p.m., Mara says, "not much is happening." At 6:30, she wants to try more LSD, but 300 mgs is already a substantial dose. Allan decides to go with the MDMA instead. An hour later Mara's pain has diminished slightly, but is still not completely gone. At 8:00, Mara smokes pot. Within minutes, she begins to shake. Tremors are now ripping through her body.

"The pain," she says, "it's burning, it's burning . . . but it's amazing how good the rest of my body feels."

Not much happens after that. At 9:00 p.m., Mara wants to go to sleep. The session is over. Marilyn can't hide her disappointment.

"No glorious cure," she says, "no dramatic end to the pain, no spark of enlightenment, and no talk of what to do next."

A week later Mara tells her nurse she's losing her resolve. "I'm worried about my parents," she says, "I suck at good-byes." A week after that, her will has broken. "I can't do this any more. I want to go fast." But there was one thing she wanted to do before she goes fast — more MDMA.

That session takes place in early September. At 2:35 p.m., Mara lies down in bed, stares up at the angels, and swallows 135 mgs of MDMA. An hour later she doubles down and takes another pill. Soon afterwards, her breathing calms, spasms subside, and then her pain is gone. By 4:30, Mara is alert.

"Call Dad," she says.

Marilyn and David Howell divorced years ago, but David lives in the area and has always been close to his daughter. Most nights, he comes by and reads to her. Most nights, Mara worries about him, worries about him more than she worries about her mom. Tonight, the moment he arrives, she starts to well up.

"It's so special," she stammers, "I get to have my mother and father with . . ."

But Mara can't finish that sentence.

Instead, she decides, if there was ever a time for indulgence . . . She sends her father to the store for chocolate. Marilyn goes to the kitchen for a moment. With her parents are out of the room, Mara looks at Allan and starts to cry.

"I'm their only child . . ." but she still can't finish that sentence.

David returns with Dove bars. Such a glorious indulgence. The music is lively. The Temptations are singing "My Girl," and Mara wants to dance. Her mother lifts one arm, her father takes the other. They move her body to the beat, swaying in time, one family together, one last dance. Finally, Mara can finish that sentence.

"How beautiful it is to die," she says, "with my mother and father with me."

10.

It's a cold October night in 2009. Rick Doblin is in his kitchen, eating dinner with his wife and their three children. He's telling a story about the time Lilah, his thirteen-year-old daughter, won a DARE-sponsored writing contest at school (as in, "DARE to Keep Your Kids Off Drugs"). His youngest, Elinore, eleven, was concerned about him. "She thought everything was going wrong in my life," he remembers. "My teenage son wasn't doing drugs. My eldest daughter had just won a DARE contest. She took my hand and looked me in the eye and said, 'Daddy, I don't want to do it now, but in the future, I promise, I'll smoke lots of pot.'"

Then the conversation turns to Mara Howell and her treatment. As the psychedelic community is small, Doblin has heard about Mara's story. "I wish it was legal," he says, "but I like the fact they're doing it in the home, that it's integrated into her hospice care, that they have co-therapists and are not limited by treatment protocols to one substance at one specific dose. They're using the entire psychedelic tool kit at the levels the situation demands. That's the future."

How long until we get to the future is another open question. The majority of current research is Phase II trials, but to actually legalize these drugs, Phase III trials are required. These are multi-centered trials with large patient populations and will take some time to set up and more time to run. The main reason trials take so much time to set up has nothing to do with the government. "The greatest problem," says Grof, "has always been recruiting patients." Doblin points out that while a few scientists may be aware that there has been a psychedelic sea change, that information has yet to trickle down to mainstream doctors. But it will, and soon.

Doblin finishes his dinner in a hurry. He needs to go pack. Tomorrow he leaves for Israel, where he's consulting on a PTSD/MDMA study, and then to Jordan, where — "Talk about peace in the Middle East," he jokes — they're doing more of the same. On his way out of the kitchen, he tells a quick story about an aerobics class he used to attend, where the teacher always showed up stoned and encouraged her students to do the same. His eleven-year old interrupts him.

"But Daddy," she shouts, "I don't want to do stoned aerobics."

Doblin shakes his head and smiles.

"Story of my life," he says.

11.

An hour after Marilyn and David dance with their daughter, the Ecstasy begins to wear off and Mara's symptoms return. Everyone in the green room tries to figure out what to do next. MDMA's effects can be prolonged, so some psychedelic therapists will administer ongoing low doses during life's final stages both for pain relief and lucidity. Marilyn and Allan go a different route. They decide to alternate sedation days with drug days, for what they believe is the maximum physical, emotional, and spiritual benefit. On his way out the door, Allan leaves enough MDMA for another session.

Mara spends the next day asleep. She can no longer eat or drink. The following morning, Marilyn can't wake her, but her daughter's pain is obvious. At noon, Mara becomes slightly alert. Marilyn asks her if she wants to try more MDMA. It takes Mara a long time to answer.

"Yes," is all she says.

Marilyn puts a tablet under her tongue. Mara falls back asleep. An hour later her breathing steadies and her muscle spasms cease, but Mara still isn't awake. Marilyn calls Allan for advice and he suggests giving her a second tablet. Marilyn takes his advice, but two more hours pass and Mara remains comatose. Marilyn calls David and tells him to come over. When he arrives, she says, "I don't think she's going to wake up again."

They spend the next few hours holding their daughter's hands, telling her stories, not knowing what else to do. Then Marilyn is seized by a peculiar notion. On his deathbed, Aldous Huxley had himself injected with LSD, believing the drug would facilitate a "good death." His wife, Laura, administered the dose. A few weeks back, Allan had dropped off a copy of Laura Huxley's *This Timeless Moment,* her posthumous biography about Aldous's life and his passing. Marilyn picks up the book and begins to read aloud.

> All too often, unconscious or dying people are treated as if they were "things," as though they were not there. But often they are very much there. Although a dying person has fewer and fewer means of expressing what he feels, he is still open to receiving communication. In this sense the very sick or

> the dying person is much like a child: he cannot tell us how he feels, but he is absorbing our feeling, our voice, and most of all our touch. . . . To the "nobly born" as to the "nobly dying" skin and voice and communication may make an im- measurable difference.

Later Marilyn learns that *nobly born* is a phrase from the Ti- betan Buddhist tradition. She now holds onto the fact that this tradition "places the greatest importance on one's state of con- sciousness at the time of death." Back then, Marilyn didn't know what to think. She was in the green room, beneath "those fucking angels," beside her dying daughter. "And for reasons I still can't fathom," she says, "I'm reading to her from Laura Huxley."

And then her dying daughter starts to move.

Mara slides her right hand out from beneath the covers and places it directly inside her father's palm. Then she lifts her chin and opens her eyes and turns straight toward him. In the past year, she's lost so much weight that her skeletal aspects have been showing through, but in that moment they vanish. David watches the transformation and can't believe what he's seeing.

"She became angelic," he says later. "She looked radiant." He also said: "I knew exactly what was going on. She held my hand for about fifteen seconds, and then this look of absolute relief came over her face. Absolute peace. And then she died."

David had experimented with drugs in his younger days and was never too keen about Mara's decision to try psychedelic therapy. "I'll be honest, I had a lot of misgivings about the whole thing."

But not anymore.

"It was a gift," he says, "to get to spend that little bit of time with her."

And her death?

"I don't know what to say about that. I think her death was a miracle."

Sympathy for the Devil

THE TROUBLED SCIENCE OF LIFE EXTENSION

In 2006, an editor called to ask if I would investigate a strange claim made by baseball player Jose Canseco — that steroids were the wonder drug of the future. But baseball bored me; everyone knew that steroids were cancer-causing, testicle-shrinking horrors; and anti-aging medicine — which is what Canseco meant by "the wonder drug of the future" — was somewhere between sci-fi fantasy and crackpot city. I wanted nothing to do with the story. But my editor could be very convincing.

"I'll pay you to do the research," he said.

"I'll take one for the team," I replied.

My plan was not Woodward and Bernstein. This wasn't about following the money. All I needed to do was convince my editor that these drugs were deadly. In the midst of the biggest steroid scandal in history, I mean, how hard could that be? So I read a few articles in medical journals. And then I read a few more. Next I started talking to experts. And kept talking. Damn if this wasn't turning into Woodward and Bernstein.

When I started, I was certain that everything I uncovered would be negative. The articles would be thick with warnings about the dangers of these substances and the experts would toe the same line. But that's not what happened. Not even close. After poring through the literature and speaking to the experts and, well, following the money, I discovered that just about everything I knew about steroids was wrong. Instead of bad drugs, I'd encountered big lies — one of the greatest misinformation campaigns in history, a stealth war of propaganda and politics, and one that has cost millions of lives.

Even stranger, as it turns out, Jose Canseco might actually be right. Steroids appear to be a cure for some of our most intractable diseases and an actual first step toward legitimate anti-aging medicine. They are the wonder drug of tomorrow, and, like everything else in this book, they are here today.

1.

The road to the future is paved in blood — my own. Not too long ago, a nurse went a little crazy with my hemoglobin. Somewhere in the middle of the second vial, I got too dizzy to pay attention, but it felt like she took pints, quarts, gallons, whatever comes after gallons, gleefully mining my veins for any secrets they might conceal. The blood was sent to a medical lab that ran a battery of tests and then, the results were shipped to a doctor named Ron Rothenberg. Besides the blood work, getting in to see Dr. Rothenberg also required signing a ten-page waiver, filling out a twenty-page health and lifestyle questionnaire, and the profound willingness to look my medical future square in the eye.

Rothenberg is of medium size, smooth-skinned and strong-shouldered. With sandy brown hair, dark eyes, and darker eyebrows, he looks like a Jewish version of a Latin American soap star, which is to say he looks nothing like his fifty-nine years. He is open about his age, just as he is open about the fact that he feels twenty-five, but unlike most who brag of their youthful virility, because of the way Ron Rothenberg now makes a living, his virility is perhaps no idle claim.

Rothenberg runs the California Health Span Institute in Encinitas, California, and to the limited number of people who know of him and understand the world of anti-aging medicine, he is considered something of a pioneer — which is saying something when you consider that the Western tradition of anti-aging medicine dates back to the 1500s, when Ponce de León accidentally discovered Florida while looking for the Fountain of Youth.

Rothenberg was not trained in anti-aging medicine, because, at the time he was trained, anti-aging medicine was not something one could get trained in. Instead, he graduated from Columbia Medical School in 1970, moved out West, learned to surf, and completed his residency at Los Angeles County–USC Medical Center. He received an academic appointment to teach emergency medicine at the University of California, San Diego in 1977, and became a full professor in 1989. Throughout, Rothenberg kept surfing.

Back in 1975, he was one of the first Americans to venture to Bali to try his hand at those now-legendary Indonesian waves. He has a house down deep in Baja, right in front of one of the better breaks in Mexico. Surfboards hang on his office walls, as do pictures of him riding overhead waves with a charging stance akin to that of Greg "The Bull" Noll. These pictures were taken in 2006, when Rothenberg was fifty-eight, but it was a few years before this — around the time he turned fifty — when his interest in surfing pointed him toward the then-emerging field of anti-aging medicine.

"Around the half-century mark, I saw all these changes in my body," says Rothenberg. "I felt fuzzy — like I was losing my edge. My energy was low, my libido was low, things didn't look as good as they used to. When I went surfing, I got winded on the paddle-out. I wasn't used to getting winded. I read a *Newsweek* article about the anti-aging properties of DHEA and started to wonder if there was something I could do about the way I was feeling and the changes my body was undergoing."

Rothenberg got in touch with the then nascent American Academy of Anti-Aging Medicine and began reeducating himself. "Most doctors are frozen in time," he says. "They stop learning when they get out of medical school. Unfortunately, one of the first things they teach you in medical school is that nearly half of what you'll learn there is wrong — only no one is exactly certain which half." One of the things Rothenberg learned in medical school was that time marches on and aging is an unstoppable process — turns out, this was part of the half that was wrong.

How wrong is still a matter of debate, but few disagree that the version of anti-aging medicine as practiced by Rothenberg and his cohorts represents one of the more radical departures in Western medical thought to surface in centuries. "Traditional medicine is reactive, disease-based medicine," says Dr. Robert Goldman, chairman of the American Academy for Anti-Aging Medicine. "Anti-aging medicine is the opposite. It's about finding the problem and fixing the problem before it occurs. If sports medicine is about optimizing the body for maximum athletic performance, then anti-aging medicine is about optimizing the body for living in general."

Goldman believes that anti-aging is the future of medicine. And Ron Rothenberg was one of the first to venture into that future. He became the tenth doctor in the world board-certified in anti-aging medicine and, in 1998, among the earliest to begin seeing patients. Truthfully, he had been self-medicating for a little while before then, and his earliest patients were fellow doctors who noticed that Rothenberg seemed younger, faster, and stronger, and wanted some of that magic for themselves. His prescription for them was very similar to his prescription for me — and this is where the road to the future takes a sharp left turn — because the basis for both prescriptions was hormones. Though, as Rothenberg likes to point out, "There's a joke in the medical community: When someone has something nice to say about the work we're doing, they use the word *hormones*. When they don't have something nice to say, they call them *steroids*."

And these days, plenty of people have plenty of not nice things to say about steroids.

2.

Oh, the trouble started a long time ago — and we'll get to that story — but its more recent incarnation arrived in 2006, when former baseball star Jose Canseco published *Juiced*, his book about "wild times, rampant 'roids, smash hits, and how baseball got big." In *Juiced,* Canseco claimed that 80 percent of ballplayers were using steroids, and then proceeded to name names. It was also in *Juiced* where Canseco argued that steroids are the wonder drug of tomorrow. "[Soon] everyone will be doing it," he writes. "Steroid use will be more common than Botox is now. Every baseball player and pro athlete will be using at least low levels of steroids. As a result, baseball and other sports will be more exciting and entertaining. Human life will be improved, too. We will live longer and better. And maybe we'll love longer and better, too."

The government, of course, has been delivering the exact opposite message for years—with the website for the National Institute of Drug Abuse (NIDA) being one example: "Steroid abuse may lead to serious, even irreversible, health problems. Some of the most dangerous consequences that have been linked to steroid abuse include kidney impairment or failure; damage to the liver; and cardiovascular problems including enlargement of the heart, high blood pressure, and changes in blood cholesterol leading to an increased risk of stroke and heart attack (even in young people)."

Unfortunately, as has often been the case with drug policy, the gap between politics and science is considerable. "As used by most people, including athletes, the adverse effects of anabolic steroids appear to be minimal," says Dr. Mauro Di Pasquale. "Steroids do not cause cancer. They don't cause kidney failure. There have been thousands of steroid studies and about a hundred of those point out bad side effects. But if you look at those studies carefully, there's no one-to-one correlation, and a one-to-one correlation is the hallmark of good science."

And Di Pasquale would know. A former world champion power-lifter, he is also a medical doctor—a family practitioner for over twenty-five years—and one of our foremost authorities on performance-enhancing drugs. In the early 1990s, when World Wrestling Federation founder Vince McMahon decided it was time to get his empire off the juice, Di Pasquale was the one who got the job. He later became the medical director to the World Bodybuilding Federation and the acting medical review officer for NASCAR, helping both sports develop their stringent drug-testing policies.

With steroids, Di Pasquale points out, it can be hard to wade through the propaganda. "Consider the apocryphal idea that steroids produce 'roid rage," he said. "What we know is that steroids produce an incredible amount of energy — but you need to think about the kind of people taking steroids. If really competitive and aggressive people start taking drugs that give them more energy, then common sense says that sooner or later you're going to have problems. But are steroids the problem, or the fact that this person didn't know how to control their anger long before the steroids came along?"

Which is not to say steroids aren't without complications. When teenagers take them, because their bodies are still producing significant amounts of natural hormones, the results can be disastrous. In adults, there are also issues — especially at higher doses. Weightlifters, for example, ingesting ten times the normal amount will see excessive hair growth in unwanted places, premature baldness, development of breasts (in men), and an enlarged clitoris (in women). Men are also at risk for testicular atrophy. It is also worth pointing out that these conditions tend to go away once they stop using steroids. As far as long-term effects — negative or positive — until very recently, almost nobody had studied them.

One of the first such investigations was undertaken by UCLA orthopedic surgeon and sports medicine specialist Nick Evans. In the early 1990s, when the original Steroid Control Act was passed (an updated version was re-passed in 2004), much was said about the dire consequences of sustained abuse, but there was little science backing up such claims. So Evans got curious. He figured if anyone knew anything about the long-term consequences of steroids, it would be weightlifters. Evans discovered that nobody had ever bothered to ask them. "It's the craziest thing you've ever seen," he says. "It was like scientists bought into all the negative hype and propaganda and never bothered to walk into a gym and talk to a bodybuilder."

Evans had no problem talking to bodybuilders. He talked to plenty. In 1996, in the *British Journal of Sports Medicine*, he published the results of those conversations: "Gym and Tonic: A Profile of 100 Steroid Users." This was followed by an even more rigorous look at 500 long-time juicers. In both studies, Evans's findings agree with Di Pasquale's conclusions. Even in long-term abusers, he found no concrete links between these drugs and the dangerous side effects — like those listed on the NIDA website — with which they're often associated. In fact, the only real concern he has is for those people taking super-high doses for years at a time. "The issue is the heart," he explains. "The heart is a muscle, and steroids increase muscle size. If the heart starts getting bigger, it becomes less efficient at doing its job, and, over time, that can cause big problems."

But Evans also feels that if steroid users had access to proper medical advice, many of these problems could be avoided. Though, because of America's current drug stance, very few have access to such advice. This is also among the reasons that Evans finds America's steroid policy slightly ridiculous — not because he believes that people should be taking steroids, rather because of the reasons most people are taking steroids.

"There's this idea out there that the only people who use these drugs are professional athletes — that regulating steroids will clean up professional sports and make the problems go away. That couldn't be farther from the truth. There are three million steroid users in the United States. In both of my studies, I found that eighty percent of them are using for cosmetic purposes."

Cosmetic purposes means people are taking steroids to look and feel younger, stronger, and more virile — which is much the same reason people choose elective plastic surgery. But, unlike the masking effects of, say, liposuction, steroids do their work

from the inside out. They don't just hide the passage of time—
they appear to turn back the clock.

3.

If you want to understand the role steroids play in anti-aging
medicine, it helps to start with metabolism. Defined as "the
chemical processes that occur within a living organism in order
to maintain life," metabolism refers to things like energy production, cell division, and waste disposal. In the early 1900s,
researchers noticed a connection between these processes and
aging. It seemed that larger animals with slower metabolisms
outlived smaller animals with faster metabolisms. Two decades later, a series of experiments with fruit flies and cantaloupe
seeds expanded this idea into the "rate-of-living theory," which
states that the faster an organism lives, the shorter its life span.
Then, in 1935, veterinary nutritionist Clive McCay found that
limiting caloric intake in lab animals—which slows metabolic
rate—decreased and delayed the onset of age-related diseases
and significantly extended life span. Chemist Denham Harman
provided a little molecular respectability to this notion in 1954,
postulating that oxygen radicals or free radicals are both by-
products of metabolism and responsible for the damages associated with aging and death.

A blizzard of other scientists have since built upon this work,
leading to an ever-increasing number of big ideas about the
causes of aging, with free radicals among them. Another notion
is that the accumulation of excess glucose in our tissues screws
up the cells' ability to function normally. Then there are telomeres, the end segments of a DNA strand, which are naturally
lost in normal cell division. Over time, after we've lost too many
telomeres, our cells lose their ability to divide into new cells.
Without these new cells, we can't rebuild body tissue, and when

we can't rebuild body tissue, we age. But the theory that has provided the most interesting results has to do with hormones.

The thinking goes that all animals are extremely efficient machines throughout their reproductive years, but afterward — because their evolutionary purpose has been accomplished — start to break down. Scientists believe this breakdown is triggered by a loss in hormones, which has been directly linked to everything from mental fuzziness and low libido to a variety of age-related disease like Alzheimer's, arthritis, osteoporosis, diabetes, and cardiovascular disease. "The old idea," says Rothenberg, "was that our hormones decline because we age. The new idea is that we age because our hormones decline."

So the anti-aging world hit upon an obvious solution: Replace the missing hormones.

Testosterone is one of the main hormones that needs replacement (pretty much every steroid on the market works by mimicking testosterone, so when people say steroids, much of the time, they mean testosterone), as it starts to decline in most people by their late twenties. Technically, testosterone is both an anabolic and androgenic steroid. Anabolic means it builds tissue up; androgenic refers to any hormone that impacts the development and maintenance of male sexual characteristics.

The earliest known research into this hormone dates back to 1767, when a Scottish scientist failed to learn much of anything by transplanting the testicles of a rooster into the abdomen of a hen. A hundred years later, German zookeeper and professor Arnold Berthold picked up this thread and castrated a series of cockerels and afterward reported that the animals' most definitive male sexual characteristics vanished alongside their testicles. Gone were the flamboyant comb, the aggressive behavior, and any interest in the opposite sex. But — and this was the finding that marked our first step down the road toward anti-aging medicine — he also found that these changes could be reversed by injecting his castrati with an as-of-yet-unnamed substance extracted from their testicles.

Two decades after Berthold's breakthrough, our first steroid controversy arrived when noted French neurologist Charles-Édouard Brown-Séquard began injecting himself with extract of animal testes — mostly guinea pigs and dogs, but sheep were sampled too — and finding the effects so rejuvenating that he spent his remaining years championing this potion as a way to prolong life. While extract of guinea pig testes wasn't exactly a hot seller, in the early 1930s, Dutch pharmacologist Ernst Laqueur managed to isolate 10 milligrams of crystalline testosterone from 100 kilograms of bull testicles, and that changed everything. Suddenly, researchers could pick apart testosterone's chemical structure; suddenly, they could experiment. Synthetic versions soon followed, as did reports of Swedish athletes taking Rejuven, a performance enhancer that worked via a small dose of testosterone. At the 1936 Olympics, there were rumors of German competitors — fueled by Hitler's dreams of Aryan perfection — taking even larger doses.

By the early 1940s, testosterone was being touted as everything from a way to increase sex drive in aging men to a way to increase productivity in society. The real dam broke in 1945, when science writer Paul de Kruif published *The Male Hormone*. Bullish about testosterone and the impact it would have on our economy and our health, de Kruif foretold riches for the drug's manufacturers and increased vigor and extended life for its consumers. And all of this was big news. Critics loved the book. *Newsweek* gave it a full-page review; *Reader's Digest* published an excerpt. It was the moment that anti-aging medicine went mainstream.

That moment didn't last for long.

4.

The trouble started in the 1960s, when female Eastern Bloc athletes started looking a little too buff and doing a little too well at the Olympics. Steroids, it was suddenly clear, threatened the level playing field of sport, jeopardizing the foundation of athletic competition and, by extension, the very big business surrounding it.

By 1975, steroids were added to the Olympics' list of banned substances. College and professional football soon followed, with other sports eventually getting in line. But it was already too late. Athletes had heard about the performance-enhancing powers of testosterone, and the bans weren't enough. Something else needed to be done. And that something, well . . . this is when things got a little strange.

"The organized-sports establishment decided to 'solve' the problem by educating athletes," says Rick Collins, our foremost legal authority on steroids and author of *Legal Muscle*, the de facto bible on the subject. "They devised a strategy: Convince athletes that anabolic steroids don't build muscle. It was a lie, of course, so they needed a credible source to sell the message. They picked the American College of Sports Medicine (ACSM) to spread the news, a bit like the Ministry of Truth spread false propaganda in George Orwell's classic *1984*."

This wasn't yet *1984*, this was still 1977 — but the ACSM took to issuing proclamations: "Steroids have no effect on lean muscle mass; the effects athletes are seeing are the result of water retention; the effects are all placebo." These claims held sway until the *real* 1984, when there was so much anecdotal evidence to the contrary that the ACSM finally had to admit that, yes, those 300-pound beasts playing left tackle could only have gotten to be 300-pound beasts with the help of anabolic steroids.

Next the ACSM came up with a different approach — tell the athletes that steroids are bad for them. Make them sound horrible. Magnify every negative side effect from every study that had ever been run. When in doubt — prevaricate. "One California physician associated with the NFL," wrote Collins in *Legal Muscle*, "made the completely unsupported assertion that 'young athletes who take heavy doses of anabolic steroids should expect to die in their thirties and forties.'"

But then another fact came to light—high school kids were starting to use steroids. Congress had to act. Some say their actions were motivated by an authentic desire to help, some talk of the drug war's relentless need for new bad guys, some about the fact that "save our children" always fills political war chests. Others bring up the multibillion-dollar industry that is professional sport and the heavy lobbying power that comes with those billions. In truth, it was probably all this and then some.

Whatever the case, in 1988, the Anti-Drug Abuse Act was passed, which made trafficking in steroids illegal, and a variety of subcommittees were formed to hear testimony about whether or not the drug should become a controlled substance. Among those who testified were Charles Yesalis, Penn State professor of health and human development and the world's leading steroid authority at the time. "Steroids do have a medical use," Yesalis told Congress. "From an epidemiologic point of view of the health dangers, I am much more concerned about heroin; I am much more concerned about cocaine; I am much more concerned about cigarettes than anabolic steroids."

The American Medical Association, the Drug Enforcement Agency, the Department of Health and Human Services, and the Food and Drug Administration—the four regulatory agencies that are supposed to have control over the drug-scheduling process—all testified against turning steroids into a controlled substance. It didn't matter. Senator Herbert Kohl spoke for many when he said, "Steroid users set an intolerable example for our nation's youth." It should also be mentioned that, at the time he was speaking, Senator Kohl was also the owner and president of the Milwaukee Bucks.

In 1990, Congress again upped the ante, this time passing the Anabolic Steroids Control Act—which criminalized these drugs. Five years later, a Los Angeles doctor named Walter Jekot was arrested for procuring and prescribing steroids for bodybuilders. His case went to the Supreme Court, where he pled guilty and served five years in federal prison. At the time, much of this was front-page news; what was significantly less publicized was that because of his imprisonment, Walter Jekot is widely considered the AIDS epidemic's first martyr.

5.

If you talk to anti-aging doctors about their work, it won't be long before a healthy dose of paranoia creeps into the conversation. "All it takes is a whiff of a hint that I'm prescribing steroids for nonmedical reasons and they'll shut me down and send me to jail," said one doctor, who asked, not surprisingly, to remain anonymous. And he wasn't alone. Almost half of the physicians interviewed for this story asked for the same. And in explaining their reticence to be named, most of them brought up Walter Jekot — their sad reminder of the dangers of taking a stand.

To understand this story, you need to know that until 1990, steroids were a prescription drug available to anyone with a note from their doctor. Since the 1960s, Jekot had been writing such notes for some of his patients, primarily athletes. He was still writing notes in 1982, when scientists identified a strange virus plaguing the gay community. A number of Jekot's patients turned out to be HIV-positive, and a few of those patients were the same ones using steroids. By 1984, Jekot noticed that those HIV-positive, steroid-using patients were still alive, while everyone else seemed to be dropping like flies. These users weren't succumbing to AIDS wasting syndrome; in fact, many of them looked downright healthy. In 1984, Walter Jekot became the first doctor to prescribe anabolic steroids as a treatment for AIDS.

Other doctors soon followed suit and before long there was a pile of experimental data and an established treatment protocol. Stories of this protocol spread quickly around the West Coast, but didn't get national attention until 1995, when another HIV-positive doctor, Michael Dullnig, published an article in *Muscle*

Media magazine talking about his own experience with steroids. In the early days of HIV research, doctors used the immune cell CD4 as a marker of health. Normal, HIV-negative people have a CD4 count between 1,000 and 1,500, while AIDS is defined by a CD4 count below 200. When he started taking steroids, Dullnig had a CD4 count of four. He should have been dead within weeks. Instead, he regained forty pounds and lived and told his story in *Muscle Media.*

Because of Dullnig's advice, an HIV-positive chemical engineer named Nelson Vergel also began taking steroids. "I put on thirty-five pounds during the next year or so. My immune response also improved, especially my CD8 T-cells, which went from 900 to 2,500 [as it turns out, CD8 cells — which are the immune cells boosted by steroids — are a much better indicator of health in HIV-positive people]. My symptoms basically disappeared. I never looked or felt better in my life, even when I was HIV-negative."

This testimony appears in *Built to Survive: HIV Wellness Guide,* which Vergel coauthored with Los Angeles nutrition expert turned AIDS researcher Michael Mooney. The book is a step-by-step guide to beating back AIDS with nutrition, exercise, and steroids. It soon became the basis for both good medicine and epic struggle. "It was a crusade of sorts," Mooney said. "Everyone we knew was dying, and a lot of these people were dying because of thirty years of antisteroid propaganda."

Walter Jekot got caught in the middle. The government ignored his HIV work and claimed he was distributing the drugs to athletes and bodybuilders, and that was enough for the court. "They wanted to make an example out of someone," says Mooney. "They chose Jekot. Was it a bad choice? Well, they scared the shit out of a lot of good doctors, and they spread a lot of bullshit about steroids that bad doctors believed as truth. It almost goes without saying that if things had gone differently, there'd be a few million HIV-positive people who'd still be alive today."

It also goes without saying that if things had gone differently, then a whole lot of anti-aging doctors would feel a lot less insecure about the work they do.

6.

When I met with Dr. Rothenberg to discuss the results of my blood work, his job was to examine my hormonal health and make suggestions. We started out looking at my cholesterol and my triglycerides; next I got a short lesson on the dangers of trans fats. "My advice here is pretty simple," says Rothenberg. "Fruits, vegetables, meats, fish are all fine. Frozen foods and canned goods — that's the danger zone. Avoid the center aisles at the grocery stores and you'll live longer."

We work our way to C-reactive proteins, which are a great measure of inflammation in the body and the impact of age. "Chronic inflammation is both the cause and the effect of most of the diseases of aging," says Rothenberg. "While acute inflammation may save your life (by cutting off blood flow to a wound), silent inflammation is what kills you." My C-reactive proteins are okay, but there's need for some DHEA, and that's when things start to get controversial.

DHEA is a cousin of testosterone and estrogen and has been called everything from the fountain-of-youth hormone to the snake oil of the modern world. It is the most abundant steroid in the body, but production slows in our twenties. By age seventy, we make roughly 20 percent of the DHEA we had in our youth. As DHEA is a precursor to all major sex hormones, its decline is partially responsible for a sluggish sex drive. Research also shows that DHEA is useful in combating inflammation, depression, cognitive decline, Type II diabetes complications, cancer, arthritis, osteoporosis, and heart disease, but naysayers claim it's worthless or dangerous or both. And while DHEA is currently available in most health food stores, those naysayers — many of whom are reputable doctors and researchers — also caution that we don't know enough about how the hormone works over time and that it should be classified as an investigational drug at best. Some go as far as saying that its wide availability is a disaster in the making. It was also these same DHEA detractors who worked very hard — unsuccessfully — to add it to the list of substances banned by the 2004 Steroid Control Act.

Another substance that sits squarely on that list is human growth hormone (HGH), and Rothenberg does suggest that I could benefit from a little extra HGH. Long used to stimulate growth in children, in adults HGH has been shown to be improve immune function, well-being, hormone repair, and — though this has never been directly proven — increased athletic performance. A little extra HGH means a self-administered daily shot, at a cost somewhere between $3,000 and $10,000 per year, though cheaper sublingual versions are now available.

As it turns out, my testosterone levels are fine. In a few years, maybe a boost would be in order, but that boost is a far cry from the megadoses that bodybuilders are putting in their body. The real eye-opener, though, isn't about what I need now; it's about what I might want then. "If you can hold on for a few more years," says Rothenberg, "you won't believe what's coming."

Stem cells are, of course, the biggest promise. "We're talking about cloning your exact DNA to repair your DNA. And this stuff isn't in the future — it's just about ready for prime time." He tells me that right now, vaccines for almost all major cancers are working their way through the drug pipeline. "I don't know what we'll have access to in America and what we won't. You may have to go to Switzerland to avoid having chemotherapy, but it's coming."

And then there's the future of hormones. Not only are other methods of delivery soon to be available — making syringes a thing of the past — but there are a bevy of gene technologies in development. "We're talking about DNA repair at an incredible level," says Rothenberg. "If your body has stopped producing the desired amount of testosterone, pretty soon we're going to be able to insert genes that double production."

How effective these technologies will be or how controversial the hubbub they will produce remains to be seen, but anti-aging doctors figure that if we can hold on for ten to fifteen more years, then we're looking at a life span of 120 years. And all those later years won't be spent in a wheelchair and a nursing home. Thanks to the wonders of hormones, what's on the table here is a geriatric second childhood. Unless, of course, Congress decides that anti-aging medicine is a serious threat to the seniors' golf tour — and then, well, all bets are off.

The Final Frontier

THE POLITICS OF STEM CELLS

Of all the stories in this book, this one is the most historical. It is about the breakthrough known as stem cells, the promise of which is considerable. But that's not the real reason I included it in the collection. Instead, I've chosen this story because of how well it elucidates an important point—how incredibly difficult innovation really is.

History is often a tale of victory. We remember the winners, forget the losers, and rarely think about how messy the battleground became along the way. Technological history is no different. Everyone knows Thomas Edison invented the lightbulb—few remember that it took him over 1,000 tries to get it right.

This story, then, is a view from the trenches. It's about the science of stem cells, for certain, but it's also about how politics, culture, and religion impact that science. It's about deception and morality and deception in the name of morality. And, of course, it's about money. In short, since the central theme of this book is the transformation of science fiction into fact, this story is a look at all the nonscientific forces that can turn such transformation into blood sport.

One final note: While stem cell technology has advanced considerably since this story was written, all of the issues presented here are still with us. This fight is far from over.

1.

Irv Weissman's home is about twenty minutes from Stanford University, hidden from the road by a tall stand of trees. Inside, the rooms are spacious, and the living room more so. The ceiling is high and broad-beamed; the furniture Western chic: chairs hewn from tree branches, tables built from tree trunks. Spread out in front of the fireplace is a bearskin rug. This bear has seen better days. Weissman is talking about those days and, more specifically, about how they came to an end.

"We ate him," he says. "Rare. We were a little nervous about it, because most wild bears have trichinosis, but what the hell."

Weissman doesn't look the bear-eating sort. He's of middle height, middle weight, mildly balding, with fine clothes, a jovial aspect, and a long, wispy beard. He looks like a Russian poet or an aged food critic. But, beneath this exterior, he's just a boy from Montana. Which is to say he comes from a culture of bear eaters.

Boys from Montana are raised by that big-sky country as much as they are by their parents. Weissman now works at Stanford, but still owns property in Montana. He goes back as often as he can, though with his schedule, that's not often enough.

Many of the reasons Weissman does not get back to Montana can be found on his resume. At Stanford, he's a much-lauded professor of cancer biology and pathology. In 2002 alone, he won the American Cancer Institute's distinguished scientist award; the Van Bekkum Stem Cell Award; and was selected to the National Academy of Science's Institute of Medicine. For the years prior to 2002 his resume lists more of the same, and this list goes on for three pages — in ten-point font.

On that resume, the only nonscientific pursuits listed are

Weissman's positions as external director of Montana Trout Un-limited and external director of the Montana Land Reliance. In 1994, he was voted Montana Conservationist of the Year. If you ask him about his passion for the state he will say: "People from Montana are open and friendly, and anyone who lives there is only two generations from the land."

Irv, himself, is two generations from the land. His grandfather arrived at Ellis Island in the early portion of the last century, didn't much like what he saw, so decided to walk across the coun-try. He stopped walking in Montana. You could make the case that his grandfather was among the first Jewish homesteaders in Montana and not run into much argument, except that home-steading proved too much for his grandfather. Technically, Irv's grandfather was a charter member in one of the smallest self-help groups in history: failed Jewish homesteaders of Montana.

After homesteading, his grandfather tried his hand at min-ing, rag picking, scrap selling, and fur trapping. He eventually opened a hide shop that became a hardware store that became five hardware stores. The first store was in Great Falls, Montana, where Irv was born.

Irv's own father was tough as well, locally known as the "man of steel, man of iron." When Irv was in the second grade, he opened the paper to find a story about a man who stabbed his father with a knife. Wounded, his father still beat the man silly. This toughness seems to run in the family. The only fear Irv ad-mits to is spiders.

Irv's father went into the family business. The hardware stores were called Weissman and Sons, but they have since closed down because, well, the sons had other ideas. When Irv was ten years old, he read Paul de Kruif's book *Microbe Hunters* about the trail-blazing work of Louis Pasteur and Paul Ehrlich and other early bacteriologists. For an entire generation of scientists this book proved seminal. Irv was no different.

Inspired by *Microbe Hunters* and still in high school, Weiss-man got a job at a local lab doing transplantation research. He

published two papers, both on cancer and transplantation, before turning eighteen. He smiles at the thought of them, mainly
because these are the same subjects he still puzzles over today, so
many, many years later.

After high school, Weissman entered Dartmouth College, but
found he didn't fit in with the East Coast Jews or the East Coast
non-Jews and soon transferred to Montana State University in
Bozeman, where he could study premed without having to worry
about, as he explains, "how a Jew from Montana was supposed to
behave on the East Coast."

In 1960, he left Montana again, this time for Stanford Medical School, where, one way or another, he has stayed for the duration. At Stanford, Weissman's early research focused on how
the cells of the immune system fight cancer. He spent much of
his time studying the relationship between blood cells, cancer,
and radiation. Because of data that emerged after the explosion
of the atomic bombs over Hiroshima and Nagasaki, scientists
knew that exposing the human body to radiation wiped out both
blood cells and cancer cells. They also knew that after irradiat-
ing the body (chemotherapy), you could perform a bone marrow
transplant, replacing cancer-riddled marrow with marrow from
a healthy, cancer-free donor, and the result was always the same:
something in that cancer-free bone marrow would begin producing all sorts of healthy new cells.

It was quite a puzzle.

"We knew there must exist a very rare cell inside the bone
marrow that gave rise to all types of cells," explains Weissman.
"But it was only a theory. No one had ever isolated that cell. Still,
I started wondering if it was possible to tease it apart from all the
others."

His effort to do just that began in the late 1960s. For decades,
Weissman sorted cells in his lab—essentially pouring mouse
blood through a long series of high-tech strainers. With each
pass, a different kind of cell was removed. Out came the T cells,
out came the B cells, the red blood cells, the white blood cells,

and so on and so on until there was only one kind of cell left. Finally, in 1988, Weissman managed to do something that no one else had ever done, something that most people didn't even think was possible: He isolated a cell that gave rise to all varieties of blood cells, a precursor cell capable of radical transformation, or, technically, a hemotopietic stem cell. As a result of this discovery, Irv also became one of the first people on the planet to realize the astounding promise of these cells.

This has made him a very controversial man.

2.

If you've been living down in a cave or deep in a desert, perhaps you haven't heard about stem cells but, otherwise, news of Irv's discovery and its pluripotent ramifications have been hard to miss. Stem cells are our rawest materials, the original parts warehouse from which developing embryos build all the other cells that eventually form the body. Unlike specialized cells, which can only become one thing—a liver, say, or a nose—stem cells can turn into any other kind of cell. From a morphological perspective, they are the ultimate multi-tool. Medically, they're a marvel.

When Weissman started working with mouse stem cells, he realized, nearly from the beginning, that he was on to something that could potentially save millions of lives. "I knew that if I could ever do this in humans," he says, "I would be able to use chemotherapy to wipe out cancer cells and then transplant in new stem cells that would be completely disease-free."

Cancer wasn't the only thing on his mind. Weissman also knew that a great number of terrible diseases—Alzheimer's, diabetes, Parkinson's, many others—are caused by misbehaving cells. Thus, by replacing those misbehaving cells with healthy stem cells, it seemed possible that we could cure these diseases. In America, 1.3 million people have cancer; 4 million have Alzheimer's; 1.5 million have Parkinson's; 17 million have diabetes.

This doesn't include those in need of a new kidney or bladder or spinal cord—which stem cells can also be used to grow. That's a lot of lives to save.

What Weissman didn't get, especially at first, was that his own government would politicize these cells, essentially deciding that saving those millions of lives was a bad idea. What he didn't understand then, but has come to understand since, is that without his rugged Montana perseverance, he might never get the chance to save those lives.

It's a kerfuffle, all right.

As R. Alta Charo, professor of law and medical ethics at the University of Wisconsin, Madison and member of President Bill Clinton's Bioethical Council, says: "The stem cell debate is a debate about everything but what it's about." Which is to say, the stem cell debate is not, actually, about stem cells.

So what is this debate really about? Plenty. It's about President George W. Bush trying to win a second-term election after not actually winning the first. It's about the son (Bush Jr.) not making the same mistakes as the father (Bush Sr.) and losing the support of evangelical Christians. Then there's the right to life and a woman's right to choose and whether the Supreme Court should deny the former to uphold the latter or vice versa. And that's just the front end of this list. There's also the values of the American people, the morals of the religious right, the economic potential of the biotech industry, the tension between church and state, the question of state's rights, and a host of other nitpickery in between. In short, in the colorful history of Science versus Politics, stem cells have become the biggest knock-down, drag-out, hellspat since Chuck Darwin told us we came from apes.

3.

If you want to drill down into this spat, then the first thing you need to understand are the five ways scientists currently obtain stem cells. The principal method is cloning or somatic cell nuclear transfer, wherein the DNA-containing nucleus of a somatic cell—that is, an adult, already specialized cell—is transferred into an *enucleated* egg cell, sort of like sucking all the filling out of a jelly donut and squirting it into the hollowed out core of a chocolate éclair.

Sort of, but not quite.

Once inside its new home, the somatic nucleus reprograms the egg cell, which begins to divide and birth new cells, and all of them now carry the DNA of the original somatic cell—which is how, for example, researchers cloned Dolly the Sheep. Where somatic cell nuclear transfer gets tricky is that this same process can be used to clone humans (an issue we'll return to later).

The second method is *parthenogenesis*, the Greek word for virgin birth, in which an unfertilized egg is tricked into cell division and then mined for stem cells. The third idea is *hybridization*, or using existing stem cell lines (meaning cell lines that researchers have already isolated) to create new cell lines via genetic manipulation. And while both of these notions are exciting, no one really knows if either will work. So, for now, both are off the radar.

In the remaining two methods, fetal stem cells are culled from aborted fetuses or embryonic stem cells are removed from unused embryos taken from in vitro fertilization clinics. And it is these final two methods that have put stem cells into the middle of America's reproductive rights debate.

"Every year since *Roe v. Wade*, thousands of women have been having abortions," explains Alta Charo. "That's thirty years—an entire generation of women who have experienced the ability to choose. That's a huge demographic imperative. The evangelical right is fighting against a culture of tolerance for embryonic destruction, and they're losing that fight every time a woman knows she can make a choice."

While opponents have been trying to oust *Roe v. Wade* for

thirty years, one of the main reasons it's held fast is the idea that a human embryo does not have the same rights as a human being. Thus, to overturn the decision, you need significant evidence showing that the American people have changed their minds and now feel that embryos are people too — an idea that is more than a little problematic.

For starters, while the Bush administration and the evangelical right are waging war against stem cells, neither has said a peep about fertility clinics. Yet, during the normal process of in vitro fertilization, embryos are destroyed by the boatload. Current techniques cull twenty or so embryos for every one that's implanted. The remainder are frozen for short-term insurance (to make sure that implantation took), then eventually discarded. But it's bad politics to piss off sterile parents and the billion-dollar industry they support, so both the Bush administration and the religious right have stayed mum on pregnancy, yet become exceptionally vocal about stem cells.

Then there's that other problem — embryos really aren't people too. "When I'm trying to explain this issue to a reporter or a congressman," says Irv Weissman, "I run a little experiment. I'll walk up to a stranger on the street and ask them to draw an embryo. Invariably, every time, without fail, they draw a fetus with a face. But a fetus with a face is not an embryo."

An embryo is a scientific term used to describe the period of time from when a zygote is formed until the time it begins to have discernible organs — meaning that the word *embryo* was literally created to distinguish it from a fetus. It is nothing like the cartoons that people draw. There's no face. Nothing even vaguely human. Under a microscope, it looks like a tightly wound ball of waxy string.

To come at this from the other direction, the current medical definition of death is the cessation of brain function. This means that the opposite of death — the beginning of life — must be the emergence of brain function. Scientists believe that the earliest signs of an active nervous system are the development of pain responses, which show up around the nineteenth week of pregnancy, or long after an embryo has become a fetus.

If you ignore these facts and still want to prove to the Supreme Court that both the scientific community and the American public have changed their minds about the status of the embryo, then you need precedents. The evidence would have to show that in related — but not abortion-specific — cases the embryo is now being afforded the same protections as both a fetus and an adult human.

To this end, President George W. Bush stacked a bevy of antichoice judges in the lower courts and appointed a pro-life attorney general in John Ashcroft. Then, in October 2002, the administration changed the section of the Health and Human Services charter that regulates research done on human subjects. The old charter granted legal protection to adults and fetuses. The new version protects embryos as well. Next, while women's groups had been lobbying the government to provide health care for pregnant women, the Bush administration extended the reach of the State Children's Health Insurance Program to cover both embryos and fetuses but, oddly, not pregnant women. Bush also lobbied for a ban on partial-birth abortions — which would criminalize a procedure now used primarily in extreme, life-threatening situations — and reinstated Ronald Reagan's gag rule, barring federally funded family planners from discussing abortion or providing abortion services.

"The point of these things," says Allison Herwitt, director of government relations for the National Abortion and Reproductive Rights Action League, "was to weave embryonic rights into law. These were not individual occurrences. They were a well-crafted strategy to end legal abortions. And one of the next steps in that strategy is to outlaw stem cell research — not because the research itself is in question, but because banning the way that research is conducted can help them to achieve their true goal."

4.

Under a microscope, stem cells are even less impressive than embryos. They grow in tiny clusters — when magnified tenfold, individual cells are still smaller than pinheads — and look not unlike slimy, slightly metallic grapes. "It's almost funny," says Dr. Larry Goldstein, "that something this dull-looking could cause such a fuss."

Goldstein, another scientist in the middle of the stem cell storm, is a handsome, plainspoken man in his late forties. As a professor of cellular and molecular medicine at the University of California, San Diego, Goldstein oversees twenty-three researchers and several thousand mice. His work involves trying to decode how proteins, lipids, and organelles move through the neurons and brain cells, which is information that could help us cure Alzheimer's, Huntington's and Lou Gehrig's disease. But to get this information, he needs stem cells.

Currently, much of Goldstein's work involves nonhuman-derived stem cells, which are not technically a point of contention. "But five years from now," he says, "if I want to actually cure these diseases, I'll need access to human embryonic stem cells, and I want to make sure they're available."

The issue of stem-cell availability is another front in this battle. In the summer of 2001, just after his first State of the Union, President Bush issued an executive order restricting federal research money to seventy-eight previously harvested lines of stem cells. These lines were cultivated between 1998, when human embryonic stem cells were first isolated, and that 2001 moment further research was nixed. "The problem," explains Weissman, "is that all seventy-eight lines come from people who utilize in vitro fertilization clinics. IVF clinics serve a very specific segment of the American population. The stem cell lines are taken from rich, white, infertile people. One of the fundamental principles of bioethics is distributed justice. That means when scientists work on medical cures, they want to develop cures for everyone — not just rich, white, infertile people."

The impact of Bush's order was considerable. Almost immediately, University of California, San Francisco stem cell pioneer Roger Pedersen packed his bags and his lab and moved to England, a country with no restrictions on this research. Other nations, including Israel, Japan, France, and Australia, have also declared their friendliness to the work. Singapore took an even more aggressive stance, calling itself an "international center for stem cell study," then breaking ground on a $15 billion research park and quickly poaching top US scientists — including, for example, Edison Liu, once a leading scientist at America's National Cancer Institute and now the head of Singapore's new Genome Institute.

These developments have proven especially troubling for California, which is far and away the nation's leader in biotech research. To give this a little context, in 2002, Californian biotech firms were granted over 19,000 patents. The next closest state was New York, with 6,100. Yet California also took a $12 billion dollar hit in the dot-com crash of 2001 and is running an annual budget deficit close to $35 billion. In other words, now and moving forward, the biotech industry is absolutely critical to California's survival.

To combat the brain drain and bring more biotech money into California, state Senator Deborah Ortiz (D-Sacramento) introduced Senate Bill 253, which allows the use of state funds and private donations for stem cell research within California. It was signed into law on September 20, 2002, with Governor Gray Davis telling reporters: "By signing SB 253, we have opened the door to important life-saving research in California . . . We fully expect stem-cell research to attract world-renowned scientists to our state. Currently, there are 2,500 biomedical companies in California that employ 225,000 people. During 2000, this industry paid its employees $12.8 billion. While this life-saving research will continue to bring the necessary funding into the state, it will more importantly save lives."

Not interested in losing their own shot at the "necessary funding" and almost immediately after the bill's passage, four other states — Rhode Island, New Jersey, Louisiana, and Pennsylvania — enacted similar legislation. Both Massachusetts and New Mexico are now considering similar proposals. Ironically, the use of states' rights to bypass federal control has lately been a Republican tactic, especially favored by evangelical Christians in their attempts to ban abortions (and block gay marriage), but here co-opted by liberal Democrats. Another tactic long favored by conservative Republicans in their attempt to oust lefty values from the crevices of government has been the creation of special-interest lobbying groups and their ruthless application of pressure.

As it turns out, two can play at that game.

5.

Jerry Zucker is the creator of his own brand of movies, a genre of wacky comedy that began with *Kentucky Fried Movie*, was perfected in *Airplane!*, and includes both the *Naked Gun* and *Police Squad* franchises. Without question, he's Hollywood royalty. But unlike other Tinseltown royals, Zucker has never been especially political. That would change.

In 2000, Zucker found out that his eleven-year-old daughter, Katie, had juvenile diabetes. Immediately, he began researching the disease. A year later, he started hearing stories about stem cells and how they might be able to not just provide better treatment for Katie, but could actually provide a cure for the disease. This was also when he heard that the Bush administration was working hard to halt this work. "As a director," says Zucker, "I tend to be calm. I try not to get carried away or lose my cool. I don't want to be another Hollywood maniac. [But] what was going on with stem cells made me very angry."

Through sad circumstance, Zucker and his wife, Janet, got to know producer Douglas Wick (*Gladiator*, *Stuart Little*, and *Work-*

ing Girl), and his wife, Lucy Fisher, the former vice chairman of Columbia TriStar Motion Picture Group. Wick and Fisher also have a daughter with juvenile diabetes. In the summer of 2002, this foursome formed the stem cell research advocacy group Cures Now, hired a lobbyist, and went to Washington. They took their daughters and Caltech biologist David Anderson along. It was, as Zucker explains, an educational crusade meant to exert considerable pressure: "We would walk in to a senator's office with my daughter and her insulin pump attached to her belt and ask them what was more important — my daughter's life or the life of a couple of cells?"

Cures Now had an impact. One of their early converts was Utah Republican pro-life advocate Orrin Hatch. Centenarian Strom Thurmond also joined their cause. And Senate Minority Leader Tom Daschle agreed not to put a Senate stem cell bill on the floor for a vote until Cures Now had a chance to talk to everyone who would listen.

A lot of that talk has involved Zucker and Co. trying to separate fact from fiction. Over the past few years, there has been a concerted effort among stem cell foes on the religious right and within the Bush administration to conflate therapeutic cloning (which produces stem cells) with reproductive cloning (which produces carbon-copy humans). This is also where Leon Kass comes into the story.

Dubbed "The President's Ethics Cop" by *Time,* Kass is a University of Chicago bioethicist and was head of Bush's influential Council on Bioethics, which is charged with advising Congress and the administration on stem cells. A few years back, Kass wrote a now-famous article for the *New Republic,* "Preventing a Brave New World or Why We Should Ban Human Cloning Now," explaining the mechanics of somatic cell nuclear transfer — the main way scientists obtain stem cells.

> What is cloning? Cloning . . . is the production of individu-
> als who are genetically identical to an already existing indi-

vidual. The procedure's name is fancy — "somatic cell nuclear transfer" — but its concept is simple. Take a mature but unfertilized egg; remove or deactivate its nucleus; introduce a nucleus obtained from a specialized (somatic) cell of an adult organism. Once the egg begins to divide, transfer the little embryo to a woman's uterus to initiate a pregnancy. Since almost all the hereditary material of a cell is contained within its nucleus, the re-nucleated egg and the individual into which it develops are genetically identical to the organism that was the source of the transferred nucleus.

Scientifically, Kass is correct, except — and this is a big except — the somatic cell nuclear transfer process actually stops short of transplanting that egg into a woman's uterus. What Kass knows, but is choosing not to acknowledge here, is that once that new egg begins to divide, it can be used to either create stem cells or to create a carbon copy human. But it's an either-or. Using somatic cell nuclear transfer to create stem cells actually destroys the embryo. Moreover, almost no one wants to see the technology used for reproductive cloning. Pretty much every mainstream scientist, including Irv Weissman and Larry Goldstein, are seriously opposed to this procedure. But, because the subject is tricky and the news media tends to prefer sexy headlines to complicated reporting, Kass's conflation had an impact.

In the spring of 2001, a pair of cloning bills was introduced — one in the House, one in the Senate — that outlaw all forms of cloning (both reproductive and therapeutic), with severe penalties of up to $1 million and ten years in prison for either doing research in this field or receiving medical treatment based on that research. This means, if the French invent a stem cell–based cure for Alzheimer's, and you go to Paris for treatment and then try to reenter the United States, well, you go straight to jail.

The original House bill went nowhere, but it was quickly rewritten and reintroduced by Dave Weldon (R-Florida) and became known as the Weldon Bill. The debate surrounding the bill should have been about stem cells. It should have been about the facts. Instead, because of conflation, it was about the ramifications of human cloning, or, more specifically, eugenics, the commodification of humanity, setting a proper moral example, and — of course — the Nazis. The House passed the Weldon Bill in three hours.

6.

Irv Weissman's kitchen is a sprawling affair. It is large and rectangular and filled with a full compliment of shiny stainless steel appliances. On the evening of December 11, 2002, Weissman stands among those appliances, wearing a long chef's apron and a serious expression. He has a wineglass in one hand and a long wooden ladle in the other and is staring intensely at the goose he is preparing for dinner.

Seated around a long table are Weissman's guests, which tonight include his sister Lauren, once a Hollywood producer and now the executive director of Cures Now; Leroy Hood, another top scientist and the man who invented the DNA sorter that sequenced the human genome; and Ann Tsukamoto, a scientist with StemCells, Inc. The group has gathered to celebrate an announcement made the day prior at Stanford, when the institution declared its plans to capitalize on $12 million of anonymously donated seed money and build a $120 million Institute for Stem Cell Biology to be headed up by Weissman. In other words, in the war over stem cells, Stanford just declared itself the Western Front.

And make no mistake, the research they plan to do there is much needed. Building on Weissman's previous work with blood-forming stem cells, the Stanford institute will initially focus on discovering the stem cells that become the other major organs of the body — that way, if these organs become cancerous, they'll have new ways to fight the disease.

"It's not only new ways to fight the disease," says Weissman, taking a break from goose-cooking duties to join the conversation. "That's only the first step. We also know that there are cancer-forming stem cells. If we can isolate these, we can get to the very root of every type of cancer. This would give us new, biologically specific targets for drugs. And because the institute is in this state, California will be the first place these therapies will come out. Our biotech companies will produce them, and Californians will get the first crack at these treatments."

As expected, Stanford's announcement sparked a firestorm. The media jumped on the news, with the dangers of human cloning getting heavy play. The Associated Press, the first outlet to cover the story, began its article: "Stanford has said its new cancer institute will conduct stem cell research using nuclear-transfer techniques—work that many consider to be cloning of human cells." ABC News followed suit: "The president believes that the creation and destruction of embryos for the purpose of research or reproduction is morally wrong. He is against cloning of any kind and feels there are other biomedical research avenues."

Of course, Leon Kass also issued a press release. "Stanford has decided to proceed with cloning research without public scrutiny and deliberation," he wrote, then went on to say that the President's Council on Bioethics wants a four-year moratorium on therapeutic cloning and does not endorse the Stanford Institute. Oddly, no such moratorium has ever been recommended and Kass issued this statement without consulting anyone else on the council—so no one besides Kass was ever asked if they supported the institute.

Not that any of this is surprising. After all, what's a little deception in the face of the bigger war—a war that is far from over. The cloning debate rages at all levels of the government, recently refueled by the UFO-worshipping Raelians' 2003 announcement that they had created the world's first human clone. Never mind that, just prior to that announcement, the Bush administration blocked a worldwide U.N. ban on reproductive cloning that might have stopped the Raelians in their supposed work. The ban was vetoed because it did not also include therapeutic cloning and was insufficient for the religious right. Meanwhile, a middle-of-the-road estimate of how many Americans will die from diseases that stem cell research might soon cure is 130 million.

Back at the stove, Weissman lays down his spoon and nods his head: "This goose is cooked."

Hacking the President's DNA

THE CONSEQUENCES OF PLAYING GOD

Cowritten with Andrew Hessel and Marc Goodman

A couple months after I finished the first draft of this book, I sent it to author Howard Bloom for feedback. In his response, Howard went off on the kind of delicious, head-spinning tangent for which he is famous. Along the way, he also managed to sum up both the ideas in this chapter and the ideas in this book as a whole.

Technically, this chapter is about the upstart field of synthetic biology—a technology with both incredible and dangerous implications. But before we get to those dangers, it's worth pausing to consider what's really going on here. Synthetic biology unlocks one of the universe's deepest secrets—the mystery of life, the formula for creation. It is quite a long step forward.

Or, as Howard Bloom so eloquently puts it: "It's time to abandon the Greek idea that hubris is bad and face a simple fact—hubris is what the cosmos seems to want from us. We humans are pushing beyond the boundaries of what this cosmos has ever achieved. And that is what the cosmos seems to ache for. She has torn up her old rules over and over again. Once upon a time this universe made a big bang from nothing; then she made quarks and leptons from a raw rush of time, space, and speed. But that didn't satisfy her. She ripped up the rules again and made atoms, galaxies, stars, life, and mind. In our acts of invention, we are not defacing nature; we are upgrading her. And radical self-improvement is what nature has been about for 13.8 billion years. That's what this book is about. It's about humans who have the audacity to change the nature of reality. It's about humans who have the audacity to join in nature's creative process, in her quest for more than mere self-improvement, in her quest for self reinvention. Radical self-reinvention."

1.

This is how the future arrived. It began innocuously. In the early 2000s, businesses started to realize that highly skilled jobs formerly performed in-house, by a single employee, could more efficiently be crowdsourced to a larger group via the Internet. Initially, offerings were simple. We crowdsourced the design of T-shirts (Threadless.com) and the writing of encyclopedias (Wikipedia.com), but it didn't take long for the trend to start making inroads into the harder sciences. Pretty soon, the hunt for extraterrestrial life, the development of self-driving cars, and the folding of enzymes into new and novel proteins were being done this way. With the fundamental tools of genetic manipulation — tools that cost millions of dollars not ten years ago — dropping precipitously in price, the crowdsourced design of biological agents was just the next logical step.

In 2008, casual DNA design competitions with small prizes arose; then, in 2011, with the launch of GE's $100 million cancer challenge, the field moved onto serious contests. By early 2015, as personalized gene therapies for end-stage cancer became medicine's bleeding edge, viral design sites began to appear where people could upload information about their disease, and virologists could post designs for a customized cure. Medically speaking, it all made perfect sense: Nature has done eons of excellent design work on viruses. With a little, relatively simple retooling, they were perfect vehicles for drug delivery.

It didn't take long for these sites to be flooded with requests that went far beyond cancer. Diagnostic agents, vaccines, antimicrobials, even designer psychoactive drugs — all appeared on the menu. What people did with these biodesigns was anybody's guess. No international body had yet been created to watch over them.

So, in December 2015, when a first-time visitor named Captain Capsid posted a challenge on the viral design website 99Virions, no alarms sounded; it was just one of the hundred design requests submitted that day. Captain Capsid might have been some consultant to the pharmaceutical industry, and the challenge just another attempt to understand the radically shifting R&D landscape — really, he could have been anyone — but the problem was interesting nonetheless. Plus, Capsid was offering $500 for the winning design, not a bad sum for a few hours work.

Later, 99Virion's log files would show that Captain Capsid's IP address originated in Panama, although this was likely spoofed. The design specification itself raised no red flags. Written in SBOL, an open-source language similar to XML and popular with the synthetic biology crowd, it seemed like a standard vaccine request. So people just got to work, as did the automated computer programs that had been written to "auto-evolve" new designs. These algorithms were getting quite good, now winning over 30 percent of the challenges.

In less than twelve hours, 243 designs were submitted, most by these computerized expert systems. But the winner, GeneGenie27, was actually human — a twenty-year-old Columbia University undergrad with a knack for virology. His design was quickly forwarded to GENeBAY, a thriving Shanghai-based biomarketplace. Less than sixty seconds later, an Icelandic synthesis startup got the contract to turn the 5,984-base-pair blueprint into actual, doubled-stranded DNA. Twenty-four hours after that, a package of 10 mm fast-dissolving microtablets was dropped in a FedEx envelope and handed to a courier.

Two days later, Samantha, a sophomore political science major at Harvard University, received the package. Thinking it contained a new, synthetic psychedelic, she slipped the tab into her left nostril and walked over to her closet. By the time Samantha had finished dressing, the tab had started to dissolve and a few strands of DNA had crossed into the cells of her nasal mucosa.

Some party drug—all she got was the flu.

Later that evening, Samantha had a slight fever and was shedding billions of virus particles. These particles would continue to spread around campus in an exponentially growing chain reaction that was—other than the mild fever and some sneezing—absolutely harmless. This would change when the virus crossed paths with cells containing a very specific DNA sequence, a sequence that would act as a molecular key to unlock secondary functions that were not so benign. This second sequence would trigger a fast-acting neurodegenerative disease that produced memory loss, extreme paranoia, eventually death. The only person in the world with this sequence was the president of the United States, who was scheduled to speak at Harvard's Kennedy School later that week. Sure, there would be thousands of sniffling people on campus, but the Secret Service probably wouldn't think anything was amiss.

It was December, after all—cold and flu season.

2.

Does the scenario we've just sketched sound like nothing beyond science fiction? If so, consider that since the turn of the twenty-first century, rapidly accelerating technology has shown a distinct tendency to turn the impossible into the everyday in no time at all. A few years back, IBM's Watson, an artificial intelligence, whipped the human champion, Ken Jennings, on *Jeopardy*. As we write this, soldiers with bionic limbs are fighting our enemies and autonomous cars are driving down our streets. Yet most of these advances are small in comparison to the great leap forward currently underway in the biosciences—a leap with consequences we've only begun to imagine.

More to the point, consider that the Secret Service is already taking extraordinary steps to protect presidential DNA. According to the *Daily Mail*, in May 2011, when Barack Obama stopped off for a pint of Guinness at Ollie Hayes's pub in Moneygall, Ireland, his service detail quickly removed the glass from which he'd drunk. According to the *Daily Mirror*, Secret Service agents carried a special bag used to hold all the objects with which he had contact. (In actuality, the Navy is responsible for presidential food preparation and laundry, so the collection job is theirs.) More important, these actions were not isolated; the president's bedsheets, drinking glasses, and any other objects with which he has contact are routinely gathered — they are later destroyed or sanitized — to try to keep would-be malefactors from stealing his genetic material.

And the US isn't only playing defense. According to a 2010 release of secret cables by Wikileaks, former Secretary of State Hillary Clinton has directed our overseas embassies to surreptitiously collect DNA samples from foreign heads of state and senior UN officials. Clearly, the United States sees strategic advantage in knowing the specific biology of world leaders; it would be surprising if other nations didn't feel the same.

Currently, while there has been no reported use of an advanced, genetically targeted bioweapon, the authors of this piece — including experts in genetics and microbiology (Andrew Hessel) and global security and law enforcement (Marc Goodman) — are convinced we are not far from the possibility. As the recent work with highly virulent bird flu demonstrated, no giant breakthroughs are required. All of the enabling technologies are in place, already serving the needs of academic R&D groups and commercial biotechnology organizations. And these technologies are getting exponentially more powerful, particularly those that allow for the easy manipulation of DNA.

The evolution of cancer treatment provides one window into what's happening in the biosciences today. All cancer drugs kill cells. Today's chemotherapies are offshoots of chemical warfare agents; we've turned weapons into cancer medicines, albeit crude ones. As with carpet bombing, collateral damage is a given. Now, because of advances in genetics, we know that each cancer is unique, and research is shifting to the development of personalized medicines — designer therapies that can exterminate specific cancerous cells in a specific way, in a specific person. Forget collateral damage, these therapies are focused like lasers. The Finnish pharmaceutical Oncos Therapuetics has treated over two hundred patients using just such methods. But it wouldn't take much at all to subvert them, turning personalized medicines into personalized weapons.

In the coming years, criminals will doubtless dedicate significant resources to exploiting these biological advances, just as they've exploited a panoply of earlier technologies. Today bio-crime is in its infancy. Yet thanks to the accelerating growth rate in biotechnology, it could soon become as problematic as cyber crime, perhaps even more so.

We used to measure the gap between paradigm-shifting technological breakthroughs in centuries. Today, we measure them in years. For most of us, this is very good news. For the Secret Service, the story is different. Its job, difficult to begin with, may soon become impossible. Our next commander-in-chief will be our first commander-in-chief to have to deal with genetically based, made-to-order biothreats.

3.

If you really want to understand the nature of what's happening in the biosciences today, then you need to understand the rate at which information technology is accelerating. In 1965, Gordon Moore famously realized that the number of transistors on a computer chip had been doubling every year since the invention of the integrated circuit in 1958. Moore, who would go on to cofound Intel, used this information to predict the trend would continue "for at least ten years." He was right. The trend did continue for ten more years, and ten more after that, and ten more after that. All told, his prediction has stayed accurate for nearly six decades, becoming so durable that it's now known as Moore's Law and used by the semiconductor industry as a guide for future planning.

Moore's Law originally stated that every 12 months (it was later updated to every 12–24 months), the number of transistors on an integrated circuit will double, which means that computers will get twice as fast for the same price—an example of exponential growth in action. While linear growth is a slow, sequential proposition (1 becomes 2 becomes 3 becomes 4, etc.), exponential growth is an explosive doubling (1 becomes 2 becomes 4 becomes 8, etc.) with a transformational effect. In the 1970s, the most powerful supercomputer in the world was a Cray. It required a small room to hold and cost roughly $8 million. Today, the iPhone that sits in your pocket is a million times cheaper and a thousand times more powerful than a Cray. This is exponential growth at work.

In the years since Moore's observation, scientists have discovered exponential growth in dozens and dozens of technologies. The expansion of telephone lines in the United States, the amount of Internet data traffic in a year, the bytes of computer data storage available per dollar, the number of digital camera pixels per dollar, the amount of data transferable over optical fiber—just to name a few—all follow this pattern. In fact, exponential growth is so prevalent, researchers now suspect it underpins all information-based technologies—that is, any technology (like a computer) used to input, store, process, retrieve, and transmit digital information—and this includes biology.

Over the past few decades, scientists have come to see that the four letters of the genetic alphabet—A (adenine), C (cytosine), G (guanine), and T (thymine)—can be transformed into the ones and zeroes of binary code, allowing for the easy, electronic manipulation of DNA. With this development, biology has turned a significant corner, morphing into an exponentially advancing information-based science. As a result, the fundamental tools of genetic engineering, tools specifically designed for the manipulation of life — tools easily co-opted for the destruction of life — are now radically falling in cost and rising in power. Today, anyone with a knack for science, a decent Internet connection, and enough cash to buy a used car has what it takes to become a bio-hacker.

Of course, these developments greatly increase several dangers to our society. The most nightmarish involve bad actors creating weapons of mass destruction, or careless scientists unleashing accidental plagues. These are very real concerns that urgently and obviously need more attention. Personalized bioweapons, the focus of this story, are a subtler and less catastrophic threat and, perhaps for that reason, society has barely begun to consider them. Yet we believe that they will be put into use much more readily than bioweapons of mass destruction. For starters, while criminals might think twice about committing a massacre, murder is downright commonplace. Within a few years, politicians, celebrities, leaders of industry, or just about anyone, really, will be vulnerable to murder by genetically engineered bioweapon. Many such killings could go undetected, confused with death by natural causes; many others would be difficult to pin on a defendant, especially given disease latency. Both of these factors are likely to make personalized bioweapons extremely attractive to anyone bearing ill will.

Moreover — as we'll explore in greater detail — these same scientific developments pave the way for an entirely new kind of personal warfare. Imagine inducing paranoid schizophrenia in the CEO of a multinational conglomerate to gain a competitive business advantage, for example, or infecting shoppers with the urge to impulse buy.

We have chosen to focus this investigation mostly on the President's biosecurity because the president's welfare is paramount to national security — and because a discussion of the challenges faced by those charged with his protection will illuminate just how difficult (and different) "security" will be in the coming years.

4.

So what does it take to attack the president's DNA? A direct frontal assault against his genome requires, of course, first being able to decode genomes. Until recently, this was no simple matter. In 1990, when the US Department of Energy and the National Institutes of Health announced their intention to sequence the human genome, it was considered the most ambitious life sciences project ever undertaken. A fifteen-year timetable was established and a budget of $3 billion was set aside. Progress did not come quickly. Even after years' worth of hard work, many experts believed that neither the time nor the money budgeted for the job would be enough to complete it.

Opinions started to change in 1998, when the entrepreneurial biologist Craig Venter and his company Celera got into the race. Taking advantage of the exponential growth in biotechnology, Venter relied on a new generation of gene sequencers and a novel, computer-intensive approach called shotgun sequencing to deliver a fully sequenced human genome in less than two years, for just under $300 million.

Venter's achievement was stunning; it was also just the beginning. By 2007, just eight years later, the cost of sequencing a human genome had dropped to $1 million. In 2008, it was $60,000, and in 2011, $5,000. Over the next few years, the $1,000 dollar barrier looks likely to fall. At the current rate of decline, within five years, the cost will be below $100. In the history of the world, no other technology has dropped in price and increased in performance so dramatically.

Still, it takes more than just a gene sequencer to build a sophisticated, personally targeted bioweapon. To begin with, a would-be attacker must collect and grow live cells from her target (more on this later), so cell-culturing tools are a necessity. Next, a molecular profile for the cells must be generated, involving DNA sequencers, microarray scanners, mass spectrometers, and more. Once a detailed genetic blueprint has been built, the attacker can begin to design, build, and test a pathogen, a process that starts with genetic databases and software and ends in virus and cell-culture work.

Putting all this equipment together isn't trivial, yet, as researchers have upgraded to new tools, large companies have merged and consolidated operations, and smaller shops have run out of money and failed, plenty of used lab equipment has been dumped onto the resale market. As a result, while all of the gear needed to engineer a personalized bioweapon would cost well over a million dollars new; used, on eBay, it can be had for as little as $10,000. Strip out the analysis equipment — since these processes can now be outsourced — and a basic cell-culture rig can be cobbled together for under $1,000.

Biological knowledge, too, is becoming increasingly democratized. Websites like jove.com (Journal of Visualized Experiments, or JoVE) provide thousands of how-to instructional videos. MIT offers advanced online courses. Many journals are going open-access, making the latest research freely available. Or, if you want a more hands-on approach, just enmesh yourself in any of the dozens and dozens of do-it-yourself biology (DIY Bio) organizations that have lately sprung up to make genetic engineering into a hobbyist's pursuit — which is no small development. Bill Gates, in a recent interview, told reporters that if he were a kid today, forget about hacking computers, he'd be hacking biology. And, for those with neither the lab nor the learning, there are dozens of service providers willing to do all the serious science for a fee.

Since the invention of genetic engineering in 1972, the high cost of equipment and the high cost of getting enough education to use that equipment effectively kept most with ill intentions away from these technologies. Those barriers to entry are now gone.

"Unfortunately," said former Secretary of State Hillary Clinton in a December 7, 2011, speech to the global review board for the Biological Weapons Convention, "the ability for terrorists or other nonstate actors to develop and use these weapons is growing. Therefore this must be a renewed focus of our efforts, because there are warning signs and they are too serious to ignore."

5.

The radical expansion of biology's frontier raises an uncomfortable question: How do you guard against threats that don't yet exist? Genetic engineering sits at the edge of a new era. The older era belonged to DNA sequencing, which is simply the act of reading genetic code — identifying and extracting meaning from the ordering of the four chemicals that make up DNA. But now we're learning how to write DNA, and this creates possibilities both grand and terrifying.

Again, Craig Venter helped usher in this shift. In the late 1990s, while working to read the human genome, he also began wondering what it would take to write one. He wanted to know: What does the minimal genome required for life look like? Back then, DNA synthesis technology was too crude and expensive to consider writing a minimum genome for life or, more to our point, constructing a sophisticated bioweapon. And gene-splicing techniques, which involve the tricky work of using enzymes to cut up DNA from one or more organisms and then stitch it back together, were too unwieldy for the task.

Exponential advances in biotechnology have obliterated these problems. The latest technology — known as synthetic biology, or synbio — moves the work from the molecular to the digital. Genetic code is manipulated using the equivalent of a word processor. With the press of a button, DNA can be cut and pasted, effortlessly imported from one species into another. Single letters can be swapped in and out with precision. And once the code looks right? Simply hit send. A dozen different DNA print shops can now turn these bits into biology.

In May 2010, with the help of these new tools, Venter answered his question, creating the world's first self-replicating, synthetic chromosome. To pull this off, he used a computer to design a novel bacterial genome (over a million base pairs in total). Once the design was complete, the code was emailed to Blue Heron Biotechnology, a Seattle-based company that specializes in synthesizing DNA from digital blueprints. Blue Heron took Venter's blueprint of As, Ts, Cs, and Gs and returned a vial filled with freeze-dried strands of the DNA. Just as one might load an operating system into a computer, Venter then inserted the synthetic code into a denucleated bacterial cell. The new cell soon began generating proteins or, to use the computer term popular with today's biologists, it "booted up," starting to metabolize, grow, and, most important, divide, based entirely on the instructions from the injected DNA. As this replication proceeded, each new cell carried only Venter's synthetic instructions. For all practical purposes, it was an altogether new life form, created from scratch. Venter called it "the first self-replicating species we've had on the planet whose parent is a computer."

But Venter's work merely grazed the surface. Increasing technical simplicity and plummeting costs are allowing synthetic biologists to tinker with life in ways never before feasible. In 2004, for example, Jay Keasling, a biochemical engineer at Berkeley, stitched together ten synthetic genes from three different organisms to create a novel yeast that can manufacture artemisinic acid, the precursor to the antimalarial drug artemisinin, natural supplies of which are extremely low. The work would have been next to impossible without synthetic biology.

Meanwhile, Venter's company, Synthetic Genomics, is working on a designer algae that consumes CO_2 and excretes biofuel; it is also trying to develop synthetic flu-fighting vaccines made in days instead of the six to eight months now required. Solazyme, a synthetic biology company based in San Francisco, is making biodiesel with engineered microalgae. Material scientists are also getting into the act; DuPont recently designed an organism that utilizes corn syrup to create a widely used polymer base for plastics manufacturing, saving 40 percent on energy costs.

Other synthetic biologists are playing with more fundamental cellular mechanisms. The Florida-based Foundation for Applied Molecular Evolution has added two new bases to DNA's traditional four (A, T, G, C), creating a new genetic alphabet. At Harvard, geneticist George Church has supercharged evolution with his Multiplex Automated Genome Engineering (MAGE) process, which randomly swaps multiple genes at once. Instead of creating novel genomes one at a time, MAGE creates billions of variants in a matter of days.

Finally, because synbio makes DNA design, synthesis, and assembly so easy, we're already moving from the tweaking of existing designs to the construction of entirely new organisms — species that have never been seen before, species birthed entirely in our imagination. Since we can control the environments these organisms will live in, we will soon be generating living creatures capable of feats impossible in the "natural" world. Imagine organisms that can thrive in battery acid or on the surface of Mars, or enzymes able to polymerize carbon into diamonds or nanotubes. The ultimate limits to synthetic biology are hard to discern, and have yet to be explored.

All of this means that our interactions with biology, already complicated, are about to get a whole lot worse. Intentionally or accidentally, mixing code from multiple species together or creating entirely novel organisms could easily have unintended consequences. Even in labs with high standards for safety, accidents happen. If those accidents involve breaches in containment procedures, a harmless bacterium could become an ecological catastrophe. A 2010 synthetic biology report by the US Presidential Commission for the Study of Bioethical Issues said as much: "Unmanaged release could, in theory, lead to undesired cross-breeding with other organisms, uncontrolled proliferation, crowding out of existing species and threats to biodiversity."

Just as worrisome as bioerror is the threat of bioterror. While the organism Venter created is harmless, the same techniques can be used to construct a known pathogen or, worse, engineer a much deadlier, optimized version. Viruses are particularly easy to manufacture, a fact made apparent in 2002, when Dr. Eckard Wimmer, a Stony Brook University virologist, created the polio genome out of mail-order DNA. At the time, the 7,500-nucleotide synthesis cost him about $500,000 and took several years to complete. Today, a similar effort would take about a week and cost about $1,500. By 2020, if trends continue, it will take a few minutes and cost roughly $3. Governments the world over have spent billions trying to eradicate polio; imagine the damage terrorists could do with a $3 pathogen.

6.

During the 1990s, the Japanese cult Aum Shinrikyo, most infamous for its deadly 1995 Sarin gas attack on the Tokyo subway, maintained an active and extremely well-funded bioweapons program. When police raided the cult's facilities, they found ebola, anthrax, cyanide, and proof of a decadelong research effort costing at least $10 million — demonstrating, among other things, the clear value terrorists see in pursuing bioweapons. While Aum did manage to cause considerable harm, its attempts to unleash mass destruction, thankfully, never came to fruition. "Aum's failure suggests that it may, in fact, be far more difficult to carry out a deadly bioterrorism attack than has sometimes been portrayed by government officials and the press," wrote William Rosenau, a Rand Corporation analyst, in a 2001 article for *Studies in Conflict and Terrorism*. "Despite its significant financial resources, dedicated personnel, motivation, and freedom from the scrutiny of the Japanese authorities, Aum was unable to achieve its objectives."

That was then.

Now, two trends have changed the game. The first emerged in 2004, when the International Genetically Engineered Machines (iGEM) competition was founded at MIT. iGem's goal is for teams of high school and college students to build simple biological systems from standardized, interchangeable parts. These standardized parts, known as BioBricks, are chunks of DNA code with clearly defined structures and functions, allowing them to be easily linked together in new combinations, a little like a set of genetic LEGO bricks. These designs are collected in the Registry of Standard Biological Parts, an open-source database accessible to anyone who is curious.

Over the years, iGEM teams have not only pushed technical barriers but creative ones as well, turning bacterial cells into everything from photographic films to hemoglobin-producing blood cells to miniature hard drives, complete with data encryption. By 2008, students were designing organisms with real-world applications; the contest that year was won by a team from Slovenia for their designer vaccine against *Helicobacter pylori*, the bacteria responsible for most ulcers. The 2011 grand prize winner, a team from the University of Washington, completed three separate projects, each one rivaling the outputs of world-class academics and the biopharmaceutical industry.

As the sophistication of iGEM research rose, so did the level of participation. In 2004, 5 iGEM teams submitted 50 potential BioBricks to the Registry. Two years later, it was 32 teams submitting 724 parts. By 2010, iGEM mushroomed to 130 teams submitting 1,863 parts — and the Registry database was over 5,000 components strong. As the *New York Times* pointed out: "iGEM has been grooming an entire generation of the world's brightest scientific minds to embrace synthetic biology's vision — without anyone really noticing, before the public debates and regulations that typically place checks on such risky and ethically controversial new technologies have even started."

The second trend to consider is the progress terrorist and criminal organizations have made with just about every other information technology. Since the birth of the digital revolution, all sorts of rogue actors have been early adopters and cunning exploiters. Phone phreakers like John Draper (aka Captain Crunch) discovered back in the 1970s that AT&T's telephone network could be fooled into making free calls with the help of a plastic whistle given away in cereal boxes (thus Draper's moniker). In the 1980s, early desktop computers were subverted by a sophisticated array of computer viruses for malicious fun — then, in the 1990s, for information theft and financial gain. The 2000s saw purportedly uncrackable credit card cryptographic algorithms reverse engineered and mobile smartphones repeatedly infected with malware. On a larger scale, denial-of-service attacks have grown increasingly destructive, crippling everything from individual websites to massive financial networks. In 2000, "Mafiaboy," a lone fifteen-year old Canadian high school student, managed to shut down the websites of Yahoo, eBay, CNN, Amazon, and Dell.

In 2007, Russian hackers swamped Estonian websites, disrupting financial institutions, broadcasting networks, and government ministries (including the Estonian Parliament). A year later, before the invasion by Russian military, the state of Georgia saw a massive cyberattack paralyze their banking system and disrupt cell-phone networks. Iraqi insurgents subsequently repurposed Skygrabber — Russian software developed to steal satellite television and available for $29.95 — to intercept the video feeds of US predator drones, giving them the information needed to monitor and evade American military operations.

Lately, organized crime has even taken up crowdsourcing, outsourcing areas of their illegal operations — printing up fake credit cards, money laundering, even murder — to those with greater expertise. With the anonymous nature of the online crowd, this development makes it all but impossible for law-enforcement to track these efforts.

Added together, the historical data is clear: Whenever novel technologies enter the market, illegitimate uses quickly follow legitimate ones. A black market is soon to appear. Thus, just as criminals and terrorists have exploited all other forms of technology, they will undoubtedly soon be turning their attention to synthetic biology, the latest digital frontier.

7.

In 2005, as a way to begin preparing for the point when terrorists do turn their attention to synthetic biology, the FBI hired former University of Southern California, Keck School of Medicine gene therapist turned Amgen cancer researcher Edward You. Special Agent You, now a supervisory special agent in the Weapons of Mass Destruction Directorate, knew that biotechnology had been expanding too quickly for the FBI to keep pace and decided the only way to stay ahead of the curve was to outsource the problem to those at the leading edge. "When I got involved," You says, "it was pretty clear the FBI wasn't about to start playing Big Brother to the life sciences. It's not our mandate and it's not possible. All the expertise lies in the scientific community. Our job has to be outreach education. We need to create a culture of security in the synbio community, of responsible science, so the researchers themselves understand that they are the guardians of the future."

Toward that end, the FBI started hosting free biosecurity conferences, stationed WMD outreach coordinators in fifty-six field offices to network with the synbio community, and even became a major iGEM sponsor. In 2006, after reporters at the *Guardian* successfully mail-ordered a crippled fragment of the smallpox virus genome, suppliers of genetic materials decided to develop self-policing guidelines. According to You, the FBI sees the fact that these guidelines emerged organically as proof that their approach is working. Others are not so sure, pointing out that these new rules don't do much more than ensure a dangerous pathogen isn't sent to a PO Box.

And much more is necessary. An October 2011 report by the WMD Center, a bipartisan nonprofit organization chaired by former senators Bob Graham (D) and Jim Talent (R), warned that a biological attack within the United States was deemed probable, and specifically highlighted the dangers of synthetic biology: "As DNA synthesis technology continues to advance at a rapid pace, it will soon become feasible to synthesize nearly any virus whose DNA sequence has been decoded . . . as well as artificial microbes that do not exist in nature. This growing ability to engineer life at the molecular level carries with it the risk of facilitating the development of new and more deadly biological weapons."

Terrorists are not the only danger America needs to consider. Thirty-six nations now have dedicated synthetic biology research programs, China foremost among them. The Beijing Genomics Institute, known as BGI, was founded in 1999. It has since grown into the largest genomic research organization in the world, and is slated to receive $1.5 billion in additional funding over the next decade. Currently, BGI is the world's largest producer of genetic code, sequencing the equivalent of over 15,000 human genomes a year. (In a recent interview with the journal *Science,* BGI claimed to have more sequencing capacity than all the labs in the United States, put together.) A few years ago, during the German E. coli outbreak, BGI sequenced the culprit in just three days (versus, say, the thirteen years it took researchers to sequence the HIV virus). And BGI now appears poised to move beyond DNA sequencing and become one of the world's foremost DNA synthesizers as well.

Many feel that whomever controls synbio will control a significant chunk of the global economy over the next fifty years, but even beyond such broad fiscal ramifications, there are security concerns as well. BGI hires thousands of bright young researchers each year. The training is great, but the wages low. This means that a steady stream of talented synthetic biologists are likely searching for better pay and greener pastures. Some of those jobs will appear in countries not yet on the synbio radar (even more economic competition for the US). Some in places we don't want them to. Iran, North Korea, and Pakistan will most definitely be hiring.

8.

In his 2009 book, *In the President's Secret Service,* Ronald Kessler points out that threats against President Obama have risen 400 percent compared to President Bush. Each must be thoroughly investigated. In January 2008, for example, when intelligence emerged that the Somalia-based Islamist group al-Shabaab might try to disrupt Mr. Obama's inauguration, the Secret Service coordinated 40,000 agents and officers from some 94 police, military, and security agencies. Detailed security checks were run on employees and hotel guests in nearby buildings, bomb-sniffing dogs and chemical-sensing technologies were deployed throughout the area, and more than a dozen countersniper teams were stationed along the parade route. This is a considerable response capability, but soon it won't be enough. Currently, nothing in the Secret Service's considerable arsenal can defend against the weapons that synthetic biology makes possible.

Part of the problem is that the range of threat vectors the Secret Service has to guard against already extends far beyond firearms or explosive devices. Both chemical and radiological attacks have been made against prominent government officials in recent years. In 2004, an assassination attempt on the life of Ukrainian President Viktor Yushchenko used TCCD, an extremely toxic dioxin compound. In 2006, Alexander Litvinenko, a former officer of the Russian Security Service, was poisoned with the radioisotope polonium 210. And the use of bioweapons themselves is hardly unknown; the American anthrax attacks nearly reached members of Congress.

The Kremlin, of course, has been poisoning its enemies for decades, and anthrax has been around for a while, yet genetic technologies open the door for an entirely new kind of threat vector, in which the president's own genome can be used against him or her. This is a particularly difficult threat to defend against. No amount of Secret Service vigilance can ever fully secure POTUS's DNA, because the president's entire genetic blueprint can now be produced from the information contained within just a single cell. Each of us sheds billions of cells every day. These can be collected from any number of sources — a drinking glass, say, or a toothbrush. Physical contact will also do the trick. Every time the president shakes hands with a constituent, cabinet member, or foreign leader, he's leaving an exploitable trail. Whenever he gives away a pen at a bill signing ceremony, a few cells are left behind. These cells are dead, but the DNA is intact, and just a few cells are enough for genetic testing.

For the real work of building a bioweapon, living cells would be the true target (although dead cells may suffice within as little as a decade). These are more difficult to recover, but a sample gathered from fresh blood or saliva or even a sneeze, caught in a discarded tissue, could suffice. Once recovered, these living cells can be cultured, providing those with nefarious intentions a continuous supply of research material.

Even if Secret Service agents were able to sweep up all the president's shed cells, they couldn't eliminate the possibility of DNA being recovered from the past. DNA is a very stable molecule, often lasting for millennia. Genetic material remains on old clothes, high school tests, or any of the myriad of objects handled and discarded by a commander-in-chief long before his candidacy was announced. How much attention was dedicated to protecting Obama's DNA when he was a senator? A neighborhood organizer in Chicago? A student at Harvard law? In preschool? Even if presidential DNA was somehow fully locked down, a good approximation of the code could be made from cells of his children, parents, and siblings, living or not.

Presidential DNA could be used in a variety of politically sensitive ways, perhaps to fabricate evidence of an affair, fuel speculation about birthplace and heritage, or identify genetic markers for a bevy of diseases that could cast doubt on leadership ability and mental acuity. How much does it take to unseat a president? The first signs of President Ronald Reagan's Alzheimer's emerged during his second term. While doctors now believe it was then too mild to affect his ability to govern, if information about his condition had been made public while he was still in office, would the American people have demanded his resignation? Could Congress be forced to impeach?

For the Secret Service, this opens the door for attack scenarios worthy of a Hollywood thriller. Advances in stem cell research make it possible for any living cell to be transformed into any other cell type, including neurons or heart cells or even in vitro-derived (IVD) sperm. Any live cells recovered from a dirty glass or an old napkin or such could, in theory, be used to manufacture synthetic sperm cells. And so, out of the blue, a president could be outed by a "former lover" coming forward with DNA "evidence" of a sexual encounter, like the proverbial semen stain on the dress. Sophisticated testing could distinguish fake IVD sperm from the real thing — they are not identical — but the results might never convince the lay public. IVD sperm may also someday prove capable of fertilizing eggs, allowing for surreptitious love children to be born using standard in vitro fertilization technologies.

As mentioned, even modern cancer therapies can be harnessed for malicious ends. Personalized therapies designed to attack a single patient's cancer cells are already moving out of the laboratory and into clinical trials. Synthetic biology is poised to rapidly expand and accelerate this process by making individualized viral therapies inexpensive. Such "magic bullets" can target cancer cells with extreme precision. But what if these bullets were trained against healthy cells instead? Trained against retinal cells, the result would be blindness. Against the hypothalamus, a memory wipe is possible. And the liver? Death would come in a matter of months.

The delivery of this sort of biological agent would be very difficult to detect. Viruses are tasteless and odorless and easily aerosolized. Hidden in a perfume bottle, a quick dab on the wrists in the general proximity of the target is all an assassination attempt would require. If the pathogen had been designed to zero in specifically on the president's DNA, then nobody else present would even get sick.

Pernicious agents could be crafted to do their damage months or even years after exposure, depending on the goals of the designer. Several viruses are already known to spark cancers. New ones could eventually be designed to infect the brain with, say, synthetic schizophrenia, bipolar disorder, or early-onset Alzheimer's. Stranger possibilities exist as well. A disease engineered to amplify the production of cortisol and dopamine could induce extreme paranoia, turning, say, a presidential dove into a warmongering hawk. Or a virus that boosts the production of oxytocin, the chemical responsible for feelings of trust, could play hell with a leader's negotiating abilities, leaving the country open to an array of biodiplomatic assaults. Some of these ideas aren't even new. The US Air Force's Wright laboratory in Ohio theorized about chemical-based pheromone bombs as far back as 1994.

Of course, heads of state are not the only ones vulnerable to this coming wave of synbio threats. Al Qaeda flew planes into buildings to cripple Wall Street, but imagine the damage an attack targeting the CEOs of Fortune 500 companies could do to the world economy. Forget kidnapping rich foreign nationals as a means of profit, soon merely kidnapping their DNA might be enough. Celebrities will face an entirely new kind of stalker. As homebrew biology matures, these technologies could end up being used to "settle" all sorts of disputes, even those of the domestic variety.

Without question, it's a brave new world.

9.

Despite the rapid acceleration of exploitable biotechnology, the Secret Service is not powerless to protect the president. Steps can be taken. Establishing a crack scientific task force to continually monitor, forecast, and evaluate new risks is the obvious place to start. Deploying sensing technologies is another. Already, biodetectors have been built that can identify known pathogens in less than three minutes. These can get better — a *lot* better — but, even so, they might not be enough. Synthetic biology opens the door to finely targeted, entirely new biothreats — how can we detect that which we've never seen before?

In this, the Secret Service has one big advantage over the Center for Disease Control: Its principle responsibility is the protection of a specific person. This makes it possible to build *specific* biosensing technologies around the president's genome. We can use his living cells to build an early warning system with molecular accuracy.

Live cell cultures taken from the president could also be kept at the ready — a biological equivalent to data backups. The Secret Service already carries several pints of the president's blood with the motorcade, just in case an emergency transfusion is necessary. These biological backup systems could be expanded to include "clean DNA," essentially verified stem cell libraries suitable for bone marrow transplantation or to provide enhanced antiviral or antimicrobial capabilities. As tissue-printing technology improves, the president's cells could even be turned into ready-made, standby replacement organs.

Yet even if we were to implement all of these proposed measures, there is no guarantee that the presidential genome could ever be completely protected. As hard as it may be, the Secret Service might have to accept that they're not going to be able to fully counter all biothreats any more than they could guarantee the president will never catch a cold.

In light of this fact, one possible solution—not without its drawbacks—is radical transparency. Either release the president's DNA and other relevant biological data to a select group of security-cleared researchers or, the far more controversial step, to the public at large. These ideas may seem counterintuitive, perhaps even startling, but we have come to believe that open-sourcing this problem—and actively engaging the American public in the challenge of protecting their leader—might turn out to be the best defense available.

For starters, cost is a factor. Any in-house protection effort is going to be exceptionally pricey. Certainly, considering what's at stake, the country would bear the expense, but is this the best solution? After all, over the past five years, DIY Drones, a not-for-profit, online community of autonomous aircraft hobbyists (working for free, in their spare time), produced a $300-dollar Unmanned Aerial Vehicle (UAV) with 90 percent of the functionality of the military's $35,000 Raven. This kind of price reduction is typical of open-sourced projects, which is why open-sourcing presidential biosecurity may turn out to be the best way to pay for presidential biosecurity.

Moreover, doing biosecurity in-house means attracting and retaining a very high level of talent. This puts the Secret Service in competition with industry, a fiscally untenable position, and academia, where many of the more interesting problems now lie. But tapping the collective intelligence of the life science community—our first scenario—enlists the help of the group best prepared to address this problem, at a price we can afford (free).

Open-sourcing the president's genetic information to a select group of security-cleared researchers brings other benefits as well. It would allow the life sciences to follow in the footsteps of the computer sciences, where so-called "red team exercises" or "penetration testing," are extremely common security practices. In these exercises, the red team, usually a group of faux black-hat hackers, attempts to find weaknesses in an organization's (blue team) defenses. A similar environment could be developed for biological war games. Samples of presidential DNA (live cells) could be provided to two teams of trusted and vetted researchers. The blue team tries to develop strategies for protection; the red team tries to attack. In this way, actual risks can be assessed and real defensive strategies — for example, combination drug therapies (genetically personalized like today's cancer drugs) — can be evaluated.

One of the reasons this practice has been so widely instituted in the computer world is because the field's speed of development far exceeds the ability of security experts to keep pace. Because the biological sciences are now advancing significantly faster than computing, little short of an internal Manhattan-style project could put the Secret Service ahead of this curve, to say nothing of keeping them there. The FBI has far greater resources at its disposal than the Secret Service (almost 36,000 people work there, compared to roughly 6,500 at the Secret Service), yet, five years ago, the FBI concluded the *only* way it could keep up with biological threats was by involving the whole of the life science community in the endeavor.

So why go further? Why take the seemingly radical step of releasing the president's genome to the rest of the world instead of just a security-cleared group? As the aforementioned Wiki-leaked, State Department cables makes clear, the surreptitious gathering of genetic material has already begun. It would not be surprising if the president's DNA has already been collected and analyzed and our adversaries are merely waiting for the right opportunity to exploit the results. The assault could even be home-grown, the result of increasingly divisive party politics and the release of unscrupulous attack ads.

In the November 2008 issue of the *New England Journal of Medicine,* Drs. Robert Green and George Annas warned against this possibility, writing that soon "advances in genomics will make it more likely that DNA will be collected and analyzed to assess genetic risk information that could be used for or, more likely, against presidential candidates." It's also not hard to imagine a biological analogue to the computer hacking group Anonymous arising, with the goal of providing a transparent picture of world leaders' genomes and medical histories. Sooner or later, even without open-sourcing, the president's genome will end up in the public eye.

So the question becomes: Is it more dangerous to play defense and hope for the best, or to go on offense and prepare for the worst? Neither choice is terrific, but even beyond the important issues of cost and talent-attraction, open-sourcing, as Dr. Claire Fraser, director of the Institute for Genomics at the University of Maryland points out, "would level the playing field, removing the need for intelligence agencies to plan for every possible worst-case scenario."

It would also allow the White House to avoid the media storm that would likely occur if someone else leaked the president's genome, while simultaneously providing a "normal" presidential baseline against which future samples can be compared. In addition, this would produce an exceptional level of early detection of cancers and other metabolic diseases. And, if such diseases were found, it could likewise accelerate personalized therapies.

The largest factor to consider is time. Currently, some 14,000 Americans are working in labs with access to seriously pathogenic materials; we don't know how many tens of thousands more are doing the same overseas. Outside of those labs, with equipment now extremely cheap, the fundamental tools and techniques of genetic engineering are accessible to anyone interested. Not all that interest will be built around peaceful intentions. On December 8, 2011, Saudi Arabian prince Turki bin

Faisal, who has twice served as an ambassador to the US, called for his country to acquire WMDs, including biological weapons, to defend against Iran and Israel's nuclear ambitions.

Back in 2003, a panel of life science experts convened by the National Science Foundation for the CIA's Strategic Assessment Group pointed out that because the processes and techniques needed for the development of advanced bio agents are "dual-use"—they can be used for both good or ill—it will soon be extremely difficult to distinguish legitimate research from the production of bioweapons. As a result, the panelists argued, a qualitatively different relationship between the government and the life science communities might be needed to effectively grapple with future threats.

In our view, it's no longer a question of might. Advances in biotechnology are quickly and radically changing the scientific landscape. We are entering a world where imagination is the only brake on biology, where dedicated individuals can create new life from scratch. Today, when a difficult problem is mentioned, a commonly heard refrain is, "There's an app for that." Sooner than you might believe, "applications" will be replaced by synthetically created "organisms"—as in, "There's an org for that"—when we think about the solutions to many of our problems. Crowdsourcing the protection of the presidential genome, in light of this coming revolution, may prove to be the only way to protect the president. And in the process, the rest of us.

The God of Sperm

THE CONTROVERSIAL FUTURE OF BIRTH

Most of the innovators we've covered in these pages emerged from beyond the mainstream. Whether it's Dezso Molnar and his flying motorcycle or William Dobelle and his artificial vision implant or Craig Venter and his synthetic genome—all three are much more maverick outsider than cozy insider. And the main character in this, our final story, is no different.

Cappy Rothman started out his career as a courier for the mob—literally a bagman. But one thing led to another, and today's he's the most powerful man in the fertility industry and, by extension, arguably the person on this planet with the most influence over the future of childbirth. And this fact, in all of its staggering implications, is the point.

Our technology has begun keeping pace with our imagination. Equally astounding, access to that technology has become so democratized that maverick outsiders can now take on challenges that two decades back were the sole province of large governments and major corporations and two millennia back belonged only to the gods.

"Follow your weird," said author Bruce Sterling. Well, mission accomplished. We followed, all right. Out of the muck and onto the land. Down from the trees and over the veldt. Across oceans and continents, then skies and stratospheres. We've chased it back in time and into distant space, and don't get me started on other dimensions. We tracked it out of science fiction and into science fact and we're not done yet. Oh yeah, we followed our weird. Followed it right into Tomorrowland.

1.

The world's largest collections of stored genetic materials are found in Sussex, England; Spitsbergen, Norway; and Los Angeles, California. Sussex hosts the Millennium Seed Bank, which houses some 750 million species of plant seed. Spitsbergen, an island less than 600 miles from the North Pole, is the site of the Svalbard Global Seed Vault, which safeguards — inside a tunnel, inside a mountain — every variety of the earth's twenty-one major food crops. And Los Angeles is home to the California Cryobank, the largest sperm bank in the world, which stores enough human seed to repopulate the planet several times over. The first two of these projects are international efforts to preserve our genetic future; the last is a private enterprise run by a man known to many as the King of Sperm.

The King wears Buddy Holly glasses. He is of medium height and medium build, balding, sixty-nine years of age, with a penchant for flashy shirts and comfortable shoes. His name is Dr. Cappy Rothman and "Cappy" is not a nickname. It is the colorful moniker given to him by his colorful father — if by colorful one means mobbed up.

The King of Sperm began his career in casinos. His father, Norman "Roughneck" Rothman, ran the San Souci Club in Havana, so Dr. Rothman spent his teenage years in Cuba. One of his earliest jobs was ferrying money — in a briefcase handcuffed to his wrist — between Cuba and banks in the States. One of his later jobs was working as an organizer for Jimmy Hoffa — to raise extra cash for medical school at the University of Miami.

Medical school led Rothman to a residency at the University of California in San Francisco, where he studied under the legendary urologist Frank Hinman Jr. Hinman liked to assign his students yearlong research projects on medical mysteries. How sperm got from testicle to outside world was Rothman's assignment for his first year of medical school. In his second, it was the mechanism of erection. Both are considered infertility problems. "I loved infertility immediately," says Rothman. "There was so much we didn't know. I felt like a pioneer."

By 1975, that pioneer was board-certified in urology and took a job at the Tyler Clinic, becoming Los Angeles' first male infertility specialist. A few years later, the Tyler clinic folded and Rothman went out on his own. The California Cryobank was born.

In 1977, Rothman published the very first article on sperm banking in the *Journal of Urology*. That was also the year a prominent US senator's son was killed in a car crash. The statesman contacted Rothman and asked if his boy's sperm could be saved. In 1978, because of the work he'd done on the senator's son, he published the first article on postmortem sperm retrieval, later appearing on *Oprah* to explain the procedure.

Despite these accolades, what Rothman remembers most about starting up his business was a young couple who came to see him. "The man was infertile and the woman was angry. In the middle of that discussion, she turned to her husband and said, 'Because I married you, I'll never be a mother.' It was a statement I never wanted to hear again. Then and there, I decided to open a sperm bank."

2.

If you adjust for size, the distance sperm must swim from testicle to ovum is the equivalent to that of a human running from Los Angeles to Seattle. Because of serious concern about transmission of diseases like AIDS to unborn children, and the drastic rise of what is known as "single mothers by choice," the human seed in the King of Sperm's collection now travels much farther — serving women in all fifty states and some twenty-eight countries.

This is no thin slice of the pie.

In the United States, the fertility industry is an annual $3.3 billion business, with sperm banking accounting for $75 million of that. Thirty percent of that business flows through the California Cryobank, but even these numbers do not truly capture Rothman's influence. Frozen sperm and eggs — which the California Cryobank also stores — are the first step in assisted reproduction, so wherever the sperm-and-egg-bank business goes, so goes the rest. As Rothman himself points out, "When California Cryobank makes a decision, some six months later the rest of the industry tends to follow."

Increasingly, these decisions are no small thing. For almost four decades, the sperm banking industry has operated almost completely without outside influence. Beyond a series of somewhat bizarre FDA rulings (more on these later), there is no top-down governance. The industry is, as it has always been, self-policing. Which means that California Cryobank and a few other key players wield enormous influence over the future of childbirth.

Right now, that future is uncertain. A growing pile of ethical, legal, and biological issues now surround the industry: the problem of donor anonymity; rules involving genetic diseases occasionally passed on by sperm and egg banks; the prevention of accidental incest between half brothers and half sisters; and strange quandaries resulting from a government increasingly using science to play politics. Will the government step in is the question. Because, until they do, the people profiting most from the future of childbirth are actually the people shaping the future of childbirth.

3.

California Cryobank's headquarters sit in a two-story office building in West LA, specifically designed by Rothman to resemble a set from *Star Wars*. But it's a little bit of overkill. Seriously, who needs sci-fi window dressing, when there's actual sci-fi technology.

Outside the building, for example, stands a 6,000-gallon nitrogen tank and a backup generator capable of providing six months of emergency power. Inside, just past the receptionist, sits a large, rectangular room: the home to ten cryotanks, each containing 20,000 color-coded ampoules of sperm. Each ampoule holds up to 60 million sperm, with the color-coding determining the ethnicity of the donor. In other words, just off the lobby of the California Cryobank, is enough sperm to refertilize the earth several times over.

Just down the hall from the cryotanks are the masturbatoriums — the little rooms where prospective donors jerk off. There are three masturbatoriums to choose from: erotic, less erotic, and not so erotic. Perhaps because Rothman is a bit old-fashioned, or perhaps because the masturbatoriums were designed by a woman from the marketing department, the photographs that wallpaper these rooms, especially when measured against today's Internet porn standards, are downright tasteful.

"For some guys," notes Rothman, "it doesn't take much."

It may not take much to finish one's business in these rooms, but it takes quite a lot to get into them in the first place. To become a donor at California Cryobank, one must submit to what Rothman calls "the most rigorous prescreening process in the field."

This process begins with a college education because, without one, California Cryobank doesn't want your sperm. A long conversation follows, where donors are filled in on the obligations that come with the job — specifically its year-and-a-half-long commitment. During that commitment, donors are paid seventy-five bucks a pop, with two to three pops a week required, meaning a guy stands to earn anywhere from $11,000 to $17,000 for his services.

If those terms are acceptable, two separate semen samples are taken and analyzed. "We're looking for very fertile men," explains Rothman. Normal sperm count is 20 million to 150 million sperm per milliliter of semen. By "very fertile," Rothman means over 200 million sperm per milliliter. Sixty percent of those sperm must be motile and must look as sperm are supposed to look.

If all of this is shipshape, a three-generation genetic history is taken. More semen is obtained and screened for diseases. Most sperm banks test for 23 variations of the mutation that causes cystic fibrosis, while California Cryobank, known for their rigor, looks for 97. Jewish donors are screened for Tay-Sachs, African American donors for sickle-cell anemia. A complete physical is then taken, followed by a six-month quarantine to assure that slow-developing HIV is not lurking in the sperm — one of those ideas that originated at California Cryobank and has since spread to the rest of the industry.

After this waiting period, donors start producing. "We see them twice a week for semen, we see them once every three months for an updated battery of STD tests," Rothman says. "We get to know them pretty well along the way."

But the major problem facing the industry right now isn't how well sperm banks get to know their donors — it's how well prospective parents get to know their donors.

4.

Here in the twenty-first century, we shop for kids via catalog — "donor catalog" to be exact. These catalogs are thick, usually including a description of donor eye color, ethnicity, and education level, a psychological profile, personal essays, and even audio interviews. Occasionally, adult photos are included and California Cryobank has just added baby pictures as well. But the one thing prospective buyers are never permitted to know is the donor's name.

Donor anonymity is the bedrock of the business and, as a result, as Jane Mattes, a New York psychotherapist and founder of Single Mothers by Choice, an organization that represents the fastest-growing group to utilize frozen sperm, says, "the most crucial issue facing the industry today."

While the industry maintains continual contact with its donors during the sperm-collection phase, California Cryobank and others have no way to keep track of donors after their tour of duty is done. Illness is the problem. There are plenty of diseases that don't manifest until later in life, yet most donors are college students who have yet to get sick. Furthermore, though most sperm banks are rigorous in their predonation screenings, many donors don't know their own genetic history. Others lie to conceal it.

Add in the fact that nobody demands that cryobanks stay in contact with donors; that banks don't have to tell new clients about health concerns among donors' prior children or release any follow-up medical information about a donor; that, traditionally, sperm banks destroy donor records to preserve anonymity after the bank is done selling their sperm, and — as the saying goes — you have the makings of a quagmire.

This quagmire has led to problems, like those facing Brittany Johnson. In 1988, Diane and Ronald Johnson used California Cryobank sperm — from a man known only as Donor 276 — to conceive their daughter Brittany. The problem with 276's sperm was an exceptionally rare kidney disorder known as autosomal dominant polycystic kidney disease, a late-onset ailment that typically doesn't appear until after age forty — but one that usually requires a kidney transplant by age fifty. It is possible that Donor 276 didn't know he was a carrier (though this seems unlikely, since his grandmother died from it and his mother and aunt also suffered from it). Either way, when Brittany got sick at age six, she became what the media dubbed the "test case for sperm gone wrong."

It became a nasty fight. The Johnsons alleged that California Cryobank knew the truth about Donor 276 — though Rothman strenuously denies this — and went out of its way to conceal it.

And Brittany may not be the only sick child around. Between 1984 and 1988, Donor 276 made $11,200 for himself by donating over 300 specimens, and court documents suggest the bank sold nearly 1,500 vials of Donor 276 sperm to an unknown number of women before being taken off the market in 1991.

While the facts of this case remain murky (it was settled out of court in 2003 and some records remain sealed), the resulting hoopla brought similar problems to light. There is the widely reported story of Donor 1084 at Fairfax Cryobank in Virginia, the second largest cryobank in America, whose sperm carries a rare platelet disease and has resulted in a half dozen sick children up and down the East Coast. Also at Fairfax, Donor 2148 carried a rare genetic immune disorder that has already infected one of Donor 2148's twenty-three known children. Then there's Donor F827, from International Cryogenics in Michigan, who fathered somewhere between five and eleven children and all with a rare blood disease that leaves carriers at serious risk for leukemia.

And this list goes on and on.

The answer that many are pushing for is to ban donor anonymity. But this brings problems of its own. In 1984, Sweden outlawed anonymity, and so severe was the drop in potential donors that Swedish women began traveling to Denmark for sperm, giving rise to what is now known as reproductive tourism. And the same thing happened in New Zealand. In 2005, when England outlawed anonymity, donor numbers dropped by 84 percent. On an island of 22 million men, fewer than 200 are now willing to bank their sperm. After the law's passage, Clare Brown, chief executive of the Infertility Network UK, told reporters, "Clinics across the country are having to close because there is a shortage of donor sperm — and that constitutes a crisis."

In the US, that crisis is following an even stranger path. In 2005, while England was banning donor anonymity, a donor sperm–born teenager named Ryan Kramer decided he wanted to know his father. So he swabbed his cheek and sent the DNA sample to an online genealogy testing service and soon became the first person in history to use Internet DNA services to track down a lost parent.

There were two immediate reactions to Ryan Kramer's quest — the first by the sperm-banking industry. "We removed a bunch of information from our donor profiles," says Cappy Rothman, "making it a lot harder for people like Ryan to track down their fathers." The second was the creation of a number of organizations dedicated to chipping away at donor anonymity and a number intent on washing it away completely.

In the chipping-away category is the Donor-Sibling Registry, founded in 2000 by Ryan Kramer's mother, Wendy. "I started the website as a Yahoo message board," she says, "to give these donor kids a place to go to try and find their half brothers and half sisters." For the first two years, the registry totaled thirty-seven members; then word started to spread. By 2003, the site's popularity had grown so much that Wendy removed it from Yahoo and created a dedicated site (donorsiblingregistry.com), which now has 8,500 members.

In the washing-away category are projects like those started by Dr. Kirk Maxey, a former sperm donor and founder of the Donor Semen Archive, the Donor X Project and the Donor Y Project, a series of endeavors that use genetic markers to track both donors and the resulting children, with hopes of forcing the industry's hand.

"I think that gamete [egg and sperm] banking is by its very nature a nonprofit activity," says Maxey. "It is only a misguided perversion that has allowed it to become an industry, and that industry is the only strong advocate for donor anonymity. The malfeasance perpetrated under the guise of donor anonymity is what we are slowly but steadily bringing to light through genetic testing."

In an interview with ABC News, Maxey said he began donating his own sperm in the 1980s, and guesstimates that over the course of sixteen years he may have produced more than 200 children. While Maxey uses these figures to paint a disturbing picture of the industry he now opposes, there is no way to verify his claims.

Dr. Rothman defends the industry, saying, "We've been trying to create an industrywide donor tracking system, but it's expensive and we're trying to get other sperm banks to buy in as well. Either way, we're hoping to have something in place within a year or two."

But there's an important caveat in Rothman's avowed support for a donor tracking system, which would put an end to the destruction of former donors' records: Their names would remain anonymous to parents. Donor tracking would be used only internally to allow gamete banks to keep track of how often and where donors sell their sperm and eggs, and, as they age, to monitor donor health issues that aren't currently tracked.

As such, this form of donor tracking would be the middle ground between current practices and an outright ban on anonymity. Many industry watchdogs feel this tracking system doesn't go far enough, while others feel Rothman's sentiments — despite the fact that he publicly applauded Wendy Kramer's efforts and initiated talks to partner with her enterprise (as of yet inconclusive) — are mere lip service. Whatever the case, when it comes to donor tracking, California Cryobank may be sailing alone.

Recently, William Jaeger, vice president of Genetics and IVF Institute in Virginia, another of the nation's biggest banks, told the *New York Times* that mandatory donor-identity disclosure "would devastate the industry." Kramer has found similar attitudes elsewhere. "I've spoken to the directors of all the major sperm banks and they don't all think like Cappy," she says. "Even though my site is based on mutual consent, Northwest Andrology [one of the other major players] is very much against what I do."

Kramer contends that Northwest Andrology — whose website features a photo of a fat wad of $100 bills and touts the news that donors earn up to $16,000 — is so opposed to unveiling the donor names that "they've threatened donors on my site, making them take down their information. They're hell-bent on preserving anonymity."

5.

While anonymity is a major issue, industry watchdogs maintain that hidden beneath it is a far more insidious problem: incest. There is a growing concern that sooner or later two donor siblings are going to meet and mate without realizing that they share the same father or, in the case of egg donations, mother. "No one on the sperm-bank side wants to talk about it," says Kramer, "but there are over one million donor children in the world, and I know of several cases where unknowing siblings have ended up going to college together and having the same groups of friends. The industry says accidental incest is a statistical impossibility, but from what I've seen, it's only a matter of time."

This is no small issue. Simply put, incest is bad for the gene pool. Sleep with your brothers and sisters and mutations arise. If this pattern of intimate relations with intimate relations continues for more than a few generations, pregnancy becomes impossible. The line dies out. For this reason, in 1910, anthropologist James Frazer demonstrated that the incest taboo was universal, an idea extended by anthropologist Claude Lévi-Strauss, who felt that the incest taboo drove us to procreate with people outside of our own family and tribe — meaning this fear is actually the fundamental building block of society.

To protect this building block, some countries have laws limiting the number of women who can receive sperm from a single donor. Britain sets their legal limit at ten, Denmark at twenty-five. In the US, there are guidelines. The American Association of Reproductive Medicine suggests that a single donor sire no more than twenty-five children within an urban area with a population of 800,000, but — as there's nothing stopping a man from donating sperm at LA's California Cryobank and then traveling a few miles down the freeway and making another donation at Pasadena's Pacific Reproductive Services — these guidelines are hard to enforce.

Instead, the banks police their own limits internally. California Cryogenics, for example, draws its line at twenty kids per donor, but only 40 percent of the women who buy frozen sperm report back to the Cryobank with news of a live birth — yet they don't cap sperm sales until those live births are reported. And, because certain — think blond-haired, blue-eyed — donors are extremely popular and not all pregnancies take, banks often sell the same sperm to more than the recommended number of buyers. Furthermore, because most families order sperm for their immediate needs and then pay a storage fee to hold more in reserve for future use, there's no way to enforce the limits.

"No sperm bank knows how many children are born to specific donors," says Kramer. "They don't know who these kids are or where they are. There's no accurate record keeping."

More alarming is the charge that sperm banks have been intentionally underplaying how many kids have been sired by particular donors. The most egregious example of this is Dr. Cecil Jacobson, who ran a reproductive genetics center in Tysons Corner, Virginia. Instead of using donor sperm, Jacobson substituted his own. When he was caught, investigators found seven children sired by the doctor and — because mothers refused to submit their kids for DNA testing — seventy-five other possibilities.

Talking about this problem, San Francisco's Chloe Ohme, both a midwife and the first person in history to impregnate herself using Internet-found, mail-order sperm, says, "I've been at gatherings of single mothers and people suddenly realize their kids look a little too alike and begin comparing donor numbers and, sure enough, they match." And that's nothing compared to what Kramer noticed after she opened her donor-sibling registry for business. "Very quickly," says Kramer, "we found donors on the website with thirty and forty and fifty kids."

Unfortunately, no one really knows the scope of the problem. One of the only times the issue of sibling incest and sperm banking has been studied was in 1984, by the Law Reform Commission of New South Wales, Australia. The Commission found no danger of incest among donor offspring in the US, but based this determination on annual, nationwide, assisted-reproduction birthrates of 10,000. These days, some 30,000 women a year use California Cryobank's services — and that's only one bank out of thousands.

Not surprisingly, it's religious organizations who are most vocal about this issue. The Catholic Church feels that any form of assisted reproduction threatens the sacred covenant between man and woman, often citing the dangers of incest among its reasons. The Southern Baptist Church has also begun looking into the dangers of accidental incest. Dr. Richard Land, president of the Ethics and Religious Liberty Commission for the Southern Baptist Convention and head of the organization's public policy arm, says, "We don't share the Catholic prohibition against AIH (artificial insemination by husband), but forget the religious implications. There are good medical reasons why all states have laws against incest. It produces very real medical dangers. In the past twenty years, we've learned enough about the tyranny of biology to know that, for the most part, the nature-versus-nurture argument is dead. Nature always wins. Which means incest is a real concern, and the more children who are the product of sperm banks, the more this concern becomes a problem for everyone."

Rothman disagrees. "Incest isn't an issue. Not only is it statistically improbable, but go back 300 years and just about all of us lived in tiny villages. There was no public transit. Everyone was related to everyone else because there was no one else around to marry. We're all descendants of incest. Secondly, from a medical perspective, you're talking about the danger of one generation of incest — even if that happens, the chances of something going wrong are minute."

Still, even if incest isn't an issue, it remains a fundamental taboo — so the problem doesn't seem likely to go away.

6.

The King of Sperm has a corner office, exotically decorated. Perched by the window is a small statue of a man with, as is appropriate, enormous testicles. His balls, literally, hang to the floor. Above the statue, hanging from the ceiling, is a sizable replica of the solar system — a *Starship Enterprise* model positioned dead center. This is also appropriate.

"I'm interested in the frontiers of technology and humanity," Rothman says. "And I know there are dangers in sperm banking. I reread *Brave New World* once every three years. But I also know that infertility is the kind of problem that ruins lives. I only wish the government would recognize this fact as well."

What Rothman means is that unless the industry finds a quick way to address donor anonymity and its downstream concerns (incest among them), it's only a matter of time before the federal government gets further involved, and that's exactly what the industry most fears. "The Food and Drug Administration has become the most onerous obstacle involved in reproduction right now," says Rothman. "They're unaware of the field and — especially in the Bush years — are taking orders from an administration — which has time and again proved themselves irresponsible with science."

Take the 2001 FDA ruling that banned the importation of European sperm on the grounds that it might be contaminated with mad cow disease. "The problem," says Rothman, "is that mad cow disease is a prion disease — it's not sexually transmittable. The only way someone could get it is to eat the frozen sperm."

Nor is this an isolated incident. In 2005, because of the dangers of HIV transmission via blood transfusions, the FDA created Donor Eligibility and Determination Labeling—a set of rules pertaining to the transference of biological material from one person to the next. Sperm banking and in vitro fertilization labs must adhere to these rules, yet there has never been a case of anyone getting HIV from the transfer of reproductive material. Concurrently, they also banned sperm banks from using the sperm of any man who has had "gay sex" in the past five years—even though, again, there is no instance of AIDS being passed via purchased sperm.

As Dr. Barry Behr, Stanford University associate professor of obstetrics and gynecology, and director of Stanford's in vitro fertilization lab, says: "The government has put unreasonable and nonsensical demands on reproductive clinics."

Among those nonsensical demands, Behr points to a California law stating that all couples considering assisted childbirth must be screened for diseases like HIV, HDLV, syphilis, hepatitis, and rubella. Save HIV and HDLV, all of these results can be ignored or waived—meaning one partner can sign a form saying they understand the dangers and want to go ahead anyway—so infected material is occasionally stored at cryobanks. "The FDA demands that this material be held in a completely separate 'biohazard' location in the cryotank," says Behr. "This means we need more cryotanks, a separate labeling system, and a ton more paperwork. All of it is unnecessary. What they don't get is that every sample in the tank is still sharing the same liquid nitrogen. It's like making people with a cough live on the same street, but using only one school bus to pick up the entire neighborhood."

"Every time the government passes another law," says Rothman, "all they're doing is restricting women's reproductive freedom. I don't think the government belongs in our bedrooms. I understand that if the industry doesn't establish a donor registry, this is what's coming. But I think the American public should rise up against it. By letting the FDA tell you whose sperm you can't use, they're in essence telling you whose sperm you have to use. And I don't think we want the federal government deciding what kinds of kids the American public should be allowed to have."

Unfortunately, since few in the industry share Rothman's position on donor tracking and almost no one on the banking side wants to see donor anonymity revoked, without some sort of intervention, the dangers of accidental incest and hidden genetic disease will continue to grow. The truth of the matter is, as the famed physicist Freeman Dyson once pointed out, "If we had a reliable way to label our toys good and bad, it would be easy to regulate technology wisely. But we can rarely see far enough ahead to know which road leads to damnation. Whoever concerns himself with big technology, either to push it forward or to stop it, is gambling in human lives."

Acknowledgments

This book would never have been possible without a great number of people. In helping me decode the science and develop the ideas, I owe a debt of gratitude to Peter Diamandis, Dezso Molnar, Andrew Hessel, Mark Gordon, James Olds, Marc Goodman, and Rick Doblin. My dear friend Michael Wharton served as an indispensible first reader/editor. My amazing wife, Joy Nicholson, kept me sane and laughing throughout.

As none of these stories would have gotten written without the magazine editors who assigned the original pieces, a great thanks to Joe Donnelly at the *LA Weekly*, AJ Baime at *Playboy*, Adam Fisher at *Wired*, Ilena Silverman at the *New York Times Magazine*, Don Peck at the *Atlantic*, Rick Theis at *Ecohearth*, Gary Kamiya at *Salon*, Torie Bosch at *Slate*, Mark Frauenfelder at *Make*, and Pamela Weintraub at *Discover*.

Also, I need to thank my agent Paul Bresnick, who was the first to believe in the possibility of this book and then worked so hard to make it a reality. Everyone at Amazon has been amazing. Special thanks are due to both Julia Cheiffetz who, before she switched jobs, bought the original manuscript, and Tara Parsons, who so ably saw it through to publication. Thanks are also due to both Ryan Holiday and Brent Underwood for their digital ninjitsu. Finally, I owe a debt of gratitude to Charles Pierce, John McPhee, and David Quammen, three majestic wordsmiths who helped me see the real possibilities in science writing.

Acknowledgments

Steven Kotler is a *New York Times* best-selling author, an award-winning journalist, and the cofounder and director of research for the Flow Genome Project. His books include *Bold, The Rise of Superman, Abundance, A Small Furry Prayer, West of Jesus,* and *The Angle Quickest for Flight.* His work has been translated into more than forty languages and has appeared in over eighty publications, including the *New York Times,* the *Atlantic Monthly, Wired, Forbes,* and *Time.* He also writes Far Frontiers, a blog about the intersection of science and culture, for Forbes.com. Kotler lives in northern New Mexico with his wife and too many dogs.

www.stevenkotler.com

Index